The
School Leader's
GUIDE
to
Learner-Centered
Education

D1466121

We dedicate this book to the courageous and inspirational school leaders we have met around the world who have embraced learner-centered principles and practices in their efforts to transform their educational systems. We know you are making a difference!

The
School Leader's
GUIDE
to
Learner-Centered
Education

From **COMPLEXITY**
to **SIMPLICITY**

BARBARA L. McCOMBS
LYNDA MILLER

CORWIN PRESS

A SAGE Company

For information:

Corwin Press, Inc.
A SAGE Company
2455 Teller Road
Thousand Oaks, California 91320
E-mail: order@corwinpress.com

SAGE Ltd.
6 Bonhill Street
London EC2A 4PU
United Kingdom

SAGE India Pvt. Ltd.
B 1/I 1 Mohan Cooperative
    Industrial Area
Mathura Road, New Delhi 110 044
India

SAGE Asia-Pacific Pte. Ltd.
33 Pekin Street #02-01
Far East Square
Singapore 048763

Printed in the United States of America

Library of Congress Cataloging-in-Publication Data

McCombs, Barbara L.
  The school leader's guide to learner-centered education : from complexity to simplicity / by Barbara L. McCombs and Lynda Miller.
      p. cm.
  Includes bibliographical references and index.
  ISBN 978-1-4129-6016-8 (cloth : acid-free paper) —
  ISBN 978-1-4129-6017-5 (pbk. : acid-free paper)
  1. Educational leadership. 2. School management and organization.
  3. Educational innovations—United States. 4. Learning, Psychology of.
  5. Teaching. I. Miller, Lynda. II. Title.

  LB2831.6.M36 2009
  371.2—dc22   2008004863

This book is printed on acid-free paper.

08 09 10 11 10 9 8 7 6 5 4 3 2 1

Acquisitions Editor:	Jessica Allan
Editorial Assistant:	Joanna Coelho
Production Editor:	Appingo Publishing Services
Cover Designer:	Michael Dubowe

Contents

Acknowledgments

From Barbara:

When our first book in this series came out, we were excited to share this work with teachers and other educators. Since that time, we have seen the challenges increase in education, particularly for those individuals in leadership roles. What is exciting, however, is that many educators, visionaries, and futurists are also recognizing these challenges and offering positive suggestions for getting beyond them. For those people who have inspired me to pull together the best of what we know for school leaders fills me with gratitude for the many friends, relatives, and professional mentors who I have been blessed with throughout my life. As with our first book, it is truly in them that the ideas here had their genesis. You will see their work cited throughout this book.

Again, my deepest gratitude goes to my parents. Their unconditional love and support helped me not only believe in myself and my gifts, but also helped enhance my curiosity, creativity, and lifelong love of learning. They also helped me realize that these qualities can be nourished and further developed in all learners. And to this, I have dedicated my professional life. Beyond that, my parents inspired me to understand the concept of servant leadership and the moral principles that define truly great leaders.

Very special thanks are also due my twin sister, Beverly Kreis, for her emotional support and her excellent editorial skills. She again took what Lynda and I created and made it even better. And, of course, without my coauthor, Lynda's, special talents, teaching, and leadership background, and wonderful writing skills, this book would not have been possible.

My husband, "Columbus," and my children, Heather and Ryan, have also been a source of support and inspiration for this book. They have had to endure my long hours spent reading and writing. They deserve my very personal thanks and gratitude for putting up with me at times when I was feeling the most pressure.

My work continues to be for them and now my four grandchildren (twins, Caitlin and Elizabeth; grandson, Cadin; and new granddaughter, Kylin). My greatest hope is that the message of this book will be realized, and they will have the learner-centered educational system all our children need and deserve.

I reserve my last thanks for our editor, Jessica Allan. Her belief in this message and this book has further made my dream come true.

From Lynda:

I was the first person in my family to attend college, largely because of their belief that education was the best thing one could do to better one's life. The members of my family who lived through the Great Depression and World War II were lucky if they finished high school, after which they immediately began to work to support themselves and their families. Throughout my life in school, my parents and favorite aunt cheered me on and championed my graduating and moving on to obtain graduate degrees.

When I began publishing books and articles regarding education, my family dutifully read every book (though not the articles!). After finishing one of my books, my mother called to say she had a question for me. Curious, I asked her what her question was, to which she said, "This is certainly interesting, but isn't what you wrote just common sense?" To which I could only reply, "Of course, but, sadly, there are a great many people out there who don't think so."

Writing this book (and our previous book for teachers) is another of those instances in which my mother would probably ask, "But isn't this just common sense?" Fortunately, it seems that, now, ideas such as the ones we describe in this book are likely to be received with enthusiasm, though my mother would still be puzzled why it took so long for people to catch on. So, to my mother, I say thank you for keeping me focused on what is important, and for reminding me that, though there are those who would argue, common sense will win out.

My coauthor, Barbara, is one of those people I hope will always grace my life. Her devotion to, and understanding of, how people learn and how we can best support them in their learning continue to inspire me. I look forward to more!

I am also grateful to all those children and families from whom I have had the pleasure of learning, over and over, the infinitely varied and unique gifts each learner brings to any situation.

From Barbara and Lynda:

Thanks to Jim Patton, who steered us to Corwin Press, where we have had the pleasure of working with a group of like-minded people dedicated to furthering our ideas. We are immensely grateful to Faye Zucker, whose excitement about this series spurred us on and gave us tremendous hope that the books would reach a wide audience.

Special thanks to Jessica Allan for her efforts in getting this book published and into the hands of those who can make the difference we dream about.

PUBLISHER'S ACKNOWLEDGMENTS

Corwin Press wishes to acknowledge the following peer reviewers for their editorial insight and guidance:

Linda C. Diaz
Program Specialist for Professional Development
Monroe County School District
Key West, FL

Maria Timmons Flores
Assistant Professor
Lewis & Clark Graduate School of Education & Counseling
Portland, OR

Jean L. Krsak
Faculty
CalState TEACH
CSU Fullerton
Fullerton, CA

About the Authors

Barbara L. McCombs, PhD, is a Senior Research Scientist at the University of Denver Research Institute in Colorado where she directs the Human Motivation, Learning, and Development Center. Her current research is directed at new models of teaching and learning, including transformational teacher-development approaches. Barbara is the primary author of *Learner-Centered Psychological Principles* (LCPs), disseminated by the American Psychological Association. Learner-centered models of teaching and learning—based on the research-validated LCPs and on Assessment of Learner-Centered Practices (ALCP) teacher and student surveys validated with over 35,000 students and their teachers in grades K–3, 4–8, 9–12, and college—are being used in numerous national and international schools and colleges. Barbara and coauthor Lynda Miller's book for teachers, *Learner-Centered Classroom Practices and Assessments: Maximizing Student Motivation, Learning, and Achievement*, was published with Corwin Press in 2007.

Lynda Miller, PhD, began her professional career as a junior high school English teacher in Westminster, Colorado. Her interest in language and cognitive development led her to graduate studies, which culminated in a PhD in language development and disorders and learning disabilities. She has held teaching positions at the University of Colorado, the University of Montana, and the University of Texas at Austin, where she pursued her research on cognition, learning styles, and intelligence. Her research and teaching focused on identifying and describing students' learning strengths and abilities, and on translating that information into instructional strategies designed to support students' developing skills as motivated, self-responsible learners. Lynda is the author of numerous publications on a variety of topics, the majority of which have as the main theme a focus on the learner and learning as the essential features of successful instruction. She lives in Albuquerque, New Mexico, where she enjoys a second career as a visual artist.

Why This Is a
Time for Change

Education [is] risky, for it fuels the sense of possibility. But a failure to equip minds with the skills for understanding and feeling and acting in the cultural world is not simply scoring a pedagogical zero. It risks creating alienation, defiance, and practical incompetence. And all of these undermine the viability of a culture.

—Jerome Bruner (1996, pp. 42–43)

Bruner's words, written over ten years ago, continue to resonate today. As the world becomes ever smaller, the ability to understand, feel, and act in the cultural context of the global community takes on ever increasing importance. If our collective purpose in schooling is to create citizens capable of participating in and furthering the cultures and world in which they live, we need to radically alter our conceptions about schooling. We need particularly to alter our ideas regarding the purpose of schooling and how best to use what we know about learning and learners to design learning communities in which everyone involved is eager to learn and develop.

WHY READ THIS BOOK?

We, the authors of this book, believe that at this moment in time, the global community is at the edge of a momentous shift in thinking about the many systems that influence our daily lives. This includes our thinking about the educational, judicial, health care, social justice, welfare, and other systems that support human well-being nationally and globally. In thinking about the educational system, such a crucial shift will require a new kind of leader who has the passion and commitment needed to transform our educational system. This is a leader with the inner power to draw others to join in the process of learning and leading schools through the 21st century and beyond.

For a number of years we have lived through a time during which education, in particular, has been subjected to the industrial, corporate, or business model, emphasizing narrow content standards and curriculum, frequent high stakes testing, and student achievement as the sole indicator of learning. After experiencing the failure of this model, we are now ready to enter a kinder, more respectful age of valuing diversity, natural learning principles, and the innate human potential—from the very young to the very old—to learn and lead.

The Industrial-Age practice of viewing students as workers—and their achievement as products—creates an environment that has unintended and detrimental effects, for these reasons:

- the curriculum narrows, and real learning needed for life in this complex information and conceptual age suffers as students are pressured to achieve and given instruction on how to take tests;
- the emphasis on testing student achievement in basic reading and math skills results in cutting short or eliminating students' meaningful and creative experiences with science, health (physical and mental), economics, art, music, and drama; and
- the practice of basing instruction on one-size-fits-all curricula reflecting the content of the achievement tests required to show accountability shortchanges students' diverse talents as well as their introduction to and immersion in the types of learning, inquiry, thinking, and reflecting that underlie the creativity necessary for flexible problem solving in an ever accelerating world.

In short, the model of education currently in place is fundamentally flawed. It is based on outdated assumptions about human capacity and evidence-based, natural learning principles. The consequences are that this current model actually deprives students of the information and skills necessary to live meaningful lives as productive citizens in a global community.

Shifting from the current, industrial model of education will require visionary leaders who are dedicated to transforming schools into continuously evolving systems that are suited to the needs of a rapidly changing world. We have written this book in the hope that it will provide you with the information and ideas you need to bring about the changes necessary to create transformed and future-serving schools. It is clear that our children must be prepared and ready to solve the big issues arising in this ever more connected and rapidly changing globe.

We will be exploring three overarching questions:

- What are the leadership qualities necessary to lead a new transformational, learner-centered form of education that moves us beyond the one-size-fits-all model?
- Why are these leadership qualities needed to provide the kind of 21st-century education that our children—and we—deserve?
- What are the leadership tools and practices that can help you on your journey to creating learner-centered educational systems?

We will describe these qualities and practices while providing a vision for what it takes to lead in our existing and yet-to-be-created new models of schools. We believe our book is unique because, unlike others in the field of leadership, ours is a synthesis of what we know about learning, leading, and change, which, when considered in combination, serve as a framework for how we can successfully lead the transformation of our schools.

SCHOOLS AS LIVING SYSTEMS

You are probably already aware that many of the people thinking and writing about educational reform view learning and change as complex living systems, or ecologies, that foster the factors both inside and outside learners that influence learning. Figure 1.1 shows the primary aspects of living systems: the technical, personal, and organizational. Living systems, or ecologies, function as a result of the dynamics arising from the interactions among the three aspects of the system. None of the three aspects in isolation can function as a system, nor can the system operate unless the three aspects are fully functional. What this means is that the aspects of a living system are interdependent. In addition, to become stronger, a living system (ecology) must create strong relationships with itself so that the individuals within the system can grow through learning, change, and continuous improvement.

The people in a system and their relationships with each other—too long neglected as the heart of true system transformation—are the learners and leaders who, in concert with community, must lead the way. Balance must be restored to our systems. The change begins with uncovering the deeply held beliefs, values and shared vision of what is possible and what needs to be created together so that technical and organizational decisions flow from these values, and vision.

One of the most compelling features of living systems is that, like networks, they can amplify whatever effects they create. For instance, in a school in which learners are supported in learning, changing, and continuously improving, everyone in contact with these learners is affected similarly—family members, friends, and community members. When a student is treated as a capable, motivated learner with a voice in what she or he sets out to learn, friends of that student's family want the same for their child. As parental demand for this type of learning increases, schools become more sensitive to the learner-based model and become more likely to undertake it themselves.

Figure 1.1   Conceptual Framework: Domains of Living Systems as Levels of Interventions Related to Systemic Research on Engagement[1]

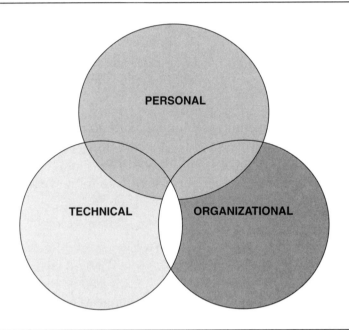

[1] The intersection between the three domains represents the core of the framework—the people as learners from each key constituent group and the values, beliefs, philosophies, and vision for their educational system.

The natural growth processes that arise within living systems underlie the kind of learning we believe our children need and deserve. These natural and organic processes reflect how humans are related, interdependent, and connected in the world in general. What is missing in most current models of education, however, is attention to the personal aspect of the ecology. Two of our goals in this book are (1) to demonstrate the importance of the *personal* aspect of any given educational system, and (2) to illustrate how you as a leader can focus on this personal aspect through a combination of moral purposes, values, and actions. Focus on the personal (including the interpersonal) serves as a rebalancing of the system (school, district, or agency) so that, in the intersection among the three aspects, people—teachers, families, administrators, students, and community members—are all seen as learners whose values, beliefs, philosophies, and visions serve as the basis for the entire system.

The prosperity of such systems requires leaders who

- know who they are as learners and as leaders;
- value everyone involved as learners;
- understand that diversity and difference mean greater opportunities for everyone in the system; and
- value personal growth and development in all learners.

WHAT DOES "LEARNER-CENTERED" MEAN?

Being learner-centered means three things. First, each learner learns through a unique combination of factors, including "heredity; temperament; experiential history; beliefs, values, and perspectives; talents; interests; capacities; and needs" (McCombs & Miller, 2007, p. 15). This means that each learner approaches any given learning situation with a set of strengths and challenges built on the history of her or his previous learning experiences, and each person's history is at least slightly different from everyone else's. For learning to be effective, it must take into account the various factors and histories associated with each learner. The people in the system must value diversity, trust the natural dispersion of talents and interests, and strive to help each learner discover and develop his or her own unique place in the world.

Second, being learner-centered means focusing on the best available evidence about learning, how it occurs, and which teaching practices are most likely to result in the highest levels of student motivation and achievement (McCombs & Whisler, 1997). What we know (and will describe in Chapter 2) is that the most highly motivated learning of all is self-motivated learning, which occurs "only when learners possess (1) choice and control about how, what, and when to learn, and (2) choice and control over what they want to achieve" (McCombs & Miller, 2007, p. 16).

Third, being learner-centered means that the content of learning—the knowledge and skills needed for our future world and present realities—must equip learners with the capacity for complex and systemic thinking; for focused inquiry and reflection on who they are and what the world needs. The curriculum is the curriculum of life, with basic skills integrated into authentic, real-world problem solving. Learning paths and learning content must be allowed to vary as students and their teachers solve real-world and complex problems in joint inquiry and with a moral and ethical concern with the future of ourselves and the world across personal, social, economic, political, and environmental boundaries.

In summary, then, learner-centered means focusing on individual learners and their learning desires, needs, and experiences, using the best available evidence and knowledge about learning and the teaching practices that best support learning for everyone—students, teachers, families, and administrators. Figure 1.2 shows our Learner-Centered Model (LCM) including the evidence-based factors that impact both learners and learning, which we will discuss in detail in Chapter 2.

The core of the LCM is that all instructional decisions begin with knowing who the learners are—individually and collectively. This is followed by thoroughly understanding learning and how best to support learning for all people in the system. Finally, decisions about what practices should be in place at the school and classroom levels depend upon what we want learners to know and be able to do. The LCM puts the *personal domain*—the learners—at the heart of a system dedicated to learning and leading. It brings the educational system back into balance with what we know about learners, leading, and living systems.

Figure 1.2 Learner-Centered Model: A Holistic Perspective

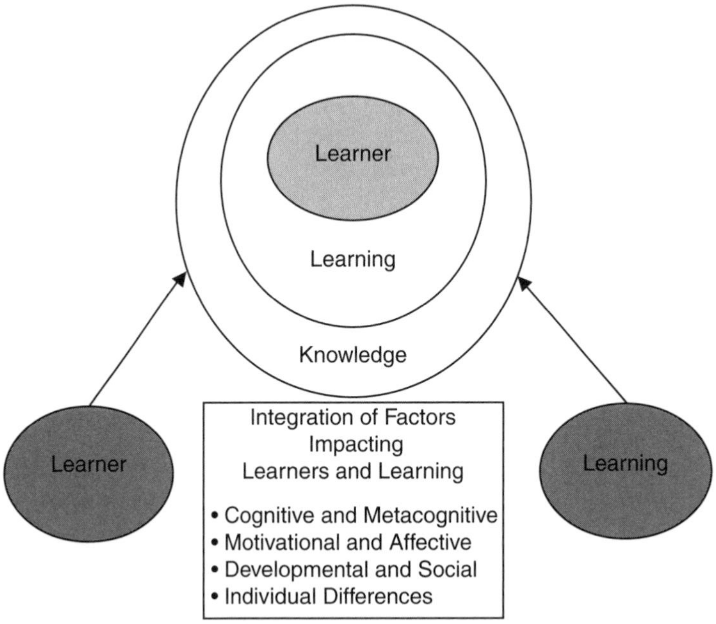

HOW THIS BOOK IS ORGANIZED

We have organized the book as both inquiry and journey toward our call for new leaders who can step up to the challenges and benefits of designing a new paradigm for learning, leading, and schooling. In this chapter, we have introduced you to the concept of learner-centered schools, viewed as living systems, and we provided a brief definition of our Learner-Centered Model, which serves as the foundation for the practical tools we provide in later chapters.

In Chapter 2 we look at what research evidence shows about effective leadership, what we know about learning and change, what it means to be learner-centered, what the learner-centered principles are, and what schooling and school leadership look like when seen as part of living systems.

In Chapter 3 we demonstrate (and ask you to reflect on) what our learner-centered model means for practice, first, by addressing the issues involved in sustaining a learner-centered model, including how to

- lead schools as moral communities;
- support learning and leading at all levels of the school community;
- negotiate political and policy environments; and
- create with others the powerful changes needed when schools are viewed as living systems.

We then present research showing the effectiveness of learner-centered models of schooling, including evidence from our own investigations of schools using the learner-centered model we described earlier in this chapter. We conclude

Chapter 3 with a description of how the learner-centered principles (introduced in Chapter 2) translate into practice at the school level and what the implications are for leadership and building communities of learners.

Chapter 4 asks you to reflect on what tools are needed for your journey to becoming a learner-centered school leader. In this chapter, we introduce you to the self-assessment and reflection process and how these can be applied at the school and classroom levels. You will have the opportunity to reflect on how these tools can support you in your own learning and leading journey. We discuss the concepts of distributed leadership, ongoing learning, change, and improvement, as well as how to identify leaders and change agents. We conclude the chapter with a summary description of the School-Level Assessment of Learner-Centered Practices (ALCP), a self-assessment and reflection assessment tool for maximizing student motivation, learning, and achievement. We show you how research has demonstrated positive relationships between learner-centered practices and the development of students' lifelong learning skills.

We devote Chapter 5 to an exploration of issues confronting school leaders and what learner-centered assessment tools can accomplish. We provide a thorough description of and examples from the ALCP, including discussion of how it was developed, how it relates to measures of lifelong learning and positive school climate, and how to take learner-centeredness to a systems level. In this chapter, you will have an opportunity to try out the ALCP survey for yourself.

Building on the material in Chapters 1 through 5, we ask you in Chapter 6 to explore how we can move educational systems to new student and system outcomes. These outcomes include those for all the learners in the system with a focus on motivating learners beyond content standards to becoming lifelong learners and forming learning partnerships. You will have an opportunity to

- identify the outcomes currently in place in your school and community and discover how they align (or not) with your state's learning standards;
- determine how your state learning standards reflect the learner-centered principles we have described here; and
- determine how the outcomes currently in place in your school and community can be expanded to include those valued by your staff and community.

You will learn what creates lifelong learners and how to identify which learning partnerships are needed in your school and community.

In Chapter 7, we explore the question of how to develop leadership qualities from within. We then describe some exciting new leadership concepts for developing leadership capacity from within. You will have the opportunity to clarify your vision for your school and identify what you need to do in order to incorporate the learner-centered model and principles into your school's practices. We provide guidelines for

- developing capacity from within your school and community;
- identifying the most successful teachers and leaders;
- forming learner-centered support groups; and
- utilizing networking and technology.

We conclude by identifying those simpler principles that can help you navigate through the complexities of a new school leadership role. We extend an invitation to build leadership capacity in everyone within your system so that, together, you can create the new learner-centered educational systems we need for the future.

In the final chapter, Chapter 8, we provide a summary of the first seven chapters. This summary is a good tool for you to use to check your understanding of the major points made throughout this book. It also is a tool for you to see how the complex topics of leadership can be reduced to simpler leadership principles and concepts.

In the following section we offer two exercises to start you on your way.

HOW DO YOU LIKE TO LEARN?

We all know something about learning, just as we all have a theory or model of learning, whether or not we can actually articulate what our model is. Although you have probably had numerous opportunities to describe how you think learning works, how recently have you stopped to consider how *you* learn? Before we describe our model of learning, we invite you to begin two exercises, which we will return to in each chapter, to discover how you learn best and to reflect on how you can use what you discover about your own learning to guide yourself along the path to creating a school (or schools) in which communities of learners collaborate to enhance the achievement of everyone.

The first exercise involves responding to the questions in Box 1.1 and then answering the three questions in Box 1.2. In each of the following chapters, we'll expand on this so you can build a detailed description of yourself as a learner. In the final chapter, you'll have an opportunity to apply what you've discovered to the question of how you can be an effective leader of a school in which everyone is a learner and collaborator for success.

The second exercise involves discovering what kind of leader you are. Jot down your responses to the prompts in Box 1.3. When you've finished, take a moment to reflect on your responses.

In the next chapters, you'll have a chance to revisit your responses and, if you wish, to revise them as you consider the ideas and processes we'll discuss in each chapter.

Box 1.1   How Do I Prefer to Learn: I

Answer each of the 14 questions below[1]. There are no right or wrong answers. Some of the responses may not express your exact feelings; nevertheless, answer as best you can. **Choose as many responses as you like for each item.** Assume that price is not a factor in choosing your responses. Ignore the letter codes for now.

1. When I walk into a stadium for a sporting event, I focus on:
    a. the athletes warming up. (p)
    b. what the spectators are wearing. (s)
    c. the conversations around me. (li)
    d. any musical sounds. (mu)
    e. how many people are there. (qu)

2. To relax, I:
    a. daydream. (ra)
    b. listen to or play music. (mu)
    c. balance the checkbook. (qu)
    d. plan a vacation. (lo)
    e. exercise. (p)

3. My favorite household chore is:
    a. mowing the lawn. (p)
    b. loading the dishwasher. (lo)
    c. balancing the checkbook. (qu)
    d. choosing the color scheme for the living room. (s)
    e. anything I can do by myself. (ra)

4. What captures my attention in a restaurant is:
    a. the amount of the bill. (qu)
    b. the presentation of the food. (s)
    c. the music. (mu)
    d. reading the descriptions of the dishes. (li)
    e. how I feel there. (ra)

5. What is my favorite thing in a restaurant:
    a. eating alone (ra)
    b. figuring the tip (qu)
    c. eating with friends (er)
    d. music (mu)
    e. looking at the décor (s)

6. What is the most important aspect when I travel:
    a. being completely alone (ra)
    b. being in a group (er)
    c. having a planned itinerary (lo)
    d. reading about where I will be going (li)
    e. playing or listening to music (mu)

7. What is the most important factor in choosing a place to live:
    a. financial considerations (qu)
    b. proximity to live musical entertainment (mu)
    c. potential neighbors (er)
    d. proximity to recreational activities (p)
    e. storage space (lo)

(Continued)

Box 1.1   (Continued)

8. I like proximity to:
    a. a library or bookstore (li)
    b. art galleries/museums (s)
    c. people to interact with (er)
    d. musical events (choir, concerts, music clubs) (mu)
    e. health club, gym, or rec center (p)

9. My favorite hobbies are:
    a. crossword puzzles (li)
    b. things I can do alone (ra)
    c. sudoku (lo)
    d. collecting music (mu)
    e. playing a computer game with great graphics (s)

10. To reduce stress, I typically:
    a. read (li)
    b. listen to or play music (mu)
    c. stretch (p)
    d. organize drawers or closets (lo)
    e. look at art (s)

11. When making a meal for a group, my favorite thing to do is:
    a. plan the menu (lo)
    b. measure ingredients and calculate the portions (qu)
    c. coordinate flowers with table arrangements (s)
    d. select music (mu)
    e. read recipes (li)

12. What do I notice most at a wedding:
    a. clothing (s)
    b. my feelings (ra)
    c. number of guests (qu)
    d. music (mu)
    e. what people are saying (li)

13. When I go to a public event such as a sporting event, concert, or play, I:
    a. estimate the collected revenue (qu)
    b. listen to the music (mu)
    c. read until the program begins (li)
    d. walk around whenever I can (p)
    e. look at faces in the crowd (s)

14. What is the first thing I think about when buying new clothing:
    a. how I look in it (ra)
    b. function/what it is for (lo)
    c. appearance (s)
    d. what others will think (er)
    e. comfort (p)

---

[1] The questions and scoring system used in this book are from Miller, L. and Miller, L. C. (1994). *The Quick Smart Profile.* Austin, TX: Smart Alternatives, Inc. Used by permission.

Note: The meanings of the abbreviations can be found in Chapter 5, pp. 142–143.

Box 1.2   How Do I Prefer to Learn: Reflection 1

In the spaces that follow each of these three questions, jot down the first thing(s) that you think of in response.

1.   What is my favorite way to relax?

2.   What do I pay closest attention to when I am anonymous in a crowd of people?

3.   What is my preferred way to reduce stress?

Box 1.3   What Kind of Leader Are You: 1

1.   Right now, these are my primary concerns about my school/district/area:

2.   I believe successful schools are based on these qualities:

3.   The most important stakeholders in schools are:

4.   My hopes for the students in my school/district/area are:

5.   My top five qualities as an educational leader are:

6.   Five things I am eager to learn in order to be a better leader are:

2

What We Know About Learning and Leading

We are born learning beings. We naturally imagine, wonder, invent, and explore our way into unknown territories and perplexing and paradoxical questions. Our curiosity and insatiable drive to know and figure things out is innate.

—Stephanie Pace Marshall (2006), p. 11.

Not many of us would question the insightful quote by Stephanie Pace Marshall, founding resident of the Illinois Mathematics and Science Academy. When we look at our current educational systems and policies, however, there seems to be a big disconnect. The natural school learning principles and assumptions—which we know intuitively and experientially—just do not fit with the unnatural design of schooling today. Just as Marshall invited her readers in her 2006 book, *The Power to Transform*, it is time to think differently about learning and schooling. It is also time to reconceive and redesign schooling (Wheatley, 1999).

This call to leadership is echoed in the work of Margaret Wheatley, internationally distinguished scholar, innovative organizational thinker, and author of the ground-breaking work *Leadership and the New Science* (2006). In a recent article for *The School Administrator*, Wheatley and Frieze (2007) argue that our current "culture of high-stakes testing" has had serious unintended consequences because it was based on a theory of learning and a theory of change that do not match what the evidence—from a variety of sources—shows.

In this high-stakes testing culture, teachers have become unsupported in their efforts to focus on individual learners, student achievement, the arts, and students as whole persons. As Wheatley and Frieze (2007) point out, in such a culture school leaders are burdened with a corporate approach that depends on "command and control leadership, a focus on results, motivation through fear and rewards" and an exclusion of any evidence except numbers (p. 17). What began as an effort to create a culture of achievement for all has resulted instead in a culture in which achievement has been subverted, leaving teachers and school leaders weary and demoralized.

Increasingly, people in leadership positions are pointing out the need to recognize our moral obligation to serve all students well by educating them holistically, focusing on learning, and recognizing their unique learning strengths and needs. As Hoffman and Burrello (2002) put it, "Schools should be concerned with honoring individuality, developing potential, and arming kids with an ability to think freely and independently" (p. 3). Because schools are defined in large part by moral purposes and values, they require a special kind of leadership that focuses on creating a set of goals, purposes, values, and commitments that motivate people to do what is necessary for every student to achieve. Although the way this leadership looks will vary from school to school and from leader to leader, a common thread is a focus on learners and learning.

Before we examine what the evidence shows about learning, we invite you to continue in Boxes 2.1 and 2.2 the exercises begun in Chapter 1, which we will return to in each chapter, to discover your leadership style based on how you learn best. These exercises will: (1) help you to reflect on how you can use what you learn about your own learning and leading styles, and (2) guide you along your path to creating a school (or schools) in which communities of learners collaborate to enhance the achievement of everyone.

WHAT KIND OF LEARNER AND LEADER ARE YOU?

This exercise involves responding to the questions in Box 2.1, and then answering the three questions in Box 2.2. As we said in Chapter 1, in each of the following chapters we will expand on this so you can build a detailed description of yourself as a learner and leader; in the final chapter, you will have an opportunity to apply what you have discovered to the question of how you can be an effective leader of a school in which everyone is a learner and collaborator for success.

We invite you to reflect on your responses to each exercise, noting any connections between how you learn and how you lead. We will revisit the importance of aligning your learning and leading styles in later chapters.

WHAT DOES EXISTING EVIDENCE SAY ABOUT LEADERSHIP?

Leadership has been the topic of many recent books and articles concerned with the state of our educational system and educational policies. All offer new

Box 2.1   How Do I Prefer to Learn: 2

Answer each of the 14 questions below[1]. There are no right or wrong answers. Some of the responses may not express your exact feelings; nevertheless, answer as best as you can. **Choose as many responses as you like for each item.** Assume that price is not a factor in choosing your responses. Ignore the letter codes for now.

15.   How do I prepare to buy a new product?
    a. I read available literature. (li)
    b. I talk to someone about it. (er)
    c. I watch a demonstration. (s)
    d. I use it first. (ra)
    e. I list pros and cons. (lo)

16.   What do I enjoy about my grocery store?
    a. its attention to nutrition and health (ra)
    b. its appearance (s)
    c. its layout (lo)
    d. its attention to unit values (qu)
    e. its background music (mu)

17.   When I keep track of my daily obligations and responsibilities, I:
    a. use a calendar (paper or electronic). (lo)
    b. use a mnemonic or rhyme. (li)
    c. imagine myself doing them. (p)
    d. put it to a song. (mu)
    e. remember the number of items. (qu)

18.   In moving into a new house or apartment, the first thing I would do is:
    a. calculate its square footage. (qu)
    b. set up my music system. (mu)
    c. list what needs to be done. (lo)
    d. enjoy the solitude. (ra)
    e. show it to my friends. (er)

19.   When I go somewhere new, I bring:
    a. a book. (li)
    b. a music player. (mu)
    c. exercise clothing/equipment. (p)
    d. my calendar (paper or electronic). (lo)
    e. drawing material or camera. (s)

20.   When I am attracted to someone, I notice their:
    a. body. (p)
    b. sense of style. (s)
    c. verbal humor. (li)
    d. reasoning abilities. (lo)
    e. ability to relate to others. (er)

21.   When I want to persuade someone of something, I:
    a. present a rational argument. (lo)
    b. ask them how they feel. (er)
    c. tell them what to do. (ra)
    d. give them reading material on the subject. (li)
    e. use numbers to make my point. (qu)

22. What is my favorite entertainment?
     a. comedy (l)
     b. dance (p)
     c. musical concert (mu)
     d. spending time by myself (ra)
     e. being with friends (er)

23. I most admire:
     a. teachers. (er)
     b. financial experts. (qu)
     c. musicians. (mu)
     d. scientists. (lo)
     e. artists. (s)

24. When I plan something with my friends and/or family, I:
     a. take a vote. (er)
     b. opt for physical comfort. (p)
     c. list the options. (lo)
     d. read about it. (li)
     e. make sure I can come and go as I please. (ra)

25. I like to teach others to:
     a. meditate. (ra)
     b. write. (li)
     c. paint or draw. (s)
     d. understand music. (mu)
     e. play math games. (qu)

26. I prefer playing:
     a. bridge. (qu)
     b. Scrabble.® (li)
     c. charades. (p)
     d. solitaire. (ra)
     e. Pictionary.® (s)

27. When planning a party, I enjoy choosing the food on the basis of:
     a. the amount of food per person. (qu)
     b. how much I like it. (ra)
     c. how much others will like it. (er)
     d. the visual presentation. (s)
     e. how healthy it is. (p)

28. The kind of test I like most is:
     a. multiple choice. (lo)
     b. essay. (li)
     c. math. (qu)
     d. personality. (ra)
     e. physical fitness test. (p)

[1] The questions and scoring system used in this book are from Miller, L. and Miller, L. C. (1994). *The Quick Smart Profile.* Austin, TX: Smart Alternatives, Inc. Used by permission.

Note: The meanings of the abbreviations can be found in Chapter 5, pp. 142–143.

Box 2.2   How Do I Prefer to Learn: Reflection 2

In the spaces that follow each of these three questions, jot down the first thing(s) that you think of in response.

I.   What is my favorite hobby (or what would it be if I had the time to pursue it)?

2.   What is the one new skill I would most like to learn?

3.   What would be my ideal environment in which to learn this new skill?

and mostly hopeful views about what is needed to lead schools in turbulent times—or to change current practices to those more consistent with human learning principles and basic social and emotional needs. In the next section, we explore some of the more traditional leadership notions and why policies and practices are changing now.

Traditional Approaches to Leadership

Top-Down and Hierarchical Models

The traditional model of leadership adheres to a mechanical model of human functioning and learning based on an educational paradigm from the Industrial Age. Marshall (2006) describes the result as a sequential model of change in which

1. a vision is created;
2. a strategy is developed;
3. policy is written;
4. an implementation plan is designed;
5. a timeline of activities and desired outcomes is specified;
6. assessment and evaluation tools are designed; and then
7. the work is parceled out.

Allies are sought, rewards and incentives are specified to achieve buy-in, punishments and other sanctions are put in place, and a communication strategy is crafted to get good press.

According to Wheatley & Frieze (2006), this theory of change has the following assumptions:

● "change is top-down and requires top-level support;
● change requires careful planning and good controls;

- change happens step-by-step in a neat, incremental fashion;
- behavior can be mandated;
- rewards and punishment motivate people to change;
- large-scale changes require large-scale efforts." (p. 3)

Day (2000) maintains that, when approaches to education become rationalistic means-ends that are characterized by segmented rather than holistic approaches, many teachers and school leaders become disenchanted with their work. Day points out that, in these times of standards, accountability, and testing, successful leaders must engage in reflective practice. This allows them to ensure that their schools provide the kind of high-quality learning opportunities to support all students in the 21st century. Today's school leaders need to balance externally determined initiatives with their own autonomy and to focus on people-centered management. The key for being effective is to reflect on their own values, beliefs, and practices; those of their staff; the position and progress of their schools relative to others in their local and national contexts; current and emerging policy matters that will affect school functioning; and conditions that support teachers in their schools.

In addition, Day cites research showing that effective school administrators are transformative rather than transactional. They are invitational rather than autocratic, and they are empowering rather than controlling. Successful leaders are strongly driven by their personal values and vision, which they are constantly monitoring and reviewing. His research further indicated that effective reflection processes for leaders also include:

- knowing, understanding, and interacting empathetically with staff and students;
- recognizing and caring for the emotional well-being of staff and students;
- assessing the strengths and weaknesses of staff;
- strategically using networking to reflect on current and future practice and direction, and engaging in intelligence gathering as a means of monitoring progress;
- seeing themselves as lifelong learners and being actively involved in their own self-development; and
- encouraging teachers to engage in critical reflection, problem posing, and self-evaluation. (Day, 2001)

Effective Leaders in Traditional Systems

Working within the traditional paradigm, researchers have searched for leadership traits and actions that can promote the kind of changes that increase student learning. For example, based on a meta-analysis of 70 empirical studies that examined the effects of leadership on student achievement as assessed by quantitative measures, Waters, Marzano, and McNulty (2004) concluded that (1) leadership matters; (2) effective leadership can be defined; and (3) effective leaders know what to do, how, and why to do it. These results were based on a sample size of 2,894 schools, 14,000 teachers, and more than 1.1 million students. In addition, 21 key areas of responsibility positively correlated with higher levels of student achievement, as shown in Table 2.1.

Table 2.1   Twenty-One Areas of Leadership Responsibility That Positively Correlate With Student Achievement

1. *Culture:* fosters shared beliefs and a sense of community and cooperation.
2. *Order:* establishes a set of standard operating procedures and routines.
3. *Discipline:* protects teachers from issues and influences that would detract from their teaching time or focus.
4. *Resources:* provide teachers with the materials and professional development necessary for the successful execution of their jobs.
5. *Curriculum, instruction, and assessment:* is directly involved in the design and implementation of curriculum, instruction, and assessment practices.
6. *Knowledge of curriculum, instruction, and assessment:* is knowledgeable about current practices.
7. *Focus:* establishes clear goals and keeps these goals at the forefront of the school's attention.
8. *Visibility:* has high-quality contact and interactions with teachers and students.
9. *Contingent rewards:* recognizes and rewards individual accomplishments.
10. *Communication:* establishes strong lines of communication with teachers and students.
11. *Outreach:* is an advocate and spokesperson for the school to all stakeholders.
12. *Input:* involves teachers in the design and implementation of important decisions and policies.
13. *Affirmation:* recognizes and celebrates school accomplishments, and acknowledges failures.
14. *Relationship:* demonstrates empathy with teachers and staff on a personal level.
15. *Change-agent role:* is willing and prepared to actively challenge the status quo.
16. *Optimizer role:* inspires and leads new and challenging innovations.
17. *Ideals and beliefs:* communicates and operates from strong ideals and beliefs about schooling.
18. *Monitoring and evaluation:* monitors the effectiveness of school practices and their impact on student learning.
19. *Flexibility:* adapts his or her leadership behavior to the needs of the current situation, and is comfortable with dissent.
20. *Situational awareness:* is aware of the details and undercurrents in the running of the school, and uses this information to address current and potential problems.
21. *Intellectual stimulation:* ensures that faculty and staff are aware of the most current theories and practices in education, and makes the discussion of these practices integral to the school's culture.

Source: Waters, Marzano, and McNulty, 2004, pp. 49–50.

Waters et al. (2004) conclude that, even if leaders possess these qualities and carry out these 21 responsibilities, there are two critical variables that may contribute to whether they will be effective. The first is whether they focus their school change on the right factors for improving student learning and achievement: that is, a challenging curriculum and learning goals, effective feedback, parent and community involvement, a safe school environment, collegiality and professionalism. This includes teachers who use effective instruction and classroom management strategies, and students who have the background knowledge, motivation, and positive home environment to be successful. The second critical variable is whether their stakeholders are prepared for and in support of the kind of changes being made; that is, are the changes consistent with the stakeholders' prevailing values and norms.

The Waters et al. study yielded some important findings that replicate those found in several other studies (e.g., Darling-Hammond, LaPointe, Meyerson, & Orr, 2007; Davis, Darling-Hammond, LaPointe, & Meyerson, 2005; Wallace Foundation, 2006). When looking at the 21 traits more closely, the one with the largest measured effects on change was culture, which includes the leadership traits of promoting

    a. cooperation among staff;
    b. a sense of staff well-being;
    c. staff cohesion;
    d. a sense of shared understanding of purpose; and
    e. a shared vision of what the school could be like.

These are the human factors that more directly relate to positive communication and relationships. The Waters et al. evidence provides a clearer way to understand leadership that conforms to principles of natural learning in living systems such as education.

Current Evidence about Leadership

Coles and Southworth (2005) make the case for a new kind of leadership that goes beyond the management of standards and testing to the creation of learning for all within the system to better prepare them for a creative and complex learning society. Future leaders need a holistic big-picture view rather than a reductionist view. This larger view—one that we argue includes an understanding of our place on this planet and how to achieve sustainability in the values and purposes that define us as humans and as learners—can help school leaders understand learning, make connections, engage in futures-thinking and critical thinking, and possess political acumen and emotional understanding. One of the biggest challenges is to sustain leadership by distributing leadership practices and developing professional learning communities.

According to Bennis (2007), because every leader has an agenda, the topic of leadership must be addressed in terms of the values and aims of the leader. In discussing what he sees as the most important qualities of a leader, Bennis says the single most important is the adaptive capacity of resilience. In addition, to be exemplary—and to get results—leaders must possess five other competencies:

- to be able to create a sense of mission;
- to motivate others to join them on that mission;
- to create an adaptive social architecture for their followers;
- to generate trust and optimism; and
- to develop other leaders.

What Are the Qualities That Define Leadership?

Vroom and Jago (2007) define leadership as "a process of motivating people to work together collaboratively to accomplish great things" (p. 18). It is a process of motivating people not only to pursue common goals but to participate in the decision-making and leadership processes. Leaders must be highly sensitive and reflective about the dynamic interplay between leaders and followers. In an earlier book, Fullan (2003) made a similar strong case that common values and goals are at the heart of effective leadership, and that school leaders need to have the courage to build new cultures based on trusting relationships. From Fullan's perspective, effective leaders need to develop professional cultures of disciplined inquiry and action.

Sternberg (2007) maintains that effective leadership is a synthesis of wisdom, creativity, and intelligence. Sternberg says that these three key components work together and are considered to be modifiable forms of developing expertise. According to Sternberg, people aren't born leaders but develop expertise in these areas as a function of the situations they are exposed to and the kinds of dispositions (attitudes) and skills they develop in these situations. In defining the three components, Sternberg notes that creativity is related to leadership success because it is the set of skills and dispositions for generating ideas and products that are relatively novel, high in quality, and appropriate for the task at hand. Creativity is related to divergent thinking which, in turn, is related to leadership success.

Sternberg (2007) describes the creative attitude as having a number of elements, which are ways of thinking found in successful leaders, as shown in Table 2.2.

Sternberg (2007) defines successful intelligence as the skills and dispositions needed for success. It is comprised of academic (or analytical) intelligence used to analyze, evaluate, and judge information, as well as practical intelligence used to solve everyday problems by applying knowledge gained from experience. Successful intelligence allows people to adapt themselves and their environment as needed.

Wisdom is defined by Sternberg (2007) as using successful intelligence, creativity, and knowledge to reach a common good. It involves applying values and balancing one's own interests and the interests of one's organization with those of others and their organizations. In synthesizing all three components, transformational leaders modify the environment to fit their vision of what it should be rather than modifying their behavior to adapt to the environment.

Which Deeper Personal Qualities Define Leadership?

Combs, Miser, and Whitaker (1999) argue that a truly effective leader must fundamentally understand themselves and other people. They need to know how to encourage high performance among staff and students. In other words, they need to understand how their own and other people's belief systems drive their personal and professional behaviors. Effective leaders also need to understand change and why many people resist it. In addition, effective leaders need

Table 2.2   The Elements of Creative Attitudes of Leaders

1. They define problems using their own judgment in alternative ways that are more conducive to solutions.
2. They are willing to take a hard look at whether their solution is the best one possible.
3. They are willing to put effort into persuading others of the value of their ideas.
4. They understand that knowledge can both help and hinder creative thinking, and they attempt to free themselves of tunnel vision.
5. They are willing to take sensible risks even if it means occasional failures.
6. They are willing to confront and surmount the obstacles that face them when taking positions contrary to the crowd.
7. They believe in their ability to accomplish the task at hand (i.e., high self-efficacy).
8. They are willing to tolerate ambiguity and long periods of uncertainty.
9. They are intrinsically motivated by the work they do and find ways to be extrinsically rewarded for this work.
10. They continue to grow intellectually and do not get stuck or stagnate in their patterns of leadership.

Source: Sternberg, R. (2007).

to understand organizations and how systems operate, and how they are reciprocally influenced by people. Combs et al. (1999) focus on how leaders can create learning organizations by developing a climate where learning and change flourish. They also make the point that learning and change occur in environments where

- learners' needs are understood, appreciated, and attended to;
- people are challenged to grow and change, not threatened to change;
- learning is accompanied by strong feeling and emotion;
- communication and feedback are frequent, are relevant, and suggest next steps; and
- collaboration, not competition, characterizes learning activities (p. 67).

Fullan (2001) believes that, to create the type of effective leadership needed in times of rapid change, a set of factors must combine in a synergistic way: having a moral purpose, understanding change, developing relationships, building knowledge, and making coherence. The first of these, moral purpose, means making a positive difference in the lives of those in our systems and the society as a whole. Having a moral purpose is more and more an important part of effective leadership in fast-changing times, as it provides a sense of stability.

Second, Fullan (2001) emphasizes that effective leaders need to understand that the change process progresses unevenly and over a period of time rather than all at once. Another critical part of the change process is that it requires strong relationships among all the stakeholders involved. Fullan describes leaders who are the most successful at implementing change as energetic, enthusiastic, and hopeful. They have high emotional intelligence, including self-awareness, self-regulation, motivation, empathy, and social skills. These leaders, because they involve all stakeholders, engender internal commitment, as opposed to imposing decisions, which results in an external commitment.

To lead in a culture of change, it is necessary to *create* a culture of change (reculturing), in which people are encouraged to seek solutions, build capacity, critically assess, and selectively incorporate new ideas and practices. Quality leadership in a culture of change is defined by Fullan (2001) as

- helping teachers to gain in required knowledge, skills, and dispositions needed to change their thinking and practices;
- developing a professional community where ongoing learning is sustained;
- leading efforts toward program coherence and alignment with desired outcomes; and
- providing technical leadership in day-to-day school management.

Fullan (2001, 2003) also believes that quality leaders must have high emotional intelligence, including self-awareness, self-regulation, motivation, empathy, and social skills.

What Are Further Insights for Global Leaders?

Steven Covey (2002) maintains that, in our global economy where the push is for quality at low cost, the only sustainable way to achieve a shift in this trend is through the empowerment of people. In high trust cultures where structures and systems are nurturing the best of human creativity and innovation, people are empowered. The opposite occurs in low trust cultures that promote high control, cynicism, and internal competition. In high trust cultures, coaches and servant leaders, described by Greenleaf (2002) as those who first want to serve (not to be served), draw out, inspire, and develop the best and highest within people—from the inside out.

Such transformational leaders create a shared vision in which people use their unique talents independently and interdependently to achieve the shared vision of the culture. They are driven by personal values and commitment to others. One of the most important qualities of a servant leader is the ability to make sense out of a complex situation and help people see ways to understand it—conceptual leadership—rather than presenting a fixed solution. The servant leader remains open to doubt and is not fanatical about a fixed solution. He or she is open to embracing uncertainty and being willing to commit to ongoing learning and capacity building, all the while allowing other people to make choices. Servant leadership also requires making oneself vulnerable and being humble. For Greenleaf (2002), the critical question is whether the people around the leader are growing—whether they are learning and changing in an unending upward spiral.

At the end of Greenleaf's book (2002), Peter Senge commends the notion of servant leadership and laments that, like so many good ideas, it hasn't caught on the way it should. He claims this is because it requires a deep commitment on the part of management. Servant leadership requires the kind of organizational learning that is collective-capacity building, and recognition that learning requires change. He also maintained that all *real* learning begins and is driven by aspirations for what the learner wants to do, and not driven by fear, which is the creation of crisis. Servant leaders understand that people who are really learning are driven by excitement, doing something new, leading toward serving people better, and/or producing a better way of life. We are particularly driven by goals that are more meaningful to us and represent something we care deeply about. For Senge, servant leadership is about community and distributing the concept throughout the organization in ways that increase the capacity of the human community to shape its future.

Hargreaves and Fink's (2004) description of sustainable leadership echoes Senge's. Their emphasis is on learning as the heart of the purpose of education. What needs to be sustained is learning that matters, is deep, that spreads, and that lasts a lifetime for all students. Hargreaves and Fink describe seven principles for sustainable leadership:

1. depth of learning and real achievement;
2. length of impact over the long haul;
3. breadth of influence in a distributed way;
4. justice in ensuring that leadership benefits all students;
5. diversity that replaces standardization;
6. resourcefulness that conserves and renews the energy of leaders; and
7. conservation that creates a better future by building on the best of the past.

These principles characterize the convictions, commitments, and moral purpose that address the kind of learning that engages students intellectually, socially, emotionally, and spiritually. Leaders responsible for sustainable learning systems acknowledge that learning is about knowing, doing, being, living together, and living sustainably—for a better future and world. The principles outlined by Hargreaves and Fink serve as emotional, moral, and spiritual leadership challenges that go beyond most cognitive and intellectual models. Sustainable leadership requires understanding human learning and human needs in the most holistic sense. The concept of sustainable leadership leads us to the moral imperative many are feeling at this time: to change the current emphasis on a piecemeal approach to education tied solely to quantitative measures of achievement.

What About the Spiritual Dimension?

Recently, in a somewhat different vein, several authors have taken what some many see as a radical approach to leadership through their discussions of the spiritual dimension of leadership. For instance, Houston and Sokolow (2007), in their discussion of the spiritual dimension of leadership, posit eight principles, shown in Table 2.3, that represent aspects of enlightened leadership, or the wisdom that comes from within.

Table 2.3   Eight Principles of Enlightened Leadership

1. Intention
2. Attention
3. Unique gifts and talents
4. Gratitude
5. Unique life lessons
6. A holistic perspective
7. Openness
8. Trust

These eight principles comprise the life-enhancing energy of mind, body, and spirit that focus on interconnectedness and interrelatedness of life at all levels. Those interested in learning more about these principles are invited to read Houston and Sokolow's book, referenced in the Resources section at the end of our book. For now, we want you to know that Houston and Sokolow's wisdom is a large part of what is required in learner-centered leadership in a transformed educational system.

THE "BIG PICTURE" VIEW: AN ECOLOGY OF LEARNING MODEL

Situating human learning principles within the larger framework of human and systems functioning helps to clarify the fundamental cause of current imbalances in our educational models and philosophies. The "industrial paradigm" that characterizes most 21st-century organizations, including schools and school systems, reflects the mismatch between principles of nature and human functioning, and institutions.

To address this mismatch, Wielkiewicz and Stelzner (2005) argue that the industrial paradigm be replaced with an ecological paradigm, which they characterize as follows:

a. effective leadership processes involve temporary resolutions of a tension between the traditional industrial approach and the neglected ecological approach;
b. specific leaders are less important than they appear because the ecological context is more important than what leaders decide to do;
c. organizations are more adaptive when there is a diversity of genuine input into decision-making processes; and
d. leadership itself is an emergent process arising from the human interactions that make up the organization (p. 326).

In general, an ecology is a complex, open system, its elements able to adapt in a dynamic and interdependent way because of its diversity. In a learning ecology, a diversity of learning options is created and delivered to students (including teachers) by way of opportunities they can use to learn through the methods and means that best support their unique situations, needs, and interests (Brown, 1999). Richardson (2002) tell us that, in a successful learning ecology, students can immediately "search for, locate, and quickly access elements of learning that address their immediate needs. Students use the ecology to construct and organize personalized, unique interactions with the content" (p. 2). Further, Richardson argues, a learning ecology supports social learning through students forming teams to collaborate on activities, or self-organizing into groups to explore learning topics.

More specifically, Table 2.4 shows the principles that define ecological systems. In the ecological perspective, leadership is an emergent process in keeping with learner-centered principles and practices that share leadership among all learners.

Table 2.4 Principles of Ecological Systems

- *Interdependence:* components with bi-directional influences, such as subgroups within the organization, families, communities;
- *Open systems and feedback loops:* dependence on inflow of materials, resources, and information from internal and external systems such as the economic, political, social, and environmental systems that surround the organization;
- *Cycling of resources:* making multiple uses of resources such as human talents without relying on a single individual;
- *Adaptation:* providing structures and processes for adaptive learning to meet challenges and changes in technology, economics, student populations, etc.

Zmuda, Kuklis, and Kline (2004) maintain that the crucial role of leaders in transforming schools is to change minds and not just practices, which occurs through dialog, debate, and reflection. Transformational leaders expose teachers to new ideas and encourage them to try them out. Table 2.5 shows the six steps of continuous improvement that Zmuda et al. (2004) recommend teachers take.

Zmuda et al. (2004) contend that systems-thinking, along with the belief in constant striving to be better, is required to make continuous improvement. Schools are seen as complex living systems with purpose, and to be competent, they must be driven by systems-thinking. Collegiality and ongoing dialogue are critical to ensure that changes are thought of in the context of their interrelationships with each other and the shared vision. In addition, data collection and analysis, continual staff development and learning, and reflection are necessary components of continuous improvement.

Wheatley (2006a) states that the new science that has emerged from physics, as well as biology and the softer sciences, has helped us to define a real world that is very different from what we've come to believe. In this new real world,

Table 2.5   Six Steps of Continuous Improvement

1. Identifying and clarifying core beliefs about the school culture;
2. Creating a shared vision of what these beliefs look like in practice;
3. Collecting accurate and detailed information about where the school is now and about gaps between current reality and shared vision;
4. Identifying what innovations will most likely close the gaps;
5. Developing and implementing an action plan that supports teachers through the change process; and
6. Embracing collective autonomy and collective accountability for closing the gaps.

there are interconnected networks, and when chaos occurs, the world (system) seeks order. Even when current structures are destroyed, the conditions are created for a new order to emerge. This self-organizing world produces networks of relationships that then evoke creativity from which strong, adaptive systems emerge with new strengths and capacities.

Wheatley's (2006a) work helps us see that leaders in the new world will need the freedom to make intelligent decisions based on how well they understand the situation rather than how well they understand the policies and procedures. They need to trust that people will invent their own solutions and to expect and value the unique solutions that emerge. Compliance to one-size-fits-all will no longer serve our local and global needs. Leaders need to know that they can rely on human creativity, compassion, caring, potential, and self-organizing capacities.

In discussing the scientific search for the basic building blocks of life, physicists find the nature of reality is relationships (Wheatley, 2006b), a scientific fact that has been largely ignored in our culture but something most needed to develop the core competencies that organizations need. Wheatley contends that by promoting healthy relationships, we free up kindness, intelligence, accountability, and learning in organizations. For leaders this means they need to make time for people to think together, share their work challenges, learn from each other, construct solutions, and discover new capabilities.

We invite you at this point to go back to your responses to the questions in Box 2.2 at the beginning of this chapter. Reflect on your responses to these questions in light of what you've read so far, and add to or modify your responses accordingly.

WHAT IT MEANS TO BE LEARNER-CENTERED

For decades, educators and researchers have argued that the basic approach to education should be one that strives to meet unique and fundamental human needs and develop human potential (Patterson, 2003). For example, William Glasser, creator of choice theory and Quality Schools, has maintained that we will not have more motivated students who work harder and learn more, nor we will have lower dropout rates, until we create more need-satisfying schools.

When schools are more personalized and need-satisfying, and not aimed at controlling students, we will be able to avoid tragedies such as the violence at Columbine High School and others. These new kinds of schools will provide environments where students can really get to know their peers and teachers and develop a sense of trust. When the focus is on standards and coverage of materials, students are bored, and they know the system isn't about them.

To develop human potential, we believe it is essential that students have an opportunity to study real world problems and learn for understanding in self-directed ways. In describing a new school paradigm, Patterson (2003) argues that decisions will be made based on what makes educational and personal sense for students rather than on administrative and teacher convenience or tradition. We believe that the type of paradigm needed is one based on research validated psychological principles of learning, motivation, development, and individual differences. This is the type of paradigm that can help students develop into the critical thinkers, self-directed learners, problem solvers, time managers, and lifelong learners needed in our complex society.

What Is Needed: Solid, Evidence-Based Principles

An educational system that embraces academic competence *and* the development of human potential and life competencies can best prepare students for democracy in a global world and for lifelong learning. To achieve a balanced and transformed view of education, we must simplify and realign our educational priorities and values based on research-validated, evidence-based principles (McCombs, 2007).

Few would disagree that we want to prepare all students for productive lives and to be lifelong learners. In spite of differing politics, most would favor solutions that are empowering and in keeping with natural learning principles and laws of human functioning. These principles and laws include the natural range and diversity in human talents, abilities, and interests. In trusting natural principles that "sort" learners into the range of skills and interests needed to support a productive democratic and global society, we move away from standardized "one-size-fits-all" educational paradigms and toward a transformed view of systems that reward and support diversity and the development of individual potential in the context of democratic social ideals. Naturally, we want these transformational solutions to be evidence-based and lead to high levels of learning and achievement. More importantly, however, we want them to embody the fullness of what it means to be human and to live with purpose and meaning.

The Learner-Centered Psychological Principles

As a grounding for such transformed practices, the American Psychological Association (APA) adopted the *Learner-Centered Psychological Principles* (Learner-Centered Principles) in 1997, largely as a response to what the APA considered ill-informed decisions being made based on *A Nation at Risk* (National Commission on Excellence and Education, 1983), which concluded that student achievement in the United States showed an alarming decline, especially in comparison with other countries such as Japan. The APA was concerned that the push toward testing and accountability was not informed by evidence regarding what best supports and fosters learning. Members of the APA Task Force working on the Learner-Centered Principles believed that psychology, as a scientific field that has studied learning for over 100 years, had a responsibility to clearly present to educators and policymakers its accumulated and research-validated knowledge base about learning and learners. The research that is summarized in the APA *Principles* derives from many fields, including psychology, education, sociology, and brain research. Research documentation can be found in Alexander & Murphy (1998); Combs, Miser, & Whitaker (1999); Kanfer & McCombs (2000); Lambert & McCombs (1998); McCombs (2000b, 2001b, 2004b); McCombs & Miller (2007); McCombs & Whisler (1997); and Perry & Weinstein (1998). Copies of *Principles* may be downloaded through the APA Web site at http://www.apa.org.

When work on the Learner-Centered Principles began, no one knew what the final product would look like or what it would be called. The Task Force saw it as a "living document" that would be revised and reissued as more was learned about learning, motivation, development, and individual differences that must be addressed to achieve optimal learning for all. The Learner-Centered Principles document is now in its second iteration and continues to be widely disseminated to educators and researchers in this country and abroad (APA, 1997).

The Learner-Centered Principles, shown in Table 2.6, serve as the foundation for the Learner-Centered Model (LCM), developed over the past decade (McCombs, 2003b, 2004a; McCombs & Lauer, 1997; McCombs & Miller, 2007; McCombs & Whisler, 1997). Based on years of research, the Learner-Centered Principles were adopted by the APA (1997) as a definition of the psychological principles with the greatest positive effect on learners and learning. The fourteen learner-centered principles, organized into four categories or domains, define what is known about learning and learners as a result of research into both. Many of these principles are consistent with recent discoveries from psychology relating to positive youth development and prevention interventions (e.g., Seligman & Csikszentmihalyi, 2000).

Table 2.6   American Psychological Association (APA) Learner-Centered
Psychological Principles[1]

The following 14 psychological principles pertain to the learner and the learning process. They focus on psychological factors that are primarily internal to and under the control of the learner rather than conditioned habits or physiological factors. However, the principles also attempt to acknowledge external environment or contextual factors that interact with these internal factors.

The principles are intended to deal holistically with learners in the context of real-world learning situations. Thus, they are best understood as an organized set of principles; no principle should be viewed in isolation. The 14 principles are divided into those referring to cognitive and metacognitive, motivational and affective, developmental and social, and individual difference factors influencing learners and learning. Finally, the principles are intended to apply to all learners—from children, to teachers, to administrators, to parents, and to community members involved in our educational system.

COGNITIVE AND METACOGNITIVE FACTORS

1. Nature of the learning process. The learning of complex subject matter is most effective when it is an intentional process of constructing meaning from information and experience.

    There are different types of learning processes, for example, habit formation in motor learning; and learning that involves the generation of knowledge, or cognitive skills and learning strategies. Learning in schools emphasizes the use of intentional processes that students can use to construct meaning from information, experiences, and their own thoughts and beliefs. Successful learners are active, goal-directed, self-regulating, and assume personal responsibility for contributing to their own learning. The principles set forth in this document focus on this type of learning.

2. Goals of the learning process. The successful learner, over time and with support and instructional guidance, can create meaningful, coherent representations of knowledge.

    The strategic nature of learning requires students to be goal directed. To construct useful representations of knowledge and to acquire the thinking and learning strategies necessary for continued learning success across the life span, students must generate and pursue personally relevant goals. Initially, students' short-term goals and learning may be sketchy in an area, but over time their understanding can be refined by filling gaps, resolving inconsistencies, and deepening their understanding of the subject matter so that they can reach longer-term goals. Educators can assist learners in creating meaningful learning goals that are consistent with both personal and educational aspirations and interests.

3. Construction of knowledge. The successful learner can link new information with existing knowledge in meaningful ways.

    Knowledge widens and deepens as students continue to build links between new information and experiences and their existing knowledge base. The nature of these links can take a variety of forms, such as adding to, modifying, or reorganizing existing knowledge or skills. How these links are made or develop may vary in different subject areas, and among students with varying talents, interests, and abilities. However, unless new knowledge becomes integrated with the learner's prior knowledge and understanding, this new knowledge remains isolated, cannot be used most effectively in new tasks, and does not transfer readily to new situations. Educators can assist learners in acquiring and integrating knowledge by a number of strategies that have been shown to be effective with learners of varying abilities, such as concept mapping and thematic organization or categorizing.

(Continued)

Table 2.6   (Continued)

4. Strategic thinking. The successful learner can create and use a repertoire of thinking and reasoning strategies to achieve complex learning goals.

    Successful learners use strategic thinking in their approach to learning, reasoning, problem solving, and concept learning. They understand and can use a variety of strategies to help them reach learning and performance goals, and to apply their knowledge in novel situations. They also continue to expand their repertoire of strategies by reflecting on the methods they use to see which work well for them, by receiving guided instruction and feedback, and by observing or interacting with appropriate models. Learning outcomes can be enhanced if educators assist learners in developing, applying, and assessing their strategic learning skills.

5. Thinking about thinking. Higher order strategies for selecting and monitoring mental operations facilitate creative and critical thinking.

    Successful learners can reflect on how they think and learn, set reasonable learning or performance goals, select potentially appropriate learning strategies or methods, and monitor their progress toward these goals. In addition, successful learners know what to do if a problem occurs or if they are not making sufficient or timely progress toward a goal. They can generate alternative methods to reach their goal (or reassess the appropriateness and utility of the goal). Instructional methods that focus on helping learners develop these higher order (metacognitive) strategies can enhance student learning and personal responsibility for learning.

6. Context of learning. Learning is influenced by environmental factors, including culture, technology, and instructional practices.

    Learning does not occur in a vacuum. Teachers play a major interactive role with both the learner and the learning environment. Cultural or group influences on students can impact many educationally relevant variables, such as motivation, orientation toward learning, and ways of thinking. Technologies and instructional practices must be appropriate for learners' level of prior knowledge, cognitive abilities, and their learning and thinking strategies. The classroom environment, particularly the degree to which it is nurturing or not, can also have significant impacts on student learning.

MOTIVATIONAL AND AFFECTIVE FACTORS

1. Motivational and emotional influences on learning. What and how much is learned is influenced by the learner's motivation. Motivation to learn, in turn, is influenced by the individual's emotional states, beliefs, interests and goals, and habits of thinking.

    The rich internal world of thoughts, beliefs, goals, and expectations for success or failure can enhance or interfere with the learner's quality of thinking and information processing. Students' beliefs about themselves as learners and the nature of learning have a marked influence on motivation. Motivational and emotional factors also influence both the quality of thinking and information processing as well as an individual's motivation to learn. Positive emotions, such as curiosity, generally enhance motivation and facilitate learning and performance. Mild anxiety can also enhance learning and performance by focusing the learner's attention on a particular task. However, intense negative emotions (e.g., anxiety, panic, rage, insecurity) and related thoughts (e.g., worrying about competence, ruminating about failure, fearing punishment, ridicule, or stigmatizing labels) generally detract from motivation, interfere with learning, and contribute to low performance.

2. Intrinsic motivation to learn. The learner's creativity, higher order thinking, and natural curiosity all contribute to motivation to learn. Intrinsic motivation is stimulated by tasks of optimal novelty and difficulty, relevant to personal interests, and providing for personal choice and control.

Curiosity, flexible and insightful thinking, and creativity are major indicators of the learners' intrinsic motivation to learn, which is in large part a function of meeting basic needs to be competent and to exercise personal control. Intrinsic motivation is facilitated on tasks that learners perceive as interesting and personally relevant and meaningful, appropriate in complexity and difficulty to the learners' abilities, and on which they believe they can succeed. Intrinsic motivation is also facilitated on tasks that are comparable to real-world situations and meet needs for choice and control. Educators can encourage and support learners' natural curiosity and motivation to learn by attending to individual differences in learners' perceptions of optimal novelty and difficulty, relevance, and personal choice and control.

3. Effects of motivation on effort. Acquisition of complex knowledge and skills requires extended learner effort and guided practice. Without learners' motivation to learn, the willingness to exert this effort is unlikely without coercion.

Effort is another major indicator of motivation to learn. The acquisition of complex knowledge and skills demands the investment of considerable learner energy and strategic effort, along with persistence over time. Educators need to be concerned with facilitating motivation by strategies that enhance learner effort and commitment to learning and to achieving high standards of comprehension and understanding. Effective strategies include purposeful learning activities, guided by practices that enhance positive emotions and intrinsic motivation to learn, and methods that increase learners' perceptions that a task is interesting and personally relevant.

DEVELOPMENTAL AND SOCIAL

1. Developmental influences on learning. As individuals develop, there are different opportunities and constraints for learning. Learning is most effective when differential development within and across physical, intellectual, emotional, and social domains is taken into account.

Individuals learn best when material is appropriate to their developmental level and is presented in an enjoyable and interesting way. Because individual development varies across intellectual, social, emotional, and physical domains, achievement in different instructional domains may also vary. Overemphasis on one type of developmental readiness—such as reading readiness, for example—may preclude learners from demonstrating that they are more capable in other areas of performance. The cognitive, emotional, and social development of individual learners and how they interpret life experiences are affected by prior schooling, home, culture, and community factors. Early and continuing parental involvement in schooling, and the quality of language interactions and two-way communications between adults and children can influence these developmental areas. Awareness and understanding of developmental differences among children with and without emotional, physical, or intellectual disabilities, can facilitate the creation of optimal learning contexts.

2. Social influences on learning. Learning is influenced by social interactions, interpersonal relations, and communication with others.

Learning can be enhanced when the learner has an opportunity to interact and to collaborate with others on instructional tasks. Learning settings that allow for social interactions, and that respect diversity, encourage flexible thinking and social competence. In interactive and collaborative instructional contexts, individuals have an opportunity for perspective taking and reflective thinking that may lead to higher levels of cognitive, social, and moral development, as well as self-esteem. Quality personal relationships that provide stability, trust, and caring can increase learners' sense of belonging, self-respect and self-acceptance, and provide a positive climate for learning. Family influences, positive interpersonal support, and instruction in self-motivation strategies can offset factors that interfere with optimal learning such as negative beliefs about competence in a particular subject, high levels of

(Continued)

Table 2.6 (Continued)

test anxiety, negative sex role expectations, and undue pressure to perform well. Positive learning climates can also help to establish the context for healthier levels of thinking, feeling, and behaving. Such contexts help learners feel safe to share ideas, actively participate in the learning process, and create a learning community.

INDIVIDUAL DIFFERENCES

1. Individual differences in learning. Learners have different strategies, approaches, and capabilities for learning that are a function of prior experience and heredity.

    Individuals are born with and develop their own capabilities and talents. In addition, through learning and social acculturation, they have acquired their own preferences for how they like to learn and the pace at which they learn. However, these preferences are not always useful in helping learners reach their learning goals. Educators need to help students examine their learning preferences and expand or modify them, if necessary. The interaction between learner differences and curricular and environmental conditions is another key factor affecting learning outcomes. Educators need to be sensitive to individual differences, in general. They also need to attend to learner perceptions of the degree to which these differences are accepted and adapted to by varying instructional methods and materials.

2. Learning and diversity. Learning is most effective when differences in learners' linguistic, cultural, and social backgrounds are taken into account.

    The same basic principles of learning, motivation, and effective instruction apply to all learners. However, language, ethnicity, race, beliefs, and socioeconomic status all can influence learning. Careful attention to these factors in the instructional setting enhances the possibilities for designing and implementing appropriate learning environments. When learners perceive that their individual differences in abilities, backgrounds, cultures, and experiences are valued, respected, and accommodated in learning tasks and contexts, levels of motivation and achievement are enhanced.

3. Standards and assessment. Setting appropriately high and challenging standards and assessing the learner as well as learning progress—including diagnostic, process, and outcome assessment—are integral parts of the learning process.

    Assessment provides important information to both the learner and teacher at all stages of the learning process. Effective learning takes place when learners feel challenged to work toward appropriately high goals; therefore, appraisal of the learner's cognitive strengths and weaknesses, as well as current knowledge and skills, is important for the selection of instructional materials of an optimal degree of difficulty. Ongoing assessment of the learner's understanding of the curricular material can provide valuable feedback to both learners and teachers about progress toward the learning goals. Standardized assessment of learner progress and outcomes assessment provides one type of information about achievement levels both within and across individuals that can inform various types of programmatic decisions. Performance assessments can provide other sources of information about the attainment of learning outcomes. Self-assessments of learning progress can also improve students' self-appraisal skills and enhance motivation and self-directed learning.

Source: Center for Psychology in Schools and Education, APA Education Directorate, 750 First Street, N.E., Washington, DC 20002, Contact: Greg White, Program Officer, Phone: (202) 336-5855.

[1] The development of each principle involved thorough discussions of the research supporting that principle. The multidisciplinary research expertise of the Task Force and Work Group members facilitated an examination of each principle from a number of different research perspectives.

The Learner-Centered Principles apply to all learners, in and outside of school, young and old. Research underlying the Learner-Centered Principles confirms that learning is nonlinear, recursive, continuous, complex, relational, and natural in humans. The evidence also shows that learning is enhanced in contexts where learners have supportive relationships, have a sense of ownership and control over the learning process, and can learn with and from each other in safe and trusting learning environments (McCombs, 2003b, 2004a). The key processes involved in developing learner-centered principles and practices are:

- building ways to meet learner needs for interpersonal relationships and connections;
- finding strategies that acknowledge individual differences and the diversity of learner needs, abilities, and interests;
- tailoring strategies to differing learner needs for personal control and choice; and
- assessing the efficacy of instructional practices to meet diverse and emerging individual learner and learning community needs.

Part of developing the Learner-Centered Principles involved looking for the match or mismatch of instructional practices with learning principles, as well as their match or mismatch with learners and their diverse needs. Once these matches and mismatches are identified, a balance of supports can then be provided with a variety of learning opportunities, content requirements, and communities of learning.

When the Learner-Centered Principles are applied to schools and classrooms, they address each of four learning domains, which we describe in the next paragraph. The resulting Learner-Centered Model (LCM) provides a systemic approach to content, context, assessment, and individual learner needs and potential. In addition, basing educational practices on the Learner-Centered Model and its associated Learner-Centered Principles provides a means for transforming education. The role of teachers changes to that of co-learners and contributors to the social and interpersonal development of students. In partnership with their teachers, students become responsible for their own learning and participate equally in determining what, how, and when they learn. The learner-centered framework adds a constant reminder that the human element cannot be left out of even the most advanced educational systems, including technology-supported networked learning communities (cf. McCombs & Vakili, 2005).

Taken together, the four domains of the Learner-Centered Principles offer a holistic way of viewing how the individual principles combine and interact to influence learners and learning. The Learner-Centered Principles reflect four domains:

- *Cognitive and metacognitive*: the intellectual capacities of learners and how they facilitate the learning process;
- *Motivational and affective*: the roles played by motivation and emotions in learning;

- *Developmental and social*: the influence of various, diverse aspects of learner development, and the importance of interpersonal interactions in learning and change;
- *Individual differences*: how individual differences influence learning, how teachers, students, and administrators adapt to learning diversity, and how standards and assessments can best support individual differences in learners.

Each of the four domains affects each learner in a unique way, as does the synergy resulting from the interaction of the domains.

Putting learners first is at the heart of learner-centered teaching. It requires knowing individual learners and providing a safe and nurturing learning environment before the job of teaching can begin. Teachers who engage in learner-centered teaching also understand that learning is a natural, lifelong process, and that motivation to learn is also natural when the learning context is supportive. If these teachers see evidence that students are not learning or do not seem motivated to learn, they do not blame the student (or the parents). To discover what may be causing the lack of motivation or learning, they look at what is *not* happening in the teaching and learning process or in the learning context and devise ways to remedy the problem(s).

Learner-centered teachers know that listening to students provides a blueprint for finding the most effective practices and for engaging students' voices in the process of learning. They encourage students to talk about how they would meet their own learning needs, satisfy their natural curiosity, and make sense of things. Our research, as well others', confirms that there are fundamental qualities of teachers that are essential to their ability to provide learner-centered practices in ways that authentically respond to student learning, motivation, and social needs. In the remainder of this chapter, we describe those qualities in the context of learning environments that we have discovered best support learners.

A LEARNER-CENTERED EDUCATIONAL MODEL

For centuries educators have been arguing that a one-size-fits-all model that standardizes curriculum and enforces testing violates biological and ecological principles. What does seem to work are alternatives based on systems theory and an ecology of learning, which we discussed briefly in Chapter 1 and earlier in this chapter. In our work with the Learner-Centered Principles, we have learned that learner-centered practices do not look the same from school to school, classroom to classroom, day to day, or even moment to moment within the same classroom. When teachers are attentive to learners and their learning needs, and when they understand basic principles of human learning, motivation, development, and individual differences, they "go with the flow" and create innovative environments that are flexible and dynamic. Teachers and school administrators we have studied who are the most learner-centered are not afraid to share power and control with students in a collaborative learning partnership (McCombs & Miller, 2007).

When translated into practice, the Learner-Centered Model consists of a variety of materials, guided reflection, and assessment tools that support teacher and administrator effectiveness and change at the individual and school levels. As support for changing their practices, our research (McCombs, 2004b; McCombs & Lauer, 1997, 1998; McCombs & Whisler, 1997) has produced a set of self-assessment and reflection tools for K–20 educators, called the Assessment of Learner-Centered Practices (ALCP). The ALCP includes surveys—for teachers, students, and administrators—that facilitate reflection and a willingness to change instructional practices. The teacher and administrator surveys offer an opportunity for reflection on how personal beliefs about learners, learning, and teaching coincide with the knowledge base underlying the Learner-Centered Principles. At the school level, they allow administrators and teachers to see the discrepancies between what they value and what they perceive to be actually in place in eight key areas of school functioning. At the classroom level, the ALCP surveys allow teachers to become aware of their students' perceptions about the frequency of their teacher's learner-centered practices. In addition, we have developed staff development workshops and videos that illustrate the learner-centered practices in diverse school settings.

In our more than fifteen years of research with the Learner-Centered Model and its associated tools, we have verified the benefits of learner-centered practices at the school and classroom levels. Research with the ALCP self-assessment surveys for teachers and students confirms that "learner-centeredness" is not solely a function of particular instructional practices or programs. Rather, learner-centeredness is a complex interaction of the programs, practices, policies, and people as perceived by the individual learners. That is, how teachers are perceived (their qualities and characteristics) as well as how instructional practices are implemented in terms of meeting student learning needs, defines learner-centeredness. Ongoing data of over 35,000 students and their teachers in kindergarten through graduate school have now been collected with the ALCP surveys (McCombs, 2001a/b; McCombs & Lauer, 1997; McCombs & Pierce, 1999; McCombs & Quiat, 2002) to evaluate programs and practices that enhance the teaching and learning process.

In our research (McCombs, 2004a/b), the qualities related to being perceived by students as engaging in high levels of learner-centered practice in domains most related to high achievement and motivation include

- high learner-centered beliefs (consistent with the APA principles) versus low non-learner-centered beliefs (more traditional);
- high levels of self-efficacy about their ability to reach and teach diverse learners;
- high reflective self-awareness; and
- high degrees of support for autonomy.

In schools and districts where the Learner-Centered Principles have been widely shared and implemented, teaching practices are achieving a more balanced approach that encourages high student learning and achievement, while also promoting learner-centered approaches. These approaches, recognized in many of the nation's most excellent schools, lead to effective schooling and to positive mental health and productivity of our nation's children, their teachers, and the systems that serve them. A summary of our results follows (from McCombs, 2007).

Grades K–3 Results

The most important finding with K–3 teachers and students is that even young children can reliably and validly assess the degree to which their teachers engage in learner-centered practices. For young children, our evidence shows that there are three types of teacher practices that correlate most closely to positive learning and motivation outcomes:

1. creates positive interpersonal relationships/climate;
2. provides motivational support for learning; and
3. facilitates thinking and learning.

Our results indicate that, when students perceived more learner-centered teacher practices, they had higher academic achievement and also reported greater interest in and liking of school and academic subjects (McCombs, Daniels, & Perry, 2008).

Grades 4–8 Results

With upper elementary and middle school students, learner-centered practices begin to have even stronger impacts on learning and motivation. Four types of teacher practice have been shown to most impact learning, motivational, and behavior outcomes:

1. creating positive relationships;
2. honoring student voice;
3. supporting higher order thinking and learning skills; and
4. adapting to individual differences (McCombs & Quiat, 2002; McCombs, 2004b; Meece, Herman, & McCombs, 2003).

At this developmental stage, students' perceptions of classroom practices are more strongly related to valued outcomes than to teachers' perceptions.

Grades 9–12 Results

For high school students, the importance and effects of learner-centered practices increase. At this level, although our research tool contains different items from the instrument used for the grade 4–8 level, the same four types of practices identified in the grades 4–8 level emerge (McCombs, 2004b). Our

findings show that students' perceptions that their teachers frequently perform the four types of learner-centered classroom practices are significantly
correlated with all motivation variables, and are particularly highly related
to student self-efficacy, epistemic (knowledge-seeking) curiosity, active learning strategies, and task mastery goals. In addition, students' perceptions that
their teachers significantly perform these four types of practices are positively correlated with classroom achievement and negatively correlated with
classroom absences.

College Level Results

For college students who are capable of further differentiating domains of
practice that are most significantly related to their motivation, learning, and
retention in higher education, our research (McCombs, 2003, 2004b; McCombs
& Pierce, 1999; Pierce, Holt, Kolar, & McCombs, 2004) has shown that there are
five domains of practice, ordered in terms of their empirical relationships to
desired student outcomes as follows:

1. establishing positive interpersonal relationships;
2. facilitating the learning process;
3. adapting to class learning needs;
4. encouraging personal challenge and responsibility; and
5. providing for individual and social learning needs.

What is significant across all levels of schooling is that the relational domain—
practices that establish positive student-teacher and student-student relationships
along with a positive climate for learning—is essential to being learner-centered
in the eyes of students. This domain of practice actually increases in importance
as students get older and the system becomes less and less about them.

WHAT ARE THE NEW NOTIONS OF
SCHOOLING AS PART OF LIVING SYSTEMS?

One of the strongest implications of the Learner-Centered Principles and
Learner-Centered Model is that education must address the whole learner. This
is certainly not a new idea. Many educators have advocated for holistic education models (e.g., Combs, 1986, 1991; Noddings, 2005). However, the evidence
base for addressing the whole learner was less clear in earlier years than it is
now, making the current case stronger in terms of positive outcomes that extend
beyond academic achievement. Noddings argues that schools were established
as much for moral and social reasons as for academic instruction, that they are
established to serve both individuals and the larger society. This means that we
want not only competent workers but graduates with sound character, social
conscience, the ability to think critically, and an awareness of global problems.
Noddings further argues that, to sustain our democracy, schools need to help
develop thoughtful citizens who can make wise civic choices.

Eisner (2005) also believes that current policies, which are focused on having clear outcomes defined by measurable standards so we can measure performance and hold schools and teachers accountable, are highly rational with logical. The problem is that these policies narrow the vision of education and deal only with intellectual capacities, neglecting the social and emotional qualities of students and situations. They promote a technical rather than organic, humanistic, or personal orientation to teaching that does not work well with living beings. Eisner argues we need to return to the vision of progressive education, as formulated by Dewey (1938), that recognized the distinctive talents of individual children and created environments to actualize those potentialities. This vision means that teachers and school leaders should design experiences that allow students to respond not just in cognitive ways, but also emotionally, imaginatively, and socially. It also means that assessment should focus on more than academic outcomes and include assessments of students' development in all these areas.

The primary issue in educating the whole child is mental health and mental hygiene. The basic argument supporting holistic education is that in human organisms, there are no independent parts; all are interconnected (Eisner, 2005). Kohn (2005) argues that, because of the uniqueness of each human being, we must accept each learner for whom they are rather than what they do because we run the risk of valuing some capabilities more than others. Kohn cites research that, when compared with students whose support from teachers is conditional, students who feel unconditionally accepted by their teachers are more interested in learning and enjoy challenging tasks. However, when teachers are under pressure to raise scores on tests that measure only the narrow curriculum of math and reading, those students who do well are usually valued more than those who do poorly. As a result, children get the message that their worth is conditional on their performance. Further, they come to understand that they are acceptable only under certain conditions, which can lead to mental health issues, striving to be someone teachers and parents will love, or rebelling in some way against what they perceive as an unfair and unbalanced system.

A Leadership Challenge

A challenge for school leaders is to capture these best practice principles in an educational systems design that prepares all learners (students and adults alike) to be lifelong learners and develop their full potentials in life. These new systems carry a much higher potential to result in a more competent, more productive, more collaborative, and more creative cadre of people who can make significant changes to existing and outdated systems in all aspects of our lives, not just the educational. To be leaders in such a movement requires all of us to be the best that we can be and to use the tools of reflection, rethinking, and renewing that are part of an ecology of learning in living systems. We believe that using learner-centered leadership practices can transform schools into networked communities of learners, in a learning partnership that is part of a continuous learning and improvement process for all those involved, not just students.

What the Evidence Tells Us About
Leadership as Part of a Transformation Process

Community building and relationships are the essence of learner-centered leadership practices. Wheatley and Frieze's (2007) new science findings indicate that the world changes because of networks of relationships formed among people who share a common vision of what's possible and/or a common cause. It does not change one person at a time, as some contend. Wheatley and Frieze point out that networks are important because they are just the beginning of the change process and must evolve into intentional working relationships that allow for the emergence of new knowledge, practices, and renewal of commitment. One example of the kind of network that can lead to change through the workings of its relationships is "Communities of Practice," in which a group of people work together over a period of time to solve problems or create innovations.

Over time (not necessarily long), the relationships in networks create ideas, solutions, and innovations; a process that is described as *emergence*. Those who study Communities of Practice believe that what emerges from the networks that form within these communities is responsible for all large-scale change in our world (e.g., Jain & Stilger, 2007). From local efforts that connect with other separate efforts, interactions and interdependences are strengthened. A "system of influence" becomes possible, which then can produce powerful cultural shifts. Within learner-centered systems, leaders form a networked learning community within which learners—students, teachers, other school staff, families, community members—form relationships and networks, to collaborate in a way that serves everyone involved. Leaders in these communities not only distribute leadership among all key constituents in the educational system; they empower each individually *and* the community as a networked learning system to engage in a lifelong learning process of continuous growth and improvement.

SELF-REFLECTIONS

At this point, you may be ready for a deep breath and a bit of time to digest what you've read, especially if some or all of what you've read so far is new information. Because taking time for self-reflection is a way to refresh and renew your own thinking and practices, we invite you to take a moment now to reflect on what you've read. You may wish to journal your thoughts as you think about the questions in Box 2.3. You may also wish to compare your responses to the earlier exercises in this chapter with what you write for the exercise in Box 2.3.

Box 2.3   What Kind of Leader Are You: 2

---

1.   How would you describe your leadership style?

2.   Thinking back on your responses to the questions in Box 2.1, do you see any clues regarding your leadership practices? If yes, what are they? (Just jot down single words—or whatever comes into your mind first.)

3.   In your current leadership position, do you incorporate any elements of a Community of Practice? List them.

4.   For what are students valued most in your school/district/area?

5.   What are the biggest problems you see in your school/district/area? List them.

WHAT'S NEXT

In the next chapter, we turn to what the Learner-Centered Model means for practice in schools. We explore the tools needed for your journey into learner-centered leadership. We discuss a variety of ways to incorporate the Learner-Centered Model and the Learner-Centered Principles, and provide examples of eight types of practices and how they translate into rural, suburban, and urban school contexts. We explore the implications of the Learner-Centered Model and Learner-Centered Principles for leadership, particularly the building of networked communities of learners. Like this chapter, Chapter 3 continues with exercises designed to help you think about and reflect on the ideas and tools you are reading about.

3

What the Learner-Centered Model Means for Practice

Ethos, understood as a metaphor for change, indicates that transforming the past by developing principals' [leaders', in our terminology] capacities for risk and imagination as they reshape their identities and reconstruct schools in tune with 21st-century needs is a challenge to principals in general as they navigate between past, present, and future.

…However, if ethos is understood as a metaphor for change, where beliefs, attitudes, and values are core components of the moral enterprise of schooling, then creating real-time learning opportunities for principals that are sustained over time is an essential dimension of their professional learning so that change and continuity are embraced as a secure and sure-footed means of risk-taking in the process of imagining alternative teaching and learning for themselves, their colleagues, and pupils.

—C. Sugrue & C. Furlong (2004, pp. 189 and 204)

Sugrue and Furlong (2004) go on to say that a major challenge in leadership is to fundamentally change the organization of schooling. Ongoing learning and inquiry into teaching and learning in the context of the common good needs to be the top priority against which concerns about a delivery system are secondary. A balance and harmony must be achieved between the past, present, and future iterations of schooling. This is particularly true in times when good leaders are hard to find. For example, Guterman (2007) provides an inside look at why there is a current shortage of qualified school principals. He reports that, in a national poll by the National Association of Elementary School Principals, the top factors that discourage teachers from pursuing the principal's job are that (1) the compensation is insufficient for the responsibilities (fifty-eight percent), (2) too much time is required for the job (twenty-five percent), and (3) the job is too stressful (twenty-three percent).

What will it take to attract and inspire fresh leaders for a different role in learning and leading the process of schooling? We believe it will take someone who feels called to make a difference in an emerging new model of schooling. We also believe it will take potential leaders having a true understanding of what it means to "learn" and "lead" in these new times. Further, as we argued in Chapter 2, it will take leaders who thoroughly understand what the scientific evidence base now has confirmed about the nature of learning and leading in ecologically interdependent systems of networks and relationships. In short, it will take people authentically committed to putting learners and learning at the core of schooling and designing delivery systems that stem naturally from that core. It will also take people with trust in the natural learning capacities and the ability of all stakeholders, including students, to join together in developing systems that nourish all learners. These systems will be sustained because of the meaningful relationships and networks of support that are created by the resulting community of learners.

Before we further our discussion of what it means to be a learner-centered leader, we invite you to continue your investigation into your own preferences and habits as a learner by responding to the items in Box 3.1. Take a moment to jot down your responses, again ignoring the letters in parentheses following each response choice.

As we indicated in Chapter 2, we'll continue to expand on the exercises in each chapter so you can build a detailed description of yourself as a learner and leader. In the final chapter, you'll have an opportunity to apply what you've learned about yourself and about leadership as we describe it in this book.

WHAT IT MEANS TO BE A LEARNER-CENTERED LEADER

We began to explore this question in Chapter 2 and now want to examine this question in further depth. Our review and synthesis of the research and our decades of combined experience in working with preK–12 systems and colleges have convinced us that a learner-centered leader has very special qualities not found in all school administrators (cf. McCombs & Miller, 2007). We have found that the best leaders share the set of qualities Art Combs (1974, 1986) identified in the best teachers, who

- are highly reflective;
- believe they can make a difference with all kinds of learners;
- see teaching and learning as a partnership between teachers and their students;

Box 3.1   How Do I Prefer to Learn: 3

29. To decide what I want to do on my day off, I:
     a. think about what I like to do. (ra)
     b. ask other people what they want to do. (er)
     c. make a list of things to do. (lo)
     d. see what my body feels like doing. (p)
     e. read about available activities. (li)

30. When going places I have never been before, I want:
     a. a map. (s)
     b. written directions in sequential order. (lo)
     c. verbal directions. (li)
     d. to have someone else help me. (er)
     e. a mileage chart. (qu)

31. The first thing I notice in a movie is:
     a. music. (mu)
     b. dialogue. (li)
     c. cinematography. (s)
     d. relationships among characters. (er)
     e. the comfort of the seats. (p)

32. I decide which movie theater to go to based on:
     a. its sound system (i.e., THX, Lucas Sound, etc.). (mu)
     b. proximity to other errands or events. (lo)
     c. price. (qu)
     d. quality and choice of the concessions. (p)
     e. the quietness of the crowd. (ra)

33. I choose my haircutting salon or barber because:
     a. I can make an appointment in advance. (lo)
     b. no one bothers me. (ra)
     c. I like how they massage my head. (p)
     d. they play music I like. (mu)
     e. the surroundings are pleasing to look at. (s)

34. I exercise because:
     a. I need to move my body. (p)
     b. I like to interact with others. (er)
     c. it gives me time to contemplate. (ra)
     d. I can listen to music. (mu)
     e. it is a part of my daily routine. (lo)

35. For the holidays that I celebrate, I most enjoy:
     a. the decorations. (s)
     b. the music. (mu)
     c. the spirituality of the event. (ra)
     d. planning the activities. (lo)
     e. getting together with my family and friends. (er)

(Continued)

Box 3.1   (Continued)

36.   I choose the music I listen to because:
      a. I personally like it. (ra)
      b. it is cool. (er)
      c. I like the lyrics. (li)
      d. it makes me want to dance. (p)
      e. I enjoy the complexity of the piece. (mu)

37.   I like to figure out the sale price of an item by:
      a. asking a sales associate. (er)
      b. calculating it in my head. (qu)
      c. using a calculator. (lo)
      d. talking myself through the "problem." (li)
      e. visualizing the "problem." (s)

38.   If I could choose a job, I would want one that:
      a. makes me feel good about myself. (ra)
      b. allows me to work with others. (er)
      c. doesn't keep me stuck at a desk. (p)
      d. lets me listen to music. (mu)
      e. lets me work with numbers. (qu)

39.   I want friends who:
      a. respect my privacy. (ra)
      b. share their feelings. (er)
      c. enjoy talking. (li)
      d. engage in physical activities. (p)
      e. share an interest in music. (mu)

40.   I select jewelry because:
      a. other people admire it. (er)
      b. it has sentimental value. (ra)
      c. it is visually attractive. (s)
      d. it is a good investment. (qu)
      e. it feels good on my skin. (p)

41.   The first thing I notice about a book is:
      a. its cover. (s)
      b. how much it costs. (qu)
      c. the writing. (li)
      d. what it helps me discover about myself. (ra)
      e. the review or recommendation of the book. (er)

42.   I get my primary information through:
      a. editorial cartoons or comics. (s)
      b. studying a subject by myself. (ra)
      c. newspapers, books, or radio. (li)
      d. internet blogs. (er)
      e. MTV or other music channels. (mu)

43. If I could buy any car I wanted, I would choose it because:
     a. it is functional and practical. (lo)
     b. it looks attractive. (s)
     c. it has a great sound system. (mu)
     d. it is physically comfortable. (p)
     e. it's a good value for the price. (qu)

44. When looking at vacation photos, I notice:
     a. how I can organize them. (lo)
     b. the quality of the photograph. (s)
     c. myself and how I look. (ra)
     d. the proportion of acceptable pictures. (qu)
     e. the people in the photos. (er)

45. What would influence my choice in buying a new sofa:
     a. others' opinions. (er)
     b. its comfort. (p)
     c. how well it looks with the rest of my furniture. (s)
     d. how well the dimensions fit in my home. (qu)
     e. its warranty and value. (lo)

46. If I were to plan a job change, I would first:
     a. make a list of pros and cons. (lo)
     b. take time to think about it. (ra)
     c. compare the salary and benefits to those of my current job. (qu)
     d. exercise to relieve stress. (p)
     e. consult with family and/or friends. (er)

47. I pick a rental movie:
     a. with another person. (er)
     b. by myself. (ra)
     c. because it is classified in a certain section, such as new releases or comedy. (lo)
     d. because I like the music. (mu)
     e. because I like the cover. (s)

48. If I were to buy computer software for relaxation or play, I would buy:
     a. image editing software. (s)
     b. game(s) I can play with other players. (er)
     c. spreadsheet software. (qu)
     d. chess. (lo)
     e. Scrabble®. (li)

49. If I were to learn a foreign language, I would choose to because:
     a. I like learning grammar. (lo)
     b. it might help me understand another culture. (er)
     c. I enjoy learning. (ra)
     d. I am attracted to how it sounds. (mu)
     e. I love language. (li)

Note: The meanings of the abbreviations can be found in Chapter 5, pp. 142–143.

- believe students should have choices and be responsible for their own learning;
- care about students and making a difference in their learning process and progress;
- are passionate about the work they are doing; and
- are experts in their fields of study.

In addition, we have learned that the best leaders also understand how all people, including children, learn, and know that leading often includes providing support for others to lead the way. Reeves (2006) contends that the most important thing school leaders need to know is how to create a team with complementary strengths. A diverse team makes decision making less risky and distributes the leadership among different talents and strengths. Reeves says (p. 28), "Distributed leadership is based on trust, as well as the certain knowledge that no single leader possesses the knowledge, skills, and talent to lead an organization..."

The Issue of Sustainable Leadership

In discussing the qualities of leadership that result in a sustainable, learner-centered model, Lambert (2005) reported on her study of fifteen schools across this country and one in Canada. Each school included a system of shared governance and distributed leadership. Their culture was vision-driven, student-focused, and concerned with improvements in inquiry-based student performance. Lambert reported that the shared characteristics of principals at these schools included

- an understanding of self and clarity of values;
- a strong belief in equity and the democratic process;
- strategic thought about the evolution of school improvement;
- a vulnerable persona;
- knowledge of the work of teaching and learning; and
- the ability to develop capacity in colleagues and in the organization (p. 63).

Sustainability, at its heart, is about trust among all the stakeholders in the school. Blankstein (2007) believes that the central issue for sustainability is courageous leadership in which the leader gets to the core issues by asking deeper questions about moral purpose and by organizing people around a shared common purpose. In his view, courageous leaders are inclusive and committed to creating opportunities for communication and for sharing their realities and dreams, which produces the emotional connections and shared responsibility that lead to desired learning outcomes.

Further, Blankstein (2007) believes that the work of everyone in the school is a problem-solving endeavor focused on sustaining success for all students. To achieve this ongoing success, everyone involved needs to develop and maintain the relationships necessary to engage all learners—students, teachers, administrators, and parents—through

- building caring connections;
- defining personal relevance;
- empowering learners through choices;
- increasing opportunities for success;
- providing immediate and accurate feedback; and
- providing multiple ways to recognize and celebrate successes.

Schools as Moral Communities

A second issue new school leaders will need to address is changing how they—and others—perceive the way schools are organized. For instance, Sergiovanni (2007) believes leaders need to see schools as social organizations and moral communities rather than formal organizations. In viewing schools as social organizations, leaders focus on shared orientations, shared beliefs, and networks of social relations. Leaders who see schools as moral communities focus not on bureaucratic and personal authority but on moral authority. They see schools as learning and caring communities with cultures of traditions, rituals, and norms that define their character and competence. These leaders protect and promote the institutional values that arise because, out of these values, a shared commitment, connection, and moral authority emerge. In schools that are moral communities, the leader helps facilitate moral connections among all learners and helps them all to become self-managing. According to Sergiovanni, this type of leadership communicates that all teachers and staff are respected, autonomous, committed, and capable, as well as morally responsible for making the school work better for its students.

Because this moral view of leadership is based on cultural norms rather than on individual psychological needs (e.g., intrinsic and extrinsic rewards), the result is a different kind of leadership—one that aims for stewardship, service, and ideas. Ideas—such as sustainability—becomes an active leadership approach that can be continued and maintained through commitment, relationships, and trust. And, because ideas can endure beyond specific people in any leadership roles or positions, they can be continued for a long period of time.

One of the most important aspects of moral leadership is passion, which Sugrue (2005) sees as the individual and collective emotional commitment to learning that can focus on continuity and purpose rather than the complex choices and demands of the position. Sugrue believes that passion is the fuel that can help leaders reshape schools to provide what is needed in developing potential in all learners. He further argues that leaders need to understand that nothing important happens quickly and that school leaders need to adopt a personality of change that is passionately committed to knowing oneself, the context, the ideas from the wider community, and the skills that are important at different points in the lifecycle of change. As in any changing system, it will become more and more important that all leaders continually create learning opportunities designed to develop and sustain future leaders in a flexible manner.

Navigating the Political and Policy Environment

Many researchers and scholars acknowledge that the new leadership models may be difficult to implement within the current educational paradigm, and they are urging educators to move beyond prescriptive standards, subject-centered coverage, and high-stakes testing to achieve enhanced and sustained levels of student learning. For example, Hargreaves, Earl, Moore, and Manning (2001) describe the difficulties of making needed changes within an opposing policy environment and stress that leaders need to take these difficulties into account as they try to effect changes. Hargreaves et al (2001). point out that, even when teachers are empowered to embark on needed changes, to be effective, leaders will need to (1) support and sometimes push teachers to implement those changes that matter, (2) take the steps necessary to ensure that teacher changes will be sustained over time, and (3) generalize the changes beyond a few teachers such that they affect the whole system. Table 3.1 lists some of the most essential changes that need to be made, along with some of the most effective support strategies. It is also important to understand that Hargreaves et al. also found that heavy-handed and imposed strategies do not work and actually cause teachers to withdraw their interest and investments in change and learning.

Table 3.1   Essential Changes and Support Strategies

Essential Changes	Essential Support Strategies
Involve students and parents in specifying the outcomes and competencies desired through the schooling process.	Build capacity to help teachers gain the knowledge, skills, dispositions, and views of self that help sustain continuous change and improvement.
Find ways to assess these outcomes and competencies.	Create professional communities that can learn together and support each other over time.
Build the integrated curriculum that will accomplish these goals in meaningful and useful ways.	Create cross-department, multi-disciplinary teacher teams that work together to achieve the desired outcomes and competencies.

Hargreaves et al. (2001) found that, in addition to providing teachers with the support necessary for them to grapple with the changes needed to change their school in ways that result in success for all learners, effective leaders give teachers the professional discretion to design their lessons and curricula in ways they think are best. For transformational and empowering leaders, it is a moral imperative to encourage professionals to be professional and to design for themselves rather than having others impose designs on them. In their research, Hargreaves et al. reported that the kinds of leadership support most desired by teachers were

- *intellectual leadership*—help in interpreting, translating, and articulating policy directions that would support their own intellectual work of change;
- *cultural and emotional leadership*—support to build collaborative work cultures, make the necessary structural changes in scheduling, and take risks by trying new things; and
- *strategic leadership*—providing the human and material resources necessary for their change efforts, including in-service workshops and conferences. In other words, providing teachers the time to plan and see other kinds of exemplary practices that energize and empower them to go beyond standards and standardization.

Hargreaves et al.'s (2001) study of teachers also concluded that effective leaders understand that teaching involves more than technical expertise; it also involves the social mission of education and the emotional bonds that teachers have with their students that gives meaning to their work. Good teachers develop students as learners, future workers, and developing citizens; they cultivate their emotional development as well as their intellectual and social development. Good leaders support and encourage teachers in all these aspects of their work, not just the technical.

Being an Exceptional Leader

A major characteristic of exceptional school leadership is preparing teacher-leaders. Gabriel (2005) describes the charge of teacher-leaders as

- influencing school culture;
- building and maintaining a successful team;
- equipping other potential teacher leaders; and
- enhancing or improving student achievement.

To accomplish these tasks, teacher-leaders need to be skillful communicators, know how to create a positive climate, and know how to develop a sense of community. It is also important that teacher-leaders know how to let go of control and to trust in the self-organizing principles of humans as they create a community of relationships. Effective leaders at all levels know that they are teachers as well as learners (Gabriel).

Wheatley and Frieze (2007) describe how the "Culture of High Stakes Testing" that emerged from NCLB was largely the old paradigm, which was based on creating a culture of achievement for all students using traditional change theory. In the old paradigm and traditional change theory, change is top down, happens step-by-step, can be mandated, and uses rewards and punishments to motivate people to change. As a result, the opposite of what was intended has occurred. The authors contend this is because change always happens through emergence and cannot be mandated in plans or strategies from on high. When small local actions begin to have powerful effects, known as emergent phenomena, new levels of capacity are built that have more power and influence than are present in separate, isolated efforts. Because they are constantly changing, emergent phenomena can't be predetermined, and system-wide change must begin by working locally.

Wheatley and Frieze (2007) suggest that leaders encourage local experi-ments, watch for and nourish supportive beliefs and community-building efforts, and encourage building connections with those who tend to work in isolation. Strengthening connections is one of the main roles of leaders—some-thing to which they need to bring institutional resources, opportunities for staff to think together and reflect on what they are learning, and ways to expand the web with new and different people.

Moving Into the Unknown

The Berkana Institute (2007), using the work of Margaret Wheatley and others, describes emergence as the process through which life creates radical change and systems of great power and influence, in contrast to more out-dated approaches that are based on planned, incremental change. Berkana has studied how emergence moves from people connecting as interdependent networks, to more intentionally working together in communities of practice, to more powerful systems of influence that result in large-scale change. That, they see, is the work of the new leader: helping to set the process of emergence in motion and nurturing its growth. From Margaret Wheatley's work over the years, Berkana has learned there are important and powerful questions that leaders can use to focus intention and energy. On their Web site, The Art of Hosting lists some potential questions, contributed in part by The Berkana Institute, on how to convene conversations:

- What gnaws at you?
- What do you care about deeply?
- How do you bring out the paradox without creating a polarity?
- How do you live with it over time?
- How do I slay the dragon of my fear?
- How do I practice what I feel?
- If I were born with a question, what would it be?
- What is sacred to you? (www.artofhosting.org/thepractice/goodques-tions/ Retrieved July 25, 2007)

What is exciting to us is the recent announcement in Britain that the gov-ernment is unveiling a new 21st-century curriculum where teachers will be given greater freedom to depart from the national subject-based curriculum (Garner, 2007). For students eleven to sixteen years old, teachers will now be able to facilitate the introduction of topics that prepare these students for adult life in the 21st century. Students will be able to learn relevant topics, making their own choices from a list of topics, and proceeding at their own speed. There will be an emphasis on creative writing and the development of teacher leadership to differentiate instruction and provide catch-up lessons in English and math, with the new time being made available through the reduction in traditional prescriptives "covering the curriculum."

Understanding How Change Really Happens in Living Systems

We understand that some (or maybe many) of you reading this book are already leaders in systems that are badly in need of major changes in order to become consistent with what we know about human nature and learning. We also know that, if this is the case, you will have to do the best you can, armed with information such as the work described in the previous section, to make the changes necessary to offset the damages of the current educational paradigm. Our major focus, however, is to help you dream big and to help those who feel called to be leaders of a major change in that paradigm to join with us and others who have already begun to define what this paradigm change looks like. So, before we begin to delve more deeply into what the Learner-Centered Model means for practice—and leadership practices in particular—we invite you to consider more thoroughly new evidence about the paradigm we need and how change actually happens in individuals and in systems.

Failures and Crises as Learning Opportunities

In an era when educational leaders must help transform an outdated paradigm, Farson (2007) makes the important point that leaders must recognize that failure is a necessary part of the process because it leads to innovation. The new leader must encourage risk-taking and failure that can lead to the kind of creative and authentic learning we care about—without punishing or penalizing failure. For Farson, the new education paradigm must make people different and not alike. It must marry each person's experience to important concepts and avoid standardization and evaluation in favor of engagement. Leaders in the new paradigm will be able to understand the natural coexistence of opposites and go in seemingly opposite directions at once in order to innovate and find even better solutions.

In understanding the need for a transformed educational paradigm, Houston (2007) describes the problem as one in which dissatisfaction with schools centers around the fact that only incremental progress has been made in reforming them despite the fact that all other things around them are exponentially changing. We need new leaders to build bridges for people to cross from where they are to where they need to be. Houston sees us moving from not only an industrial age to an information age, but also from a fast-ending information age to a conceptual age. Left-brain, logical, sequential solutions will no longer suffice in a conceptual age. We will need to add the right-brain creative, holistic skills and the kind of teachers who can help students create meanings that are relevant and necessary to solve the problems posed by living in a conceptual age. Education will need to be more about discovering and solving the mysteries of the universe, as well as understanding ourselves and the human condition. Houston believes that teachers need to be designers and storytellers; leaders need to understand and be mindful of what it will take to achieve the new kinds of asset (versus deficit) outcomes needed to accomplish goals of creativity and innovation.

The Time Has Come for New Educational Paradigms

New paradigms for education and schooling have become a topic of international concern. For example, Cheng (2007) describes three waves of paradigm shifts in the Asia-Pacific region in the past three or more decades. The first wave he calls the Effective Education Movement; the second wave, the Quality/ Competitive Education Movement; and the third wave, the World Class Education Movement. In these shifts, the focus has moved from effectiveness to quality to future relevance (Cheng). The movement of paradigms was also a shift from the focus on the internal effectiveness of institutions to a broader notion of an institution's accountability to the wider community, and now to a concern with the relevance of current systems to meet the future—an era of globalization, increased technological capabilities, and a knowledge-based economy. Cheng points out that the shifts in the Asia-Pacific region are similar to those here in the United States. That is, there is a recognition in the United States that the new paradigms will need to be dynamic, ecological, decentralized, networked, and focused on diversification rather than standardization.

In an earlier section, we referred to the work of the Berkana Institute, which is one of the virtual organizations making a difference in the preparation of new leaders. Berkana, founded by Margaret Wheatley in 1992 (The Berkana Institute, 2007), is committed to developing new leadership that can restore hope. As the board states in their 2006 Annual Report:

> The need for new leaders is urgent. We need people who can work together to resolve pressing issues of health, poverty, hunger, illiteracy, justice, environment, democracy. We need leaders who know how to nourish and rely on the innate creativity, freedom, generosity, and caring of people. We need leaders who are life-affirming rather than life-destroying. Unless we quickly figure out how to nurture and support this new leadership, we can't hope for peaceful change. We will, instead, be confronted by increasing anarchy and social and ecological meltdowns. (The Berkana Institute, 2007, p. 3)

New Views of Learning and Schooling

One of the true pioneers and leaders in the reconception and redesign of schooling is Stephanie Pace Marshall, whom we mentioned in the previous chapter. In her latest book, *The Power to Transform* (2006), she invites leaders of all types to think differently about learning and schooling. She offers a new language, new design principles, and a new framework for schooling redesign that integrate dynamic properties of living systems with generative principles of learning. Marshall (2006) argues that the new design of schooling must be life-affirming, invitational, engaging, nurturing, and potential fulfilling. She sees the current system as incapable of encouraging children to experience their rich inner lives, understand their connections to the world and one another, and embrace and celebrate their capacity to be involved in creating an emergent future.

Marshall (2006) defines the fundamental purpose of education as one of liberating the goodness and genius of children through learning and schooling that is in harmony with life and the human spirit. To do this, students need the tools to become fearless and self-directed learners who engage in holistic, systemic learning across their lifetime. Leaders of schooling systems need to help reconnect all of those involved, including the community, in ways that evoke intellectual, emotional, and spiritual potential. Leaders need to design programs, experiences, and opportunities that help all engage in this new work in ways that build capacity for authentic learning to flourish, e.g., through processes such as reflection, exploration, imagination, and connectedness. According to Marshall, the real job of leadership is to evoke and liberate rather than to prescribe—to intentionally create the generative conditions for learning that embody the creative processes for learning and life. From the very young to the very old, the human spirit is one of wanting to learn; it is also one of wanting to find meaning, purpose, connection, and contribution to the larger world.

Marshall (2006), along with other visionaries and futurists that we have mentioned, describes how science now sees the natural world as interdependent, relational, and part of a living web of connections that are holistic, abundant, creative, and self-organizing. At the heart of life is learning, a natural and creative human endeavor. Marshall argues that schooling and learning systems and the environments in which these systems reside must be models of natural creativity that nurture the joy of life itself through finding answers to the powerful questions of life and experience. Marshall's call is a call to reconnect learning to life. Both are about freedom, interdependence, creativity, novelty, relationships, exploration, and discovery.

New Views of Change

As globalization begins to shape not only what we do here in the United States but also what we do internationally, we are seeing an upsurge of creative thinking about what it takes to change systems. This new thinking is informed by recent advances in quantum physics and other natural sciences that are beginning to better understand and articulate the dynamics of change in living things. For example, scientists now see networking as a major new strategy for change (e.g., Senge, Scharmer, Jaworksi, & Flowers, 2004a).

Schools are social networks of people, where the larger network consists of connections between subgroups, such as grade or subject-matter teacher groups, student groups, and other collections of people that share expertise, information, and resources from person to person or subgroup to subgroup within various social structures (Penuel & Riel, 2007). In discussing how teacher networks can facilitate school change, Penuel and Riel summarize findings from their study of twenty-three California schools engaged in schoolwide reform:

1. It's not just how many people you talk to, but whom you talk to. *"It was ties that teachers had to 'experts'—whom we defined in our study as people with more experience in implementing their school's reform—that made the biggest difference"* (p. 612).

2. Getting help from outside one's immediate circle is valuable for obtaining new information and expertise. *"We found that teachers who took advantage of the knowledge of the teachers in other subgroups had access to more resources, to more 'social capital,' to use to make changes in their own practice"* (p. 613).

3. The goal of trying to make everyone an expert all at once does not strengthen the network; making effective expertise visible to all does work. *"Making expertise visible is partly a function of having structures that allow people to talk about their teaching practice, share their successes and struggles, and share and discuss instructional resources. It is also about publicly recognizing success and achievement in a way that encourages teachers to seek out their colleagues as resources and sources of help. To be useful, expertise has to be explicit and elaborated"* (p. 613).

4. Neither establishing a clear "chain of command" nor using the strategy of "let a hundred flowers bloom" works well to make expertise visible; success comes from "matrixing." …*"individuals participate in multiple meetings in which their school's reform is discussed. The types of meetings cross different functions in the school"* (p. 614).

5. Freeing up the time of experts to help others is particularly important, especially if professional development dollars are scarce. *"Identifying the true experts and enabling them to help others may be especially critical when dollars for formal professional development are scarce, as they are in many schools. Therefore, the informal network and the informal leaders within it may be the most important resources for facilitating implementation of a reform"* (p. 615).

Penuel and Riel (2007) believe that building trust through collegial relationships is also crucial, as it can help reduce the risk associated with making needed changes. When trust becomes a characteristic of the network as a whole, it expands the number of people resources that can be called upon in a collaborative learning and leading process.

Several decades ago, Beisser (1970), a follower of Gestalt therapy, wrote an article that still provides useful insights today about the nature of change and the role of the change agent. Called the paradoxical theory of change, this theory states:

> *"…change occurs when one becomes what he is, not when he tries to become what he is not. Change does not take place through a coercive attempt by the individual or by another person to change him, but it does take place if one takes the time and effort to be what he is—to be fully invested in his current positions. By rejecting the role of change agent, we make meaningful and orderly change possible."* (p. 1)

Box 3.2   Margaret Mead's Axioms of Change

1. When changing a complex system, it is less about planning and more about creating the conditions for change in people and contexts.

2. Risk-taking is required to be prepared for surprises as well as being well-educated in the nature of living systems, learning, and change.

3. When the system gets stuck, it is the product of human processes and what people are choosing not to see, feel, or do.

4. To move forth toward change, a power move may be required by someone who sees that he or she has the capacity to change a system.

5. The collective group or community of practice has to be able to act with a single intelligence or will that arises out of diversity of views and individuals.

6. When we have weak clusters of relationships, we create a "small world" in which every member of the network is connected to every other member through a small number of connections, usually not more than six.

7. When there is a minimum threshold of connections which include some tight clusters of relationships, there is the possibility that a movement or an idea will reach the tipping point.

One of the assumptions of Gestalt theory is that the natural human state is to be a single whole being (the self) that is in a dynamic transaction with the environment. That is, for change to happen, it is necessary to have the firm footing of being where one is now (Beisser, 1970). To change, the individual must have the ability to be flexible and adaptive in order to move with the times, while at the same time retaining individual stability and character.

One of Margaret Mead's enduring legacies is her belief in and commitment to the power of people to bring about significant changes through their collective and collaborative efforts, summarized by Hassan (2005) as a series of axioms, shown in Box 3.2.

Mead believed that:

> For a small group of thoughtful and committed people to change the world, they must believe that change is possible. They must be ready to act the moment a stuck system becomes liquid. They will only be effective if they display collective intelligence. Finally, they must live in a small world. (Hassan, 2005, p. 5)

Such groups are rapidly forming, both here in the United States and internationally. In the Department of Planning at the University College London, a group of researchers and educators has already begun the task of creating international networks based on trust deriving from the relationships of diverse people committed to shared values that are revisited and rearticulated over time (Church et al., 2003). Effective networks include processes for encouraging participation, relationship-building and trust, facilitative leadership, minimum levels of structure and control, diversity and dynamism, and decentralization and democracy. According to Church et al. the network fosters coordinated, reciprocal action that can be replicated in a number of countries.

Closer to home at the Berkana Institute, Margaret Wheatley and her colleagues (Jain & Stilger, 2007; Stilger, 2005; Wheatley, 2001b) describe a leader as anyone who wants to help at this time because they have a deep passion or desire to change some aspect of their world. In 2001, they articulated a new initiative, which they call Now Activism, to create learning circles around the world that could give rise to good human dialogue. They envisioned the circles as communities of practice in which leaders would emerge with greater skills for changing what needs to be changed. Their vision was to create a global voice that had the practices and values that could nourish and sustain the human spirit. Based on research of living systems, they posited that change happens from within, with many local actions occurring simultaneously such that as local groups networked together, a sudden and surprising global force could emerge. These global forces would occur as the result of emergence and have greater power than the sum of the parts (Wheatley, 2001b), and the leaders that emerge will be able to look at the surrounding web of relationships and system and see the whole picture (Stilger, 2005). Moving into their spiritual center allows them to hear and trust their inner voices so they become able to follow their callings. As of May 2007, this movement has involved people from over fourteen countries (Jain & Stilger).

This seems a good point at which to stop for a bit to digest what you've been reading and to reflect a bit on what all this means for you. Take a few moments to consider and respond to the activities in Box 3.3.

WHAT THE RESEARCH SHOWS ABOUT THE EFFECTIVENESS OF LEARNER-CENTERED MODELS

Now that you have had a chance to reflect on and consider the possibilities for beginning to create that new educational paradigm, we want to share some important evidence for you to consider. We believe that the new leader(s) will need to be armed with this evidence to build their confidence and courage as they make needed changes in their own thinking and leading practices. We start with a major study that analyzed the accumulated evidence of the benefits of learner- or person-centered educational models.

Large Scale Research Findings

Cornelius-White (2007) reviewed 119 studies that investigated the efficacy and associations of learner-centered instructional relationships with comprehensive student success. The studies synthesized were published between 1948 and 2004, written in English or German, and conducted in most areas of the United States, the Philippines, Brazil, Germany, Austria, the United Kingdom, and Canada. The studies involved over 350,000 students, nearly 15,000 teachers,

Box 3.3   Considering Change

1.   List the major barriers you see to bringing about change in your school/district.

2.   List three ways you can remove the barriers you listed above.

3.   List the people in your school and/or district you believe possess the qualities we've been describing as necessary to bringing about major change.

4.   List five steps you could take tomorrow to begin the process of change in your school/district.

and 1,450 separate findings from pre-school to graduate school. In this meta-analysis of person-centered education models, Cornelius-White (2007) found that person- and learner-centered education is associated with large increases in student participation/initiation ($r = .55$), satisfaction ($r = .44$), and motivation to learn ($r = .32$), all of which indicated high levels of engagement in learner-centered classrooms (p. 128). There were also positive effects on self-esteem ($r = .35$) and social connections and skills ($r = .32$), and reductions in dropout ($r = .35$), disruptive behavior ($r = .25$), and absences ($r = .25$) (p. 128). This meta-analysis also found support for the importance of student perspectives as better predictors of their own academic success than teacher perspectives on the frequency with which they performed learner-centered practices.

The major teacher variables associated with positive student outcomes include positive relationships, nondirectivity, empathy, warmth, and encouraging thinking and learning skills. Cornelius-White (2007) also found that learner-centered practices may work better with minority teachers and learners, suggesting that these universal variables are particularly important for students who traditionally do not receive this level of support. In general, the results showed that learner-centered instruction (LCI) had an overall corrected correlation average of $r = .31$ (Cornelius-White, p. 127). Cornelius-White concluded that the overall findings show that LCI is highly associated with student success.

Cornelius-White (2007) concludes that the synthesis of the research also found that what is observable is most potent in another way. Considering the 1,450 separate findings from the meta-analysis together, observers and students' perspectives yield higher associations to student success than teachers' views. In other words, the genuine, warm empathy that is central to learner-centered practices has to be perceived by, experienced, and relevant for the student, not just superficial niceness, for it to really be effective. The meta-analysis forms a solid foundation to support using learner-centered instruction in schools and classrooms. This type of instruction is part of a bigger model that focuses on the core principles of encouragement, challenge, and adaptation.

Other Substantial Results Relating to Democracy in Our Schools

The role of the new leaders needed to transform our educational paradigm moves from moral, ethical, and spiritual dimensions to an appreciation of what the future will hold for all of us. As we have mentioned, the new leaders must not only know what to do; they must know who they are and what is possible in the schooling process.

Schools as Models of Social Responsibility and Democracy

McQuillan (2005) argues that, although U.S. schools may express a commitment to preparing students for the responsibilities of being democratic citizens, most institutions define their students as passive and subordinate and treat them in undemocratic ways. He presents results of case studies of two high schools' efforts to promote learner-centered practices through student empowerment in an effort to extend research showing that empowerment strategies promote greater student participation, engagement, and responsibility in their education. The ultimate benefit would be an understanding of how to create schools that "educate for democracy" but also show where they give students the opportunities to participate in a pluralistic community and become "crucibles of democracy."

McQuillan (2005) defines student empowerment as involving the academic, political, and social dimensions where students have a say in how to understand the economic, political, and social realities that affect their lives in curricular, institutional leadership, and institutional structures and policies such that they create a social environment that supports and nurtures the safety of expressing diverse views in a context where all voices are respected. From our perspective, this is the type of approach that creates schools that model both what and who we want students to be in the world.

In his research, McQuillan (2005) found that the academic, political, and social dimensions were synergistic and mutually reinforcing, and as students and teachers become more empowered, they were more likely to empower others. Thus, all people in the system are seen as agents with appropriate distribution of power. McQuillan also found that a sense of disequilibrium is necessary (e.g., feeling that goals of schooling are not as they could be) for student empowerment to occur in schools. Change will require all people in the system to step out of their comfort zone and confront traditional structures and practices, including beliefs and values. McQuillan argues that student empowerment—a basic concept in learner-centered practices—is a promising strategy for reducing the achievement gap and should become our top educational priority in establishing a more democratic educational process. It also needs to be the basis for new paradigms of schooling.

Re-Engaging Students in Schooling and Learning

Darling-Hammond and Ifill-Lynch (2006) report that by 9th grade, forty percent of urban students fail multiple classes and that fifty percent or more students leave school without graduating. Of those who enter high school, many lack the learning and study skills they need to be good students (e.g., knowing how to take notes, study on their own, engage in classwork, and finish their homework). Consistent with research by motivation researchers (e.g., Covington & Teel, 1996; Dweck, 1999; Meece, Herman, & McCombs, 2003), to protect their self-esteem, many adolescents maintain they don't care about school and the boring or "stupid" work they have to do. Darling-Hammon and Ifill-Lynch contend that an effective approach to engaging students with their schoolwork is to create a strong academic culture that changes students' beliefs and behaviors. A big part of this culture is work that students find relevant, meaningful, and authentic, such as inquiry- and project-based learning that is part of successful approaches such as those reported by Deborah Meier (2002) at Central Park East. Involving students and making them part of the solution are also effective, along with meeting with students, alone or in teams, to emphasize their strengths and areas where they have been successful. Collaboration is a primary strategy where students and their teachers can work together, as well as helping those students who work to get credit with work-based learning plans. In short, Darling-Hammond and Ifill-Lynch propose learner-centered approaches that recognize the learning and life needs of struggling students.

In national studies conducted by the Just for the Kids organization, the number one indicator of student success is to focus on the student, followed by high-quality teaching and research-based instructional practices. Another correlate of student success is that teachers are given the materials, training, and support they need and the time to plan together, discuss student progress, and reflect on best practices (Just for the Kids, 2003). In one such high-performance school in Los Angeles, teachers work together to help students take risks so that they develop character and the skills to succeed in life (Mathews, 2004a). As with Deborah Meier who formed Central Park East School in East Harlem in 1974, the key to the success of that school and its students was the strong and educative relationships between students and adults (Mathews, 2004b). Students were taught to develop their minds by weighing evidence, seeing other ways of looking at the same data or situation, comparing and contrasting, seeking patterns, conjecturing and arguing—skills to use their minds powerfully (Meier, 2002). Current policies that do not ask students to engage in intellectual rigor and instead use their minds for factual recall will only add to the already growing dropout rate, particularly among disadvantaged and minority students (Wagner, 2003).

Addressing the Holistic Development of Learners

In a study of 120 elementary schools that engage in some form of character education, Benninga, Berkowitz, Kuehn, and Smith (2006) report that there are common qualities that support both high academic achievement and positive development of virtues related to character and citizenship. Their list of what good schools do is highly similar to those qualities of schools that can be defined as "learner-centered:"

1. They ensure a clean and secure physical environment;
2. They promote and model fairness, equity, caring, and respect;
3. They allow students to contribute to their school and community in meaningful ways;
4. They promote a caring community and positive social relationships. (Benninga et al., 2006)

Further, the adults in these schools understand their role in preparing students for future citizenship in a democratic and diverse society. Benninga et al. (2006) argue that their results support maintaining a rich curriculum that supports all aspects of student development and growth rather than narrowing the curricula to concentrate on skills measured by standardized tests.

A fundamental focus in learner-centered schools is on quality relationships. In looking at more than 1,360 pieces of data from the National Institute of Child Health and Human Development (NICHHD) on children from birth through sixth grade, O'Connor and McCartney (2007) found that, even beyond factors such as individual characteristics, mother-child relationships, family environment, school relationships, classroom environment, and culture, children's achievement was increased by high-quality teacher-child relationships. This study also cited the impressive research literature showing the beneficial effects on both achievement and behavior of child-teacher relationships that are characterized as affectionate, warm, close, low conflict, and open communication. Overall, these relationships are secure versus insecure and conform to an ecological model of development that takes into account multiple interrelated components and factors and their impact on development at given time periods and over time.

O'Connor and McCartney (2007) conclude that their findings provide strong implications for changes in teacher education programs. Whereas early childhood teachers often get instruction on how to foster high-quality child-teacher relationships, elementary teachers usually are trained to promote effective instructional interactions rather than relationships with students. Expanding this preparation may well prevent the risk factors and harmful behaviors of children whose other ecological factors can be offset by quality teacher-child relationships.

Martin (2002), in a review of alternative educational models, examined learner-centered, progressive, and holistic education. A growing number of alternative schools fit within this broad category and include democratic and free schools, folk education, Quaker schools, Krishnamurti schools, Montessori education, open schools, homeschooling/unschooling/deschooling, and Waldorf schools. This diversity of alternatives to mainstream or traditional education is in keeping with social values that include pluralism and diversity, a more sustainable world, and just democracy. The alternative models tend NOT to be rooted in an overly rational or objective way of knowing but instead emphasize interdependencies and values—and include the emotional, ecological, spiritual, physical, social, and intellectual aspects of living that are reflected in schooling.

These models address the needs of the whole child in balance with the needs of the community and society at large. They hold in common a respect for diversity and different philosophical beliefs about what it means to live, learn, love, and grow in today's society (Forbes, 1999). They are all, however, "person-centered" approaches expressed in a diversity of ways. What makes "learner-centered" transformative (holistic) is its recognition that meaning is co-constructed, self-regulation occurs through interdependence, with a focus on being, and becoming fully functioning.

Results From Our Research

In our own research with the Learner-Centered Model (LCM), which we introduced in Chapter 1, we have worked with schools in systemic change projects that begin with a school-level assessment of what all staff report as the alignment of their basic beliefs and perceptions of actual practice in the eight areas of school functioning (McCombs, 2003b, 2005; McCombs & Quiat, 2002) shown in Table 3.2. This research has confirmed the relationships shown in Figure 3.1. That is, at the school leadership level, it is essential that all staff be included in a process of self-assessing the discrepancies between (1) what they believe should be happening in their schools and classrooms and (2) what they perceive is the actual degree to which these practices are taking place.

Table 3.2   Eight Areas of Learner-Centered School Functioning[1]

- Expectations for Students
- Instruction and Management Practices
- Curriculum Structures
- Assessment and Grading Practices
- Professional Development Practices
- Parent and Community Involvement Strategies
- Leadership Style and Practices
- Policies and Regulations

[1] From the Assessment of Learner-Centered Practices (ALCP) School-Level Survey (McCombs, 1999b).

With the permission of all staff and agreements as to how to aggregate the data (e.g., by various staff positions, grade levels, departments, etc.), these results are shared and become the basis for dialogue about the best ways to resolve personal and group discrepancies. This dialogue process is one similar to that described in the preceding section. It invites and allows all staff, students, parents, and other community stakeholders to ask the probing questions, listen respectfully to all divergent views, and learn with and from each other about

Figure 3.1   A Learner-Centered Model of Relations Between Teacher Beliefs, Teacher Practices, and Student Outcomes

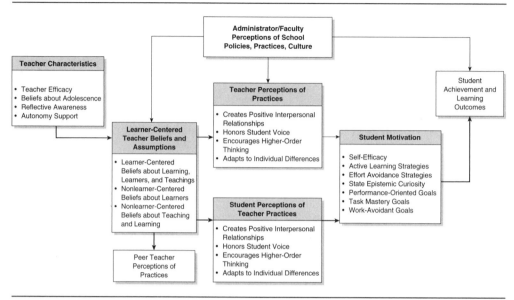

what needs to change. The result is a unique school or district-based plan that focuses staff development and ongoing learning on ways to create new learning communities and learner-centered support groups. Through individual and group networks, these groups become the communities of practice and influence that empower, support, and spread the emergence of new forms and structures to support the evolving and continuously changing new educational paradigm in practice.

The work of becoming "learner-centered" starts with the connecting of people and the honest and open exchange of values, beliefs, and perceptions through a dialogue model. Margaret Wheatley's work (2002, 2006a, 2006b), which we will talk more about in Chapter 4, provides the basis for this process. For now, look at Box 3.4, which describes an urban middle school we worked with in Texas. As you read the description, ask yourself whether you have experienced anything similar during your own career. If so, take a moment to reflect on how you handled your experience(s).

When you have finished reading the description and reflecting on your own experiences, take a moment to consider whether you agree or disagree with the process we described (or whether you agree with some aspects and not others). Write your thoughts down in your journal, and, if possible, share them with another person who is also engaged in the process of educational change. Take a few minutes to dialogue with yourself or your partner about any areas of agreement and/or disagreement. Note any unanswered questions you have at this point so you can revisit them as you continue your journey through this book.

(Text continues on page 70)

Box 3.4   A Middle School on the "Hit List"

From 1999 through 2002, we worked with a middle school in a major urban area in Texas identi-fied as a failing school. The school district had based its definition of failing schools on student performance in reading and mathematics on the state test, the Texas Assessment of Knowledge and Skills (the TAKS). School districts whose scores in either reading or mathematics were below the 80th percentile made this "hit list," as it was called by employees in the district. Schools designated as failing, at any level elementary through high school, had the option of working with outside consultants who had a comprehensive school reform model to bring up students' test scores in a three-year period. If test scores were not up to the 80th percentile by the end of the third year, the schools would be privatized and most, if not all, of the school staff dismissed or sent to other schools. This Texas model was the precursor to the policies codified in the current No Child Left Behind (NCLB) legislation.

Our Learner-Centered Model (LCM), and its associated tools, was chosen by one of the middle schools whose reading and mathematics scores were both in the 20th percentile. We met first with the district administration and school principal to discuss the change strategies, assessment tools, and instructional practices associated with the LCM. It was agreed that this middle school, which sat in one of the most impoverished and gang-ridden areas of the city, would work with us to implement the LCM over the next three years.

In the middle school itself, we met initially with faculty and administrators to introduce them to the LCM, the underlying Learner-Centered Psychological Principles (LCPs), and the various profes-sional development tools and strategies for improving student motivation and achievement. At the same time, all staff members were invited to participate in the school-level Assessment of Learner-Centered Practices (ALCP) survey. The school principal and other members of the leader-ship team had agreed that school or classroom level ALCP surveys would not be mandated if any staff person (or student in the case of the classroom level surveys) were unwilling to participate. It was emphasized that change happens because of critical relationships, and, consequently, they were not to worry about those who chose to wait to become involved. We took this step because many of them had become fearful in the punitive testing and accountability environment that surrounded Texas schools.

As it turned out, all but two nonfaculty staff people participated in the first administration of the School-Level ALCP surveys. The results were analyzed and broken into categories by grade levels (6, 7, 8) and by reading and math subject areas. Administrator and leadership team results were also compared to faculty and paraprofessional staff categories. Their findings were tabulated (see Table 3.3) and graphed (see Figures 3.2 through 3.6). School personnel were able to see value areas they agreed and disagreed upon and what they wanted to see in place at the school level. They could then see areas of consensus in perceptions of the degree to which these practices were actually occurring.

During the first semester, a series of meetings and dialogues about the findings took place. These meetings were held after school or on Saturdays, with an atmosphere of fun and socialization. Food was brought in and shared, games were played, and efforts were made for people to get to know each other at a deeper level. Even though many of these faculty and other school personnel had worked together for ten or more years—and many of them had taught the parents of the children now in the middle school—they realized that they really didn't know each other at a per-sonal level. They found out they shared many of the same interests, hobbies, and personal values.

Once this atmosphere of fun and trust was developed during the fall of that first school year, we tackled the hard questions raised by the School-Level ALCP survey results. Although some of the

(Continued)

Box 3.4   (Continued)

discussions at times became fairly "heated," the time spent involving everyone in setting ground rules for the dialogue resulted in a group that listened respectfully to each other's views. This led to the formation of various administrator-leadership-faculty-other school staff work groups. These groups were organized around their high interest and passion areas in the ALCP domains of school functioning showing the largest discrepancies in practice goals and perceptions of actual practices existed. The groups identified areas needing further staff development, and leaders emerged who were willing to take responsibility. A sense of excitement, tempered by cautious optimism, began to build.

One of the more serious issues identified early on was the feelings of fear, abandonment, and low morale being experienced by all due to the district's mandates to teach to a new curriculum, filled with "drill and kill" and ongoing testing of students. Students who were normally well-behaved had begun to act out and teachers, as well as administrators, were frustrated by increased absenteeism, student fighting, and in some cases, open rebellion to the new curriculum and testing procedures. We asked staff if they had been open with students and had explained to them why the situation had changed and how serious the consequences would be if they didn't raise their reading and mathematics scores on the state test in three years. When we were told "no," we made the suggestion that teachers go into their classrooms and explain, in their own style and wording, what was going on. Most importantly, we suggested that teachers ask students for their help in coming up with ideas for how they could make what they had to do more fun, interesting, and relevant for themselves. We asked teachers to listen carefully to what students suggested, write these ideas down, and act on them.

Students became involved in taking ownership over their ideas—good ideas such as pairing with each other and doing drills with each other, engaging in "spelling bee" type formats to learn what they would be tested on. Teachers acted on these ideas. In combination with the LCM classroom-level ALCP student and teacher assessments and reflective feedback sessions, by mid-year, the atmosphere of the school began to change from one of fear and pessimism to one of hope and optimism. By testing time that first year, everyone was ready and excited to show what they had accomplished. Miraculously, state test scores in reading and mathematics had risen to over the 40th percentile!

We continued to work with the ALCP assessments, specialized professional development opportunities, strong administrative support, and learner-centered support groups. The support groups were a venue in which to share expertise in areas of practice critical to student motivation and learning. Ongoing learning and inquiry groups were formed, and significant changes in practice began to occur in spite of the mandated use of the Texas curriculum and testing policies. By the end of the second year, test scores in both reading and mathematics were in the 60th percentile. Most exciting for all of us, the students were highly engaged and viewing themselves as partners in preventing the closure of their school. Throughout, all successes were opportunities for celebration by students, parents, teachers, and school leaders alike.

As our third school year began, it was clear that the philosophy, change model, and strategies embedded in the LCM were taking hold. All teachers were voluntarily involved in assessing their classroom practices with their students, making needed changes, and working with "expert teachers" identified by the ALCP assessment process in those areas of practice where they were struggling. At the middle school level, the areas of practice—in the order of importance in predicting student motivation, learning outcomes, and disruptive behaviors—unfolded as: (1) creating positive student relationships and a positive climate for learning; (2) honoring student voice and creating challenging learning opportunities; (3) supporting students' higher-order thinking and learning skills; and (4) adapting to individual developmental differences. In this, as in any school system, the best experts in each of these areas are the teachers who work in that system. By the third year, we knew who the experts were, and they were paired with struggling teachers who welcomed the help. They welcomed the help because a true community of practice had been created.

There's a good news, bad news, and then good news end to this story. The good news was that test scores at the end of the third year were 72nd percentile in reading and 76th percentile in mathematics. The bad news was that the then-superintendent said that wasn't good enough and to close the school down. The good news was that the superintendent was sent to Washington to be Secretary of Education, and the acting superintendent reversed the decision, stating that there was that much margin of error in measurement in the Texas test. Any school making that much progress—and having fun doing it—shouldn't be shut down. So we all rejoiced at that final good news!!

Figure 3.2   Goals of Texas Middle School

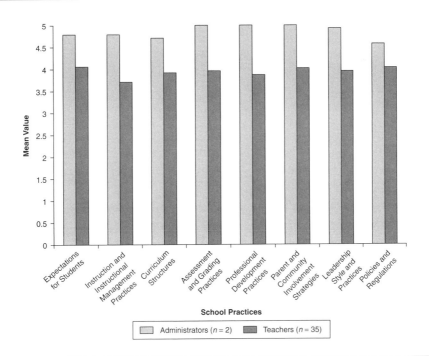

Figure 3.3   Actual Practices of Texas Middle School

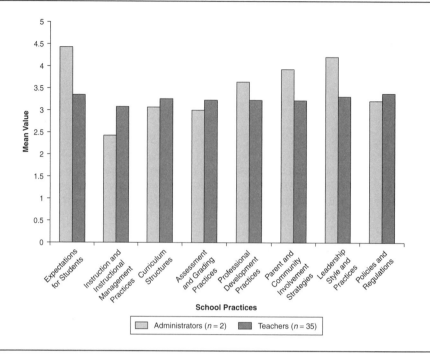

Figure 3.4   Grades 6–8: Goals

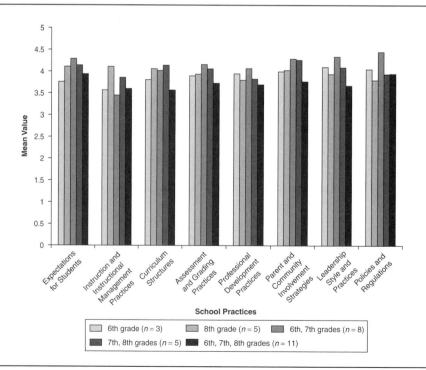

Figure 3.5   Grades 6–8: Actuals

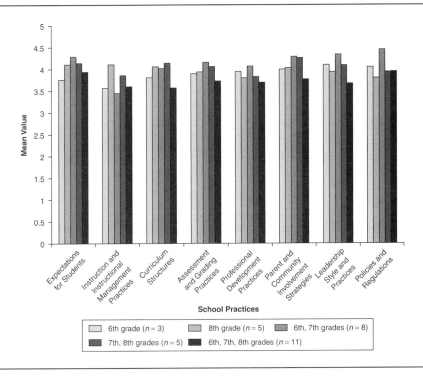

Figure 3.6   "All Grades" and Administrator Categories

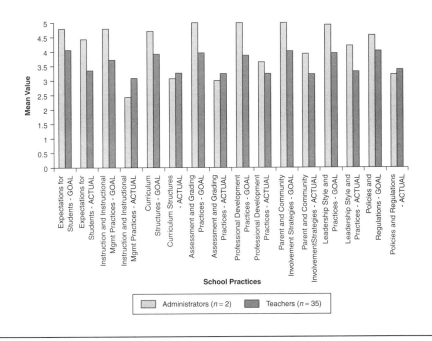

Table 3.3 School-Level Assessment of Learner-Centered Principles and Practices: ALCP School Level Practices Survey Results

School Practice Area	Texas Middle School: 2000–2001						Texas Middle School: 1998–1999							
	Administrators		Teachers (N=35)		Total		Administrators		Teachers		Total		Colorado Sample	
	Mean n=2	SD	Mean n=35	SD	Mean	SD	Mean n=5	SD	Mean n=33	SD	Mean	SD	Mean n=250	SD
Expectations for Students														
Expectations for Students—Goal	4.79	0.10	4.06	0.74	4.10	0.74	4.06	1.08	4.33	0.59	4.30	0.66	4.83	0.25
Expectations for Students—Actual	4.43	0.00	3.35	0.80	3.41	0.81	3.06	1.43	3.33	0.86	3.29	0.93	3.37	0.68
Instruction and Instructional Management Practices														
Instruction and Instructional Mgmt Practices—Goal	4.79	0.10	3.71	0.77	3.77	0.79	3.54	0.91	3.92	0.72	3.87	0.74	4.55	0.43
Instruction and Instructional Mgmt Practices—Actual	2.43	0.40	3.08	0.70	3.04	0.70	2.71	0.75	2.94	0.75	2.91	0.74	2.75	0.62
Curriculum Structures														
Curriculum Structures—Goal	4.71	0.40	3.92	0.93	3.96	0.92	3.80	1.10	4.09	0.93	4.05	0.95	4.60	0.44
Curriculum Structures—Actual	3.07	0.71	3.26	0.77	3.25	0.75	2.80	0.36	2.76	0.93	2.77	0.87	2.93	0.61
Assessment and Grading Practices														
Assessment and Grading Practices—Goal	5.00	0.00	3.96	0.82	4.02	0.84	3.51	1.09	4.04	0.95	3.97	0.97	4.38	0.60

Assessment and Grading Practices—Actual	3.00	0.61	3.24	0.87	3.22	0.85	3.09	0.46	2.92	1.02	2.95	0.96	2.56	0.80

Professional Development Practices

Professional Development Practices—Goal	5.00	0.00	3.87	1.03	3.93	1.04	3.24	1.31	4.27	0.78	4.13	0.92	4.70	0.42
Professional Development Practices—Actual	3.64	0.10	3.24	0.88	3.24	0.86	2.80	0.63	3.16	0.93	3.12	0.90	2.88	0.78

Parent and Community Involvement Strategies

Parent and Community Involvement Strategies—Goal	5.00	0.00	4.02	0.91	4.07	0.91	3.97	1.30	4.23	0.84	4.20	0.90	none	none
Parent and Community Involvement Strategies—Actual	3.93	0.30	3.22	0.85	3.25	0.84	2.91	0.71	3.19	0.88	3.16	0.86		

Leadership Style and Practices

Leadership Style and Practices—Goal	4.93	0.10	3.95	1.02	4.00	1.01	3.89	1.47	4.44	0.63	4.36	0.78	none	none
Leadership Style and Practices—Actual	4.21	0.30	3.31	1.01	3.36	1.01	3.26	0.85	3.21	0.94	3.21	0.91		

Policies and Regulations

Policies and Regulations—Goal	4.57	0.61	4.03	0.89	4.06	0.88	3.68	1.73	4.39	0.71	4.30	0.90	4.52	0.50
Policies and Regulation—Actual	3.21	0.51	3.38	0.89	3.37	0.87	2.90	0.73	3.15	1.01	3.12	0.98	2.96	0.76

HOW THE LEARNER-CENTERED PRINCIPLES TRANSLATE INTO PRACTICE AT THE SCHOOL LEVEL

As you have seen in your examination of the case study in Box 3.4, the School-Level Assessment of Learner-Centered Practices Surveys provide an important tool to begin the dialogue required for school change.

Introduction to How the Learner-Centered Principles Translate Into Different Areas of School Practice

The Assessment of Learner-Centered Practices School-Level Survey, based on *Learner-Centered Psychological Principles* (APA, 1993, 1997) (which we described in Chapter 2), addresses the comprehensive needs of the learner in ways that are consistent with the research on teaching and learning we've described in previous sections. The Assessment of Learner-Centered Practices School-Level Practices Survey is a 112-item self-assessment measure that asks administrators, faculty, involved parents, and other school and district personnel to indicate the degree to which various learner-centered practices, shown in Table 3.2, are held as Practice Goals (Beliefs and Values) and Perceptions of the Degree They Already Exist in their buildings (see Table 3.4 for how these categories appear on the survey).

Items on the Assessment of Learner-Centered Practices are rated on a five-point Likert-type scale for both the practice goals and perceived actual practice for each item in each of the eight categories. Mean ratings of goals versus practice for the eight school practice areas can be compared for different groups of respondents within a school and also with the validation sample of teachers and school administrators from diverse rural, suburban, and urban school districts. School-Level Practices Survey results indicate differences in beliefs about the value of different educational practices as well as differences in perceptions concerning the existence of these practices in respondents' current school settings. School leaders can use feedback from the School-Level Practices Survey to help plan for school restructuring and improvement and design staff development. Sample items from the School-Level Practices Survey are shown in Table 3.4.

Our findings from research with the Assessment of Learner-Centered Practices School-Level Practices Survey are that both are powerful tools for examining the sorts of discrepancies we described in our case study in Box 3.4. Our research also shows that effective dialogue and other tools and processes associated with the Learner-Centered Model work equally well in rural, suburban, and urban contexts (McCombs, 2004b). Although the degree to which the eight dimensions of school functioning in Table 3.2 are valued and observed in practice differ, in all cases the creation of communities of learners and practice can together create the system changes needed in identifying and articulating:

Table 3.4   The Assessment of Learner-Centered Practices (ALCP): School-Level Survey (K–12)©

SAMPLE ITEMS

DIRECTIONS: Each item below has two parts: (1) what practices and policies you believe your school or district **should have** in six key areas of school operation; and (2) what practices and policies your school or district **already has in place**. For each item, please think about and respond to **both parts**. Indicate the degree to which you agree with each statement as a **practice goal** and the degree to which you think it **already exists**. Blacken the responses for each item on your answer sheet that best indicates your choice on **both parts** according to the following scale:

Strongly **D**isagree -------------------- Strongly **A**gree

A	B	C	D	E
SD				SA

Remember that each statement has two parts. Mark BOTH your parts for each item.

EXAMPLE ITEM:

Practice Goal   **Already Exists**

A B C D E   Classrooms that are bright and cheery.   **A B C D E**
SD   SA   SD   SA

This survey asks you to assess your goals for school-level practices and your perceptions of what already exists in eight areas: Expectations for Students, Instruction and Instructional Management Practices, Curriculum Structures, Assessment and Grading Practices, Professional Development Practices, Parent and Community Involvement Strategies, Leadership Style and Practices, and Policies and Regulations.

YOU MAY NOW BEGIN!

PLEASE TURN THE PAGE

Table 3.4   (Continued)

Sample Items—Assessment of Learner-Centered Practices
(School Level)

<u>Practice Goal</u>   <u>Already Exists</u>

1.   Expectations for Students

1.   **A B C D E**   Students are expected to be   2.   **A B C D E**
      <u>SD</u>   <u>SA</u>   responsible for their own learning.   <u>SD</u>   <u>SA</u>

2.   Instruction and Instructional Management Practices

15.   **A B C D E**   Students are given choices in how,   16.   **A B C D E**
      <u>SD</u>   <u>SA</u>   when, and with whom they want to learn.   <u>SD</u>   <u>SA</u>

3.   Curriculum Structures

29.   **A B C D E**   Curricula is thematic and integrated   30.   **A B C D E**
      <u>SD</u>   <u>SA</u>   across disciplines and content areas.   <u>SD</u>   <u>SA</u>

4.   Assessment and Grading Practices

43.   **A B C D E**   Assessment practices foster student   44.   **A B C D E**
      <u>SD</u>   <u>SA</u>   responsibility for learning (e.g., self-   <u>SD</u>   <u>SA</u>
                               evaluation.)

5.   Professional Development Practices

57.   **A B C D E**   Teachers are given training in adapting   58.   **A B C D E**
      SD   SA   to individual differences in student   <u>SD</u>   <u>SA</u>
                               learning needs.

6.   Parent and Community Involvement Strategies

71.   **A B C D E**   Mentoring programs are available for   72.   **A B C D E**
      <u>SD</u>   <u>SA</u>   parents and community members to   <u>SD</u>   <u>SA</u>
                               work with students.

7.   Leadership Style and Practices

85.   **A B C D E**   Leadership provides learning   86.   **A B C D E**
      <u>SD</u>   <u>SA</u>   environments that allow students and   <u>SD</u>   <u>SA</u>
                               individual or group learning.

8.   Policies and Regulations

99.   **A B C D E**   Policies promote the integration of   100. **A B C D E**
      <u>SD</u>   <u>SA</u>   technology into curriculum,   <u>SD</u>   <u>SA</u>
                               instruction, and staff development.

- *Expectations for Students*—the beliefs and perceptions of actual practices in terms of understanding how students learn;
- *Instruction and Management Practices*—the beliefs and perceptions of actual practices regarding how instruction is delivered and managed;
- *Curriculum Structures*—the beliefs and perceptions of actual practices about how curriculum is organized and delivered;
- *Assessment and Grading Practices*—the beliefs and perceptions of actual practices about the types of assessments used and how students are "graded" for their performances and achievement of desired outcomes;
- *Professional Development Practices*—the beliefs and perceptions of actual practices about how teachers are treated as learners and how they achieve professional development goals;
- *Parent and Community Involvement Strategies*—the beliefs and perceptions of actual practices about the role of parents and communities and how they are involved in school redesign;
- *Leadership Style and Practices*—the beliefs and perceptions of actual practices about what constitutes leadership, who the leaders are, and how leadership emerges;
- *Policies and Regulations*—the beliefs and perceptions of actual practices regarding navigating the policy environment and what changes can be made within the policy context.

The differences in goals and actual practices across a number of schools in a single district can be illustrated as shown in the results graphed in Figures 3.7 and 3.8, respectively. These figures show how the School-Level Assessment of Learner-Centered Practices Surveys can be used at a district level to guide school leadership—at all levels—toward respectful dialogue and the formation of communities of learning and practice. You will have a chance to learn more about this process in subsequent chapters.

What the Learner-Centered Model and Learner-Centered Approaches Add

With a learner-centered approach to educational reform, the focus is on the psychological, emotional, and social needs of learners and interventions that maximize healthy development and functioning such that motivation, learning, and achievement are promoted for *all* learners. The Learner-Centered Principles, validated over several years (APA, 1993, 1997), provide a knowledge base for understanding that learning and motivation are natural processes that occur when the *conditions and context* of learning are supportive of individual learner needs, capacities, experiences, and interests.

As we indicated in Chapter 1, all living systems include three domains: personal, technical, and organizational (see Figure 1.1 on page 4). As we mentioned in our discussion there, for schools to achieve the richness and power of living systems, we believe it is essential to focus attention on the personal domain, which has been largely ignored in recent years. Attention to the knowledge base about learners and learning is critical in order to define the personal domain of

Figure 3.7   Goals of All Schools

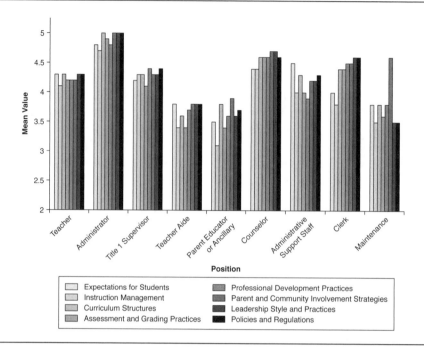

Figure 3.8   Actual for All Schools

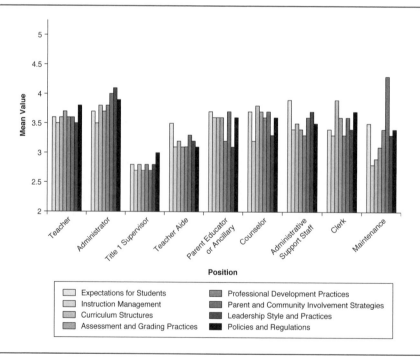

educational systems. In contrast to the technical domain that focuses on content, standards, methods for organizing/delivering instruction, and strategies for assessing the attainment of the subject matter of education, the personal domain focuses on the *human processes* that operate on and/or are supported by the standards, curriculum, instruction, and assessment components in the technical domain. In addition, in contrast to the organizational domain, which is concerned with the management structure, decision making processes, policies that support the people, and content requirements of education, the personal domain centers on personal and interpersonal *relationships, beliefs, and perceptions* that are affected by and/or supported by the organization and educational system as a whole.

Current reform efforts are concerned primarily with technical issues (e.g., high academic standards, increased student achievement, alignment of curricula and assessment) that emphasize accountability (e.g., high stakes testing, teacher responsibility for student achievement) and punitive consequences for teachers, students, and administrators when standards are not met. To bring the system into balance, as well as bring some of the joy of learning back into the educational process, we argue that the focus must also be on personal issues and the needs of all people in the system, including students and the adults who serve them in the teaching and learning process (cf. McCombs, 2003d, 2007; McCombs & Miller, 2007). We see this as a basic component of schooling, learning, and leading.

IMPLICATIONS FOR LEADERSHIP AND BUILDING COMMUNITIES OF LEARNERS

It has long been recognized that humans have a need and tendency to form social connections. According to Cacioppo, Hawkley, Rickett, and Masi (2005), humans also share common qualities such as empathy, kindness, compassion, love, friendship, and hope, all of which represent human spirituality. Because humans are social creatures, the social relationships they form serve as the basis from which these spiritual qualities emerge and/or are developed. As organizational structures—such as schools, educational agencies, or districts, among others—are themselves social structures, the people in them make meaning from the relationships they create, thus leading to the further development of spirituality.

What We Know About the Value of Networks and Communities of Learning

Increasing numbers of researchers are arguing for more complex metaphors, such as living systems, networks, and communities of learners, to describe the human mind and behavior. These more complex metaphors help us move away from the mechanical or artificial intelligence (AI) computer metaphors that have failed to adequately describe and explain the interconnectivity of human functions in creative, flexible, and innovative ways (e.g., Cacioppo et al., 2005; Caine & Caine, 2006). For instance, Summers, Beretvas, Svinicki, and Gorin (2005) argue that the benefits of faculty and students sharing academic goals and working together is clear at all educational levels. Such practices lead to the development of a sense of community, which has been shown to have a number of positive benefits, including increased student attendance at the K–12 level and student retention at the college level. The major factor underlying the benefits of collaborative learning and the development of community is that collaborative learning meets our basic human need to be connected to and in relation to others.

The idea of communities within education is far from new. When ideas such as "schools as learning organizations" began to surface in the early 1990s, Kofman and Senge (1993) began proposing that organizations should undertake "dialogue projects" in order to develop deeper patterns of reflection and communication. They recognized that, to create learning organizations, it was necessary to make basic shifts in how we think and interact.

Such shifts require a personal transformation that can occur only within the safety of a learning community because, within the community, people are able to identify any faulty thinking habits and to commit to making the changes necessary for everyone to experience ongoing learning. Through recognizing that people need community in order to develop—i.e., learn—in positive ways, the members of the community develop a commitment to support the whole—the community.

In Kofman and Senge's (1993) view, a learning organization must base its culture on the values of love, wonder, humility, and compassion. From there, practices must be instituted that provide for dialogue, generative conversation, and coordinated action. Finally, those in the organization must be supported to develop a capacity to see and work with the flow of life as a system. Concepts such as servant leadership, which we described in Chapter 2, remind us that the most basic and essential learning is learning about who we are.

From a related perspective, Niesz (2007) makes a strong case for communities of practice that interweave learning and teaching in social networks. She believes that such communities hold the promise of restoring thoughtful, professional expertise in schooling as teachers are organized into networks with the purpose of learning through inquiry. These communities of practice have been applauded by many as a social constructivist and constructivist orientation to teacher learning and professional development. As Niesz explains, these networks assume that teacher learning should endure over time, build on the experiences and knowledge of teachers, and promote opportunities for inquiry and critical dialogue through public sharing of practice and understandings. The concept of communities of practice, which we mentioned briefly in Chapter 2, was developed by Jean Lave and Etienne Wenger (1998) as four interconnected components of social learning theory:

1. *community*: where learning is belonging;
2. *identity*: where learning is becoming

3. *practice*: where learning is doing; and
4. *meaning*: where learning is experience.

Creating the Context for the Emergence of Teacher Leaders

Networks provide the social context for learning and school improvement, as well as professional development. They foster the willingness of teachers and other school staff to commit time, energy, and part of themselves to the personal and social learning process. Interpersonal relationships and experiences are shared, and, in the process, trust and respect—critical components of change—develop. Networks can function as a bridge between the two cultures of schooling and professional development (Lieberman & Miller, 2001). Furthermore, because networks are outside the bureaucratic structures of schools—i.e., they are decentralized and distributed—and because they are voluntary—i.e., they are self-initiated and self-organizing—the goals of teachers in the schooling system fall into alignment with those of the network as a consequence of shared experiences, resulting in positive school change.

Bartholomew (2007) makes a good case for the fact that most educators do not yet fully understand the importance of intrinsic motivation for academic excellence and the voluntary emergence of learning communities. Too often, educators rely on external motivators or fear-based approaches that may yield compliance and control, but clearly, from a research standpoint, do not lead to inspired, creative, and authentic learning.

Contrary to their intended result, many of these classroom management tactics quickly evolve into disincentives to learning and engagement. Bartholomew (2007) argues that teachers need to study educational motivation from the body of knowledge in psychology, sociology, linguistics, speech, and organizational management. This knowledge base yields a number of general principles about what increases motivation and engagement, including

- providing developmentally appropriate learning challenges and choices;
- establishing consistent expectations and routines;
- collaborating with students to establish their own learning goals, strategies, and achievement plans;
- setting the tone of trusting students to learn independently through coaching and feedback;
- using attentive listening to monitor student performance and engagement;
- building and expanding on the positives to encourage optimistic thinking patterns and emotions such as joy, pride, and contentment with learning potential; and
- creating climates in which students feel their input is important, they can engage in curricular and instructional choices, and they feel valued and respected.

There are few who would not agree that the quality of teaching is the most powerful influence on students' learning. Where opinions differ markedly is what defines the quality of teaching and how best to prepare quality teachers. Our research and our combined experience have led us to believe that what defines effective learning opportunities for teachers are the same principles that underlie effective learning opportunities for students—i.e., professional development based on learner-centered principles (Hawley & Valli, 2000). Although their design principles were based in part on the APA Learner-Centered Principles, Hawley & Valli also incorporate work from other researchers involved in the study of learning and effective teaching. Most important, these design principles center on involving teachers in their own identification of what they need to learn and how best to learn it. The process of professional development is seen as collaborative, continuous, and ongoing problem solving.

From our own research, we have learned that the learning that occurs in learner-centered professional development often leads to comprehensive change. That is, when teachers truly learn new information, their mental schemata and brain networks change (McCombs, 2003a, 2004b)—they literally "change their mind." To the extent that teachers can view their professional development as an ongoing learning and change process, they embark on a lifelong journey that can inspire and renew them, at the same time increasing their professional competence. We have also learned that the change in teachers can happen quickly when they are reconnected to the moral purpose that brought them to education and the teaching role, as illustrated in this story:

> *During a one-day inservice workshop we were doing for a school district in Texas, one high school English teacher, close to retirement, was clearly not happy about being there. She made every effort to disrupt the training during the morning session. By acknowledging her and encouraging her to participate in exercises that revealed how to help struggling students, we were able to support her to contribute in positive ways in the afternoon session. By the end of the day, she was excited and announced that she now felt validated and reinvested in teaching. She said she knew she could still make a difference with her students and was not going to retire at the end of the year as originally planned.*

Leadership Redefined

In this chapter we hope we have encouraged you to rethink what it means to lead in a time of rapid change in national and world conditions and events. We've discussed the need for values and vision, for courage and conceptual change, and for starting with a close look at ourselves as learners. We've also described some new theories of change and how they are connected to findings in a variety of scientific fields—all of which stress the value of relationships, networks, and collaborative partnerships that emerge as learning communities and communities of practice. All of these ideas and findings are embedded in our concept of a learner-centered form of schooling. As the exact shape, size, and specific practices emerge in each setting, leaders can rely on a set of evidence-based principles that provide the "nonnegotiables" they can use to stay the course, maintaining the vision and sustaining the energy of an ever-changing array of learners from all levels of the system.

When our focus is on change from within, when we realize we are all learners for a lifetime, and when we design systems that focus on learners and learning, some exciting things can happen. For example, Fredrickson and Losada (2005) studied the ratio of positive to negative affect in an effort to quantify what it means to flourish—to live within the optimal range of human functioning that connotes superior functioning, generativity, growth, and resilience. Their research indicated that enhancing positive affect is critical because it is associated with enhanced attention, intuition, and creativity, as well as to other positive outcomes, such as increased motivation and learning.

Further, students who have been educated in systems that emphasize control rather than autonomy are not well prepared to function successfully in the global economy or to be effective, participating citizens in the global village (McLuhan, 1989; Tomlinson, 1999). Students schooled in settings that focus on firm control of students and rote memorization learn compliance to directives, inability and unwillingness to question authority, and dependence and fragility as lifelong learners. What we need are learner-centered models of schooling that promote autonomy, personal responsibility, and trust, as well as a broader base of knowledge and resource management that allows students to be more than low-level knowledge reproducers. When they are educated in a learner-centered community, they learn to be knowledge producers and critical thinkers—just the abilities needed to participate actively and productively in local and global societies. Within learner-centered communities, they experience schooling practices in which they have an active partnership role in governance, and they engage in learning activities with challenging and caring adults. They experience and help create social justice that begins in school; they learn ethical decision-making through youth-adult empowerment experiences.

In discussing why school reform efforts have often failed, Rich (2005) argues that they are based on mistaken and misleading assumptions, many of which are familiar to educators and researchers who base their reform ideas on sound scientific principles. The mistaken views include these assumptions:

- schools are the primary source of education;
- test scores are the best measures of student achievement;
- punishment works to help students learn;
- raising standards means students will meet them; and
- better teaching in schools can close the achievement gap.

Rich argues that the success of school reform initiatives depends on the positive attitudes, behaviors, and habits that students bring into the classroom, as well as the ones they learn in classrooms and schools. Rich believes that addressing these social and emotional factors in concert with the academic factors is critical for school reform efforts to be effective.

What Students Need and Want

Cushman's work on students' perceptions of school is directly applicable to how we should be designing change (2006). She presents the voices of students who speak out for a meaningful curriculum. Compared with students in suburban schools, urban students had far fewer opportunities to participate in challenging and interesting courses. They also had fewer opportunities to participate in extracurricular activities, and as a result, they found school to be boring. These students also "…chafe against a system that shuts them out rather than recognizing and developing their potential" (Cushman, p. 34). To help get them interested in school again, many urban students express that they would like schools to be places where they have

- a voice in determining what courses are offered;
- respect for their nonacademic interests;
- inspiring role models; and
- opportunities to connect with the community.

In Cushman's (2006) study, students were not trying to avoid academic challenge but were asking for schoolwork that builds on what they know and care about. They wanted schoolwork that stretched their thinking and related to their interests. They wanted teachers who respected them and their needs, related to them as partners and co-learners, and provided role models that fostered their interest in school and academic subjects. As motivation experts have long held, students need a sense of agency, purpose, and meaning that will help them with the major task of adolescence—forming a personal identity and sense of purpose.

At the 2005 ASCD Conference on Teaching and Learning, students were asked what kind of schools they want to go to and what are the most desirable teacher qualities. A diverse group of middle and high school students provided the responses shown in Box 3.5. The problems these students identified as ones they would remove from their schools and the qualities they wanted in their school are shown in Box 3.6.

Sroka (2006) sees these student responses as embodying a spirit of teaching and learning that puts learners at the center of instructional policy and practices that address the whole learner.

Taking Dewey's (1938) view that there should be a reciprocal and organic relationship between personal life experiences and education, Pugh and Bergin (2005) synthesized the research on the influence of school learning on students' out-of-school experiences. They found that not only has little research been done in this area, but of those existing studies, findings suggest that school learning does not have that much influence on out-of-school experience. In discussing what is needed, Pugh and Bergin argue for a transformative education model that focuses on radically changing the values, character, morals, attitudes, and outlooks of individuals rather than transmitting predetermined content. This model provides transformative experiences in how

Box 3.5   Student Voices: What Schools Should Look Like and Qualities of Effective Teachers

What Kind of Schools Students Want To Go To	Qualities of Effective Teachers
Safe, healthy places	Nonjudgmental
Supportive teachers who know them and relate to their needs	Welcoming and respectful of student opinions
Where they can speak their minds and be respected	Outgoing and understanding
Where they can learn without internal or external threats	Could be confided in
	Care about their students and the content they teach

Box 3.6   Problems Students Would Remove From Their Schools and the Qualities Students Want In Their Schools

Problems Students Would Remove	Qualities Students Want In Their Schools
Bullying	Positive discipline
Discrimination	A clean, safe, welcoming environment
Dispassionate teachers and students	Teaching for understanding
Testing as a way of ranking students	An emotionally nurturing place
Grades	Quality teachers with senses of humor
Drugs	A place where creativity is valued and encouraged

students perceive and relate to objects of study (e.g., rocks, works of art). As a result students are more motivated to apply what they learn in out-of-school contexts, they expand their perception of the meaningfulness of learned concepts, and they begin to value the content for the experience it provides.

Boyle (2007) describes the dimensions needed for leaders of transformative schooling as embodied in compassion, which means putting empathy and caring into action through compassionate interventions. In this view, cultures must be created that manage and adapt to problems collectively and depend on the knowledge and leadership of the group. Leaders must be capable of a new kind of emotional intelligence, which Boyle relates to abilities to empower, heal, dialogue, inquire, self-respect, and deeply listen. Compassionate interventions apply to the total system and entail developing caring, professional learning communities that value collaboration, and capacity-building at all levels within and between buildings in the system. For Boyle, compassionate interventions lead to renewal in mind, body, heart, and spirit.

Box 3.7   What Kind of Leader Are You: 3

1.   Of the qualities of effective leaders we described on pp. 20-24, which would you say you exhibit? List each, along with an example that illustrates how you exhibit that quality.

2.   Devise a simple instrument you can use to ask your teachers what kinds of leadership support they most desire. What questions would you ask? List them.

3.   Journal your responses to Margaret Wheatley's questions on p. 50.

4.   List the problems you think the students in your school/district/agency would like to see removed from their schools.

5.   List what you think are the top five qualities students in your school/district/agency would like to see in their schools.

SELF-REFLECTIONS

We designed the exercises in Box 3.7 to help you assimilate the ideas we've been presenting so far. We hope the exercises will help you begin translating these ideas into your thinking and planning about transforming your school, district, and/or agency.

We have many challenges and exciting opportunities ahead. We hope that you, along with us, are feeling more inspired and ready to take these on.

WHAT'S NEXT

In Chapter 4, our journey will deepen into what it means to lead in these changing times. You will have an opportunity to explore additional tools from our research and further explanations of how the Assessment of Learner-Centered Practices School-Level Survey tools can help in the implementation of change and in fostering the emergence of the leaders we need for transformed models of schooling. We will explore what it takes to facilitate the emergence of networked communities of learning and practice that can give birth to new leaders throughout the educational system. We will look carefully at the processes for meaningful dialogue that are being advocated by some of our most enlightened scholars and educators. As in this chapter and in Chapter 2, Chapter 4 includes exercises designed to help you think about and reflect on the ideas and potential challenges to your thinking that we present.

4

The Tools Needed for the Journey

It is a strange thing indeed that at this time of extraordinary human challenge our vision of education should seem so little related to the questions and concerns that beset us as a society and as a community.

—H. Svi Shapiro (2006, p. xv)

In our journey so far, we have explored why the time is now for a new type of leadership and for a new paradigm for education. We have examined the evidence base for what we believe are the essential principles of leadership, learning, and human capacity which lie at the center of this new living-systems paradigm. We have specifically examined what many visionaries and futurists believe the educational system should do. We also examined leadership as a return to education's moral, ethnical, and spiritual purposes within the new educational system's design. And in Chapter 3, we began to look more closely at learner-centered principles and practices emanating from decades of research. In that chapter, we showed how these principles can provide a foundation for transformative leadership and school practices that support networked communities of learners. Now we turn to a description of specific tools you can use as you plan how to become more learner-centered in your own leadership.

TOOLS FOR THE JOURNEY WITHIN

The research is clear that the journey within oneself is the first step needed for today's school leaders. Allen and Schwartz (2007a) argue that self-leadership is a requirement for becoming an effective and inspiring leader. Developments in neuroscience have shown that self-leadership is easily definable and achievable because of the malleable nature of the brain, making it possible to develop new skills and modify old behaviors. In self-leadership it is necessary to be both a leader and a manager—to be strategic and tactical, to be a visionary, and to direct action consistent with your inner purpose.

Allen and Schwartz (2007b) point out that when the brain tries to conserve energy by resisting new neuronal connections and maintaining the status quo, the will must be activated by forming a clear purpose. It is helpful to clearly answer the question of "why am I doing this?" as well as to look at the disadvantages and then advantages of changing. Resisting an old way of doing something gives it attention, which strengthens brain paths and neuronal connections. Paying attention to a new way of doing something helps self-direct the neuroplasticity of the brain—i.e., the brain is rewired. Mental rehearsal is a good strategy, as is "acting as if" with your full attention to what you are doing.

Allen and Schwartz state,

> The person skilled at self-leadership has a strategy of who s/he is or s/he wants to be and can use 'acting as if' as one tactic to become that person. The self-leader is fully aware of his or her actions, knowing that those actions create the brain connections and habits that facilitate future behavior. The person who is not aware of his or her action and its consequences is not a self-leader. (2007a, p. 5)

Allen and Schwartz (2007a) report that neuroscientists have discovered that our every experience shapes and forms the brain. Using this knowledge, we can label the thoughts and emotions we are feeling (e.g., "I am judging that person," or "I am feeling angry") so that we become increasingly aware of them, which leads to the ability to control our behavior across a wide range of situations, including difficult or stormy ones. In other words, if we pay attention to our thoughts and feelings, we are free to become an impartial observer. However, if we are not aware of the influence of our thoughts and experiences, our brains can be molded outside of our awareness, and we can find ourselves responding in ways that are not conducive to effective leadership.

Allen and Schwartz (2007b) suggest that, because education of any kind creates a brain with more connections, people can give in to these changes, or they can co-author them, which allows us to become aware of ourselves in a new way and is an important leadership trait. This kind of self-awareness allows leaders to step back and observe practices across many different cultures, thereby increasing understanding and sensitivity to cultural differences and points of view. But the real journey starts with knowing ourselves.

Knowing Ourselves

A big part of knowing who we are starts with increasing our awareness of our own thoughts and emotions. The first set of important tools for new school leaders includes knowing the latest research and practice in the areas of thinking, emotions, and tools for increasing awareness of the impact of these self-processes on our behaviors and interactions with others.

What the Research Says About Our Thinking

Metacognition has generally been defined as one's capacity to "think about thinking" or to "be aware of and in control of one's thinking processes." More specifically, metacognition is an area of research that shows how individuals can learn about affect and ways to control thinking (McCombs, 2007). As has been argued elsewhere (Kanfer & McCombs, 2000; McCombs, 1986, 1988, 2005; McCombs & Marzano, 1990), metacognitive knowledge and skills provide the basic structure for the development of positive self-control and self-regulation of one's thinking and feelings. Developmental psychologists are increasingly emphasizing that, for optimum development of metacognitive capacities, individuals need to have a relatively well-defined and stable self-identity that can give rise to self-awareness (cf. Harter, 2006). Self-awareness is critical in that it is recognized as the basis for self-regulation (Bransford, Brown, & Cocking, 1999), which provides a link to various forms of self-control in human's perceptual, behavioral, emotional, and cognitive systems (Cervone et al., 2006).

In a survey of several investigations into psychological processes and structures underlying self-regulated learning capacities, we have identified a number of higher-order processes for controlling lower-order cognitive, affective, and motivational processes during learning (McCombs, 1986, 1989, 1991; McCombs & Marzano, 1990; McCombs & Whisler, 1988). These metacognitive processes consist primarily of self-appraisal and self-management of thoughts and feelings. That is, they involve *realizing the role of the self as agent in the learning process* (McCombs & Marzano, 1990; McCombs, 1991). Thus, the most critical aspect of metacognition for self-regulated learning is not just the awareness of who one is or could be, but rather, it is a deeper realization of the self as constructor of those current and future self-views and self-evaluations. This higher-level metacognitive understanding of self-agency allows individuals to step outside the influence of self-constructed beliefs that influence their expectations, feelings, motivation, and behavior, making possible a greater degree of self-regulation over one's thinking, feelings, and behavior.

In our earlier research (McCombs, 1991; Kanfer & McCombs, 2000), we noted that it is important to distinguish between those metacognitive thinking processes that operate within the cognitive or intellectual system, and those higher-level thinking processes that operate at higher levels of consciousness or self-awareness. Processes such as insight, creativity, wisdom, and common sense operate outside of the cognitive system and are accessed at higher levels of consciousness. At higher levels of consciousness, one understands that the cognitive system and intellectual skills and processes support the person as a whole. The self is seen as an entity that exists independently from the cognitive system, and metacognition is seen as a tool of agency. One's recognition of self-agency and the ability to control one's thinking go far in dispelling the negative impact on an individual learner of low expectations, under-achievement, and poor self-concept brought about by societal, cultural and familial influences. However, for many individuals, this type of awareness is often nonexistent, leaving her or him susceptible to any outside entity that can create and perpetuate negative expectations or feelings. To put it simply, it is important for individual learners to raise both their self-awareness of their thinking processes and their awareness of the impact of outside influences.

Tools for Understanding Thoughts, Emotions, and Behaviors

In delineating the concept of agency, Mills and Spittle (2001) and Suarez, Mills, and Stewart (1987) clarify the relationship between agency and self-awareness, or consciousness. They point out that if we do not recognize our choice to selectively use our thought system, we operate unconsciously within the limits of that thought system. That is, we operate as if those thoughts were truths, rather than a subset of actualized thoughts that exist within a larger universe of possible thoughts. McCombs and Marzano (1990) have further pointed out that unexamined self-knowledge and beliefs play a primary role in behavior only to the extent that we are not aware of our role as agent in choosing how to view their influence.

Understanding and insight involve seeing beyond our conditioned belief systems—our thoughts—and personal frames of reference. Thus, metacognitive understanding is an ongoing process of constructing progressively deeper insights or realizations that, in turn, lead to an awareness or realization of the self as agent. It is *not* simply a process of intellectually constructing a schema that includes the role of self.

The research of Mills and his colleagues (Mills, 1991; Mills, Dunham, & Alpert, 1988; Mills & Spittle, 2001; Suarez, 1988) reveals that if individuals understand thought as a function, they are empowered by experiencing voluntary control of their thinking and, in turn, their emotions and behavior. Their research shows that, while the constructivist framework has been helpful both in explaining how humans actively create and construe their personal realities and belief systems and in laying the foundation for self-determination and empowerment of the individual, it has overlooked the functional side of thought. The function of thought provides a more basic level of agency than the content of thought (beliefs, values, expectancies, goals, etc.). Thought is the immediate origin of all cognitions and is amenable to conscious voluntary control. Being aware of our agency in creating thoughts on a moment-by-moment basis is one of the most influential factors in how we experience and react emotionally to the contents of our cognitions. The implications of this research for a leader's work with all those in his or her educational systems, including teachers and students, are substantial.

To help you understand the significance of this research, we invite you to do some exercises in Boxes 4.1 and 4.2 adapted from the work of Mills and

Box 4.1   The Personal Thought Cycle Exercise

Describe a situation that you don't like when you are trying to lead others to see a new future possibility for your school. Then use the Thought Cycle diagram below to write out your thoughts, feelings, behaviors, and the results of that situation. An example might be "trying to help others see a different ways to think about a new curriculum design."

Situation: _____

_____

_____

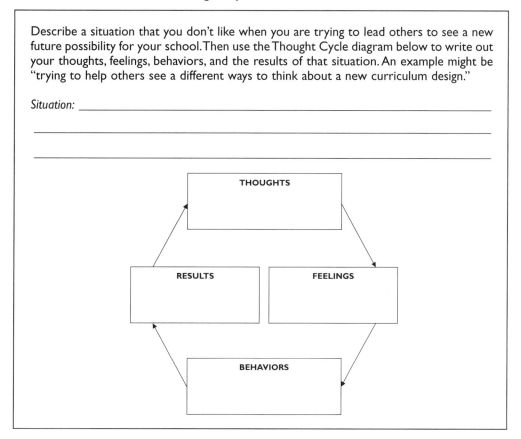

his colleagues (Mills et al., 1988; Timm & Stewart, 1990) and described by McCombs (2007). These exercises ask you to think about situations in which you might find yourself frustrated in your own leadership role and situations that have presented an interpersonal conflict as you guide others toward change. After you complete the exercises, we will show you examples of similar situations and how others have responded.

Now take a look at the how others have responded. Compare your responses with theirs and think about how a similar exercise might be used in your own leadership work (Boxes 4.3 and 4.4).

In the next section, we are going to build on these exercises as you explore how your thinking and, particularly, your beliefs and values play a significant role in your leadership style and direction.

The Role of Beliefs and Values In School Cultures

According to Noguera and Blankstein (2007), successful leadership focuses on school culture—the values, norms, attitudes, beliefs, and relationships of all members of the school community. Parents and community members are central to the process of reform and need to be involved in thoughtful

Box 4.2   The Thought Cycle Exercise in Interpersonal Conflicts

Describe a conflict situation between you and another person. This person could be a staff member or someone in your community. After describing the situation, write out your thoughts, feelings, and behaviors, and how you think the other person reacted in terms of his or her thoughts, feelings, and behaviors. Really try to put yourself in the other person's shoes. When you finish this sheet, ask yourself whether you see the person or situation differently. Then fill out another sheet like this, this time choosing to start with other thoughts that take into account your new thoughts about the person.

Situation: _____

_____

_____

```
                        ┌──────────────────────┐
                        │    YOUR THOUGHTS     │
                        │                      │
                        └──────────────────────┘
   ┌─────────────────────────┐    ┌──────────────────────┐
   │ OTHER PERSON'S BEHAVIORS │    │    YOUR FEELINGS     │
   │                         │    │                      │
   └─────────────────────────┘    └──────────────────────┘
   ┌─────────────────────────┐    ┌──────────────────────┐
   │  OTHER PERSON'S FEELINGS │    │    YOUR BEHAVIORS    │
   │                         │    │                      │
   └─────────────────────────┘    └──────────────────────┘
                   ┌──────────────────────┐
                   │   OTHER PERSON'S     │
                   │   REACTION/THOUGHTS  │
                   └──────────────────────┘
```

discussions about what new approaches are needed and what each person should do to achieve common goals. Buy-in from teachers and students is particularly important, as they are the ones who have to carry out the reforms. The importance of culture is echoed by Lindsey and Lindsey (2007) in their discussion of how schools can become culturally proficient. Lindsey and Lindsey define the "Guiding Principles of Cultural Proficiency" upon which leadership actions must be aligned:

- culture is a predominant force in the lives of people and organizations;
- people are served in varying degrees by the dominant culture;
- people have both group identities and individual identities;
- diversity within cultures is vast and significant; and
- each cultural group has unique cultural needs. (pp. 44–45)

Box 4.3   Example: The Personal Thought Cycle Exercise

Describe a situation that you don't like when you are trying to lead others to see a new future possibility for your school. Then use the Thought Cycle diagram below to write out your thoughts, feelings, behaviors, and the result of that situation. An example might be "trying to help others see a different ways to think about a new curriculum design."

Situation: At the staff planning retreat, the discussion has turned to how the curriculum can be changed to allow students more choice in answering their own questions about real world issues. The curriculum will have to be revamped to be more interdisciplinary and flexible.

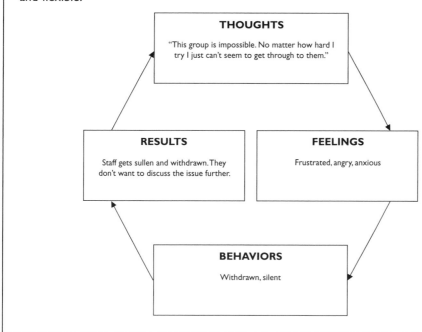

These principles provide a moral compass and commitment to lifelong learning by serving the educational needs of all cultural groups. Ongoing learning includes learning about cultural groups, their experiences, and their perspectives.

Along similar lines, Sparks (2007) maintains that the biggest responsibility of the new school leaders will be to transform organizational cultures in ways that can actualize individual and organizational potential. To do this, new leaders will have to accomplish seven actions:

1. cultivate clarity regarding values and fundamental purposes;
2. identify stretching and compelling goals;
3. communicate fundamental choices, goals, and ideas;
4. view their work as a creative process;
5. attend to the fundamental barriers that impede improvement;
6. develop and display high levels of emotional and social intelligence; and
7. focus on the small things that make the biggest difference. (Sparks, 2007, p. 13)

Box 4.4   Example of the Thought Cycle Exercise in Interpersonal Conflicts

Describe a conflict situation between you and another person. This person could be a staff member or someone in your community. After describing the situation, write out your thoughts, feelings, and behaviors, and how you think the other person reacted in terms of his or her thoughts, feelings, and behaviors. Really try to put yourself in the other person's shoes. When you finish this sheet, ask yourself if you see the person or situation differently. Then fill out another sheet like this, this time choosing to start with other thoughts that take into account your new thoughts about the person.

Situation: A parent has come in to discuss their reaction to a new district decision to allow students more freedom in the courses they take. The parent doesn't understand the new curriculum and life performance outcomes you have led others to adopt. The parent is adamant that this new policy will prevent her child from getting into the college he wants.

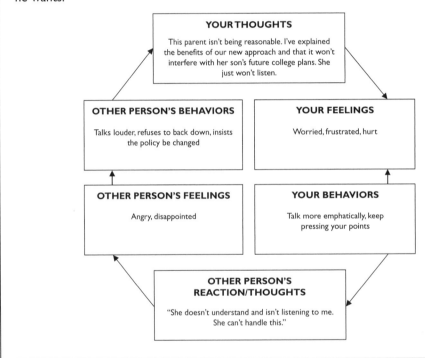

According to Sparks (2007), new leaders will have to be clear about their deepest and most cherished purposes and values for themselves and their organizations. They will need this clarity to help others move toward ambitious and compelling goals for producing genuine and sustainable change in beliefs and practices that can improve the learning of all.

New leaders will also need the ability to express their ideas in succinct and powerful ways and through many media. They will need to see schools as places for inventive and creative solutions that are generated from the inside rather than imposed from the outside. With a sense of possibility and optimism, they will need to see barriers as opportunities to look beneath the surface to the root causes of problems. The new leaders will need to understand that leading is more about who they are than what they do, and to cultivate their inner lives in ways that give them enhanced inspiration and understanding about their emotions and their ability to form quality relationships based on integrity and inner wisdom. With these qualities, the new leaders will be able to identify what contributes most—and most effectively—to the achievement of personal and organizational goals.

The Role of Vision

Schwahn and Spady (2006) contend that the type of leaders required for changing the current educational paradigm in the direction of the future will have the following characteristics:

- they are purpose-, value-, and vision-driven;
- they are visionaries;
- they rely on future forecasting; and
- they are lifelong learners. (pp. 12–13)

With these qualities they are able to provide authentic leadership that helps define the purpose of the school, district, or any educational unit, while also helping to frame its vision. This is done through visionary leadership, wherein cultural leadership is developed through ownership in a diverse culture. Capacity is developed through quality leadership, and support is ensured through service leadership. For Schwahn and Spady, these leaders ("total leaders," in their lexicon) lay the moral foundation through personal values, core organizational values, and principles of professionalism. Underlying the moral foundation are the total leaders' abilities for courage, openness, reflection, risk-taking, and habits that include inquiry, future-focusing, connection, and inclusiveness.

Using recent findings from scientific studies, Spady (2006) has developed a set of precepts of what it means to lead. These precepts focus on the nature of life as energy, with the role of the leader being to nurture, express, and model her or his understanding of the basic nature of energy as it is manifested in thoughts, words, actions, feelings, and forms. From Spady's (2006) perspective, the total leader is one who can consciously, competently, and creatively lead others through leading, learning, and living in ways that restore harmony and balance, while transforming schooling. In the transformation of schooling, attention is directed to changing those assumptions and practices that no longer positively serve learners throughout the system. These are replaced with new principles and practices based on effective learning and leading principles for living systems.

An educational leader and visionary, Spady (2007) has laid out what he sees as major differences between a reformer and transformer leadership orientation, shown in Figure 4.1 (pp. 3–4). Spady (2007) also argues that, to be a genuine leader in transformational educational change, one must see the fundamental differences between the five possible paradigms (pp. 4–5) shown in Figure 4.2.

Figure 4.1   Differences in Leadership Orientation (Spady, 2007)

Reformer Orientation ⟷	Transformer Orientation
Educentric Paradigm	Holistic Paradigm
Content-Focused Learning	Inner Focused Learning
Disciplinary Curriculum	Trans-Disciplinary Curriculum
Rational/Logical Thinking	Divergent/Lateral Thinking
Teacher-Initiated/Classroom-Based Learning	Learner-Initiated/Life Experience Learning
Graded Structure and Learning Opportunities	Nongraded Structure and Learning Opportunities
Standardized Achievement and Advancement	Personal Development, Competence and Maturity
Transmission of Accepted Knowledge and Understandings	Exploration of Unique Possibilities and Understandings
External Expectations, Control, and Rewards	Internal Motivation, Control, and Fulfillment
Premium on IQ Learning	Focus on EQ Development
Competitive Organizational Ethic	Collaborative Organizational Ethic
Quantitative Measures of Success	Qualitative Measures of Development
Closed System Thinking and Operations	Open System Thinking and Operations
Scheduled Learning Opportunities	Flexible Learning Opportunities
Getting Right Answers	Asking Deeper Questions

We would point out that today's leaders must be able to understand the perspectives of those who argue for each of these paradigms. As leaders, we need to see where people and groups fall developmentally. We need to appreciate and listen to the diversity of views and then engage in a process of respectful dialogue that leads to a change process beneficial to all stakeholders. As a way to think about the ideas we're presenting and to discover more about your own beliefs, we invite you to complete the following exercise (Box 4.5).

Next, we want to turn to some specific tools you can use to self-assess and reflect on where you see yourself regarding beliefs and values about schooling and education. You will also have an opportunity to think about how these tools might be applied in the schools, districts, or other institutions where you work.

TOOLS FOR A SCHOOL-LEVEL ASSESSMENT SYSTEM AND LEADERSHIP PROCESS

In tying together what it means to learn and lead in a new paradigm of schooling that conforms to human learning principles and ecological principles of living systems, we have explained that this is an inside-out process. What this

Figure 4.2   Five Possible Educational Paradigms (Spady, 2007)

Paradigm 1: Academic Standards

Essence of the Model: Content mastery of academic subjects
Nature of Learning: Mental processing of verbal, abstract, and symbolic material
Major Outcome Measure: Paper-pencil test performance on content "essentials"
Key Pedagogy: Curriculum transmission by content experts from approved texts
Opportunity Structure: Grade-level constrained/time-based/calendar-driven

Paradigm 2: Performance-Based

Essence of the Model: Functional competence across a range of practical skills
Nature of Learning: Hands-on practice and application of defined skills
Major Outcome Measure: Demonstrated mastery of criterion-defined tasks
Key Pedagogy: Modeling and direct feedback on increasingly complex skills
Opportunity Structure: Time-flexible/determined by rate of learning

Paradigm 3: Life Performance

Essence of the Model: Direct engagement with emerging life role challenges
Nature of Learning: Integration and application of life performance abilities
Major Outcome Measure: Demonstration of complex performance roles in context
Key Pedagogy: Undertaking life-challenge simulations of increasing complexity
Opportunity Structure: Expanded/continuous opportunity in life settings

Paradigm 4: Personal Empowerment

Essence of the Model: Personal control over one's learning and development
Nature of Learning: Intrinsic motivation fuels natural interests and aptitudes
Major Outcome Measure: Authentic exhibitions of one's developed abilities
Key Pedagogy: In-depth exploration and experience develop expertise
Opportunity Structure: Learner-responsive/developmentally-based timing

Paradigm 5: Inner Realization

Essence of the Model: Expanded consciousness of one's spiritual nature/potential
Nature of Learning: Developing one's intuitive connection to universal wisdom
Major Outcome Measure: Taking full responsibility for one's life and experiences
Key Pedagogy: Meditative exploration by quieting the conscious mind
Temporal Structure: Learner-controlled timing/group-enhanced experience

means is that change starts with individuals who brings a willingness, intention, and commitment to examining their deepest purpose, beliefs, and values. The process can then spread out to involving and inviting others to join in the journey of creating the new paradigm of education. New models that emerge will be grounded in a shared moral purpose. In this section, we first review current research that can help define leadership in a time of change and then describe tools we have developed to support this process, which begins with self-assessment and reflection.

Leading in a Time of Change

We have found that working with school leadership requires bringing to the surface the human perceptions and values of everyone involved and aligning

Box 4.5   Reflections On My Beliefs and Values: I

1. Which of the paradigms shown in Figure 4.2 best describes the system in use in your school, district, or agency?

2. Which of the paradigms shown in Figure 4.2 most closely describes what you believe should be in use in your school, district, or agency?

3. Outline a five year plan that would move your school, district, or agency from the paradigm currently in use to the one you believe should be in use.

4. Based on the five year plan you outlined in #3, what are the specific steps you need to take in the first year of the plan? List them, along with the resources (all types, not just budgetary) you will need in order to implement them.

them through a process of respectful discourse. The experience of many people in education is that they are rarely asked what they value or to examine differences in these values and perceptions among colleagues. Such differences can differ widely in any school culture. The formation of true community begins when individuals identify and articulate these and embark on a dialogue about their differences and similarities. Later in this chapter, we discuss tools that can help in this process.

Bolman and Deal (2002) stress that it is essential to understand the different realities of teachers and principals and to use different lenses or frames to reframe challenges. They emphasize that, to be a highly effective leader, one must develop powerful habits of mind—i.e., practical ways of thinking about schools and classrooms that can help leaders deal with various sorts of issues, including political, human resource, structural, and symbolic or cultural. For Bolman and Deal, reframing involves making a conscious effort to understand a situation from multiple perspectives and the realities of various constituencies in the system before finding new ways to handle the situation.

Setting the Context for Change

A new area of research is exploring what motivates individuals to redefine themselves during times of uncertainly, such as those occurring during this age of increasing globalization (Hermans & Dimaggio, 2007). These authors contend that, during such times, this type of change requires a dialogical conceptualization of self and identity. This occurs through continuous interchanges and negotiations that provide opportunities for global and local voices to be involved in new kinds of dialogue. The necessity for change can result from technological advances that often increase differences between cultures, or from oppositions that have not previously risen to the surface for both individuals and groups. Through the process of constructive dialogue, however, people can learn to adapt in ways that form new connections among diverse cultures and ideas.

Hermans and Dimaggio (2007) suggest that uncertainty does not have to produce negative experiences, as it can open and broaden possible actions. Uncertainty, because it is complex, ambiguous, unpredictable, and characterized by not-knowing, can motivate people to solve problems in ways that produce feelings of security, safety, and certainty. Uncertainty can also help people better define their local values and deepen their sense of identity, leading to increased innovation. The kind of dialogue required is one in which people are willing to recognize each other's perspective and are further willing to revise and change their initial viewpoints by taking others' perspectives into account. People recognize they are all parts of an extended self.

From our view, an enlightened leader will understand the impact of globalization in transforming schooling. He or she will anticipate individual and group reactions and be attentive to the value of collective voices and diverse views. It will be important to recognize the value of including diverse cultural groups in dialogue regarding change. Conversations must be kept constructive, while minimizing the tendency for any individual or group to dominate. The new leader will provide a context of safety, security, and certainty so that individuals are free to ask questions of each other at any time in the conversation. This requires skillful handling of the emotions that may at times cause people to want to return to the familiar in an effort to self-protect their positions (Hermans & Dimaggio, 2007). Letting the group define the rules for handling this situation not only promotes ownership, but also allows individuals to interact in new ways that are shared and appreciated by the larger community to which they belong.

Facilitating Conceptual Change

For decades, psychologists and educational researchers have studied the influence of individual learner perceptions and thinking on their emotions (affect), motivation, learning, performance, and other behaviors in a variety of learning situations (Cervone, Shadel, Smith, & Fiori, 2006; Combs, 1962; Do & Schallert, 2004; Marshall & Weinstein, 1986; McCombs, 1999a; Rogers, 1961). As we said earlier in our description of metacognition, individuals can be taught to understand their psychological functioning and agency while also learning to value themselves as learners and to value the process of learning itself. In that section, we described evidence showing that helping educational leaders understand how their thinking contributes to their emotions and, in turn, to their behavior, is an important step in helping them control negative feelings and emotions that can arise when change becomes challenging (McCombs, 2007).

Some of the evidence for this comes from P. K. Murphy's (2007) recent research on the relationship between deeply held beliefs and newly acquired knowledge within the change process. She has constructed a research-based framework for understanding the internal and individual process of conceptual change—a necessary precursor to making individual or organizational changes outside the person. According to Murphy's research, beliefs are generally held in higher status than knowledge regarding their truth. Her research shows that, even though people acknowledge that beliefs are personal and related to experiences with family, values, society, and culture, they hold a higher worth for individuals because they are shared beyond themselves with groups important to them. Although people intertwine knowledge with their beliefs, exposing them to contradictory facts or showing them the weaknesses of their existing beliefs are not likely to change their beliefs.

Murphy (2007) contends that, for conceptual change to occur, an external source or crisis must first trigger the need for change in beliefs or knowledge. Further, the person must then be aware of the consequences of holding an inaccurate understanding, and these consequences must outweigh the consequences of maintaining the inaccurate belief. The final step is that the person must be able to publicly verify that the new ideas hold up under the scrutiny of others. Murphy's work is helpful for leaders because it illustrates what is required to persuade people to change their beliefs and knowledge: to critically and analytically subject prior beliefs and knowledge to an evaluation using reason, evidence, and justification. Leaders who engage in this process for themselves model it for others and, in doing so, convey the legitimacy of "changing one's mind."

Extending Metacognitive and Reflection Activities to Teachers' Roles

How can modeling self processes in the leadership role provide a basis for similar changes in teachers' roles? In discussing how teachers can better deal with the ill-defined problems and tasks of teaching, Lin, Schwartz, and Hatano (2005) describe examples of how teachers can benefit from adaptive metacognition—i.e., changing themselves and their environment in response to a wide range of classroom social and instructional variability. Lin et al. (2005) describe how critical event-based instruction can help teachers see the need for metacognitive adaptation by becoming more aware of the novelty and hidden values in everyday recurrent classroom events. Leaders can help teachers see the need to adapt instruction through such strategies as teacher reflection on his or her goals as a teacher, what a good teacher should do in difficult situation, and how to make sure that students learn.

Lin et al.'s research identified other metacognitive strategies that can lead to adaptation, including

- helping teachers with problem finding;
- setting adaptive goals;
- identity building; and
- values clarification.

Our own research has shown that sharing research findings on the difference in student and teacher perceptions of the characteristics of an ideal student in different cultures also helps teachers see the need for adaptive metacognition. They then reflect on their own assumptions about learning and schooling, as well as how to improve their own practice, both of which help students focus on genuine learning rather than behavior (e.g., sitting still during lectures). To help students recognize the possibility of doing things in a new way, effective approaches involve supporting teachers in examining their beliefs in the context of learning about novel approaches of teachers from other schools, cultures, and countries.

Lin et al. (2005) describe a learning cycle for the critical event-based instructional learning environment. It begins with teachers exploring common events that are likely to occur in teaching. They then seek out, through reflection and adaptation, the particular but often hidden features requiring differentiated solutions, and generate ideas with others who have contrasting values and experiences. In the process, teachers learn that not all situations have a one-size-fits-all solution, adding to the novelty and complexity of what may appear as simple and familiar problem situations. Teachers are asked to consider potential sources of hidden variability in situations, with the result that, over time, the process becomes a habit of mind. They then act on this new information by changing some instructional approaches, self-assessing, and then coming back together to reflect on and share what was learned.

This learning cycle enhances critical, creative, and collaborative thinking about the complex and changing conditions affecting teaching and learning. As Lin et al. (2005) state, the critical event-based instructional learning environment also integrates cognitive skills (e.g., making decisions) and general adaptive and social abilities (e.g., reflecting and feeling). This helps teachers develop proactive metacognitive capabilities of self-assessment and reflection, which are central to the process of change in self-awareness and thinking necessary to talk with and share leadership with others.

The Self-Assessment and Reflection Process

As we mentioned in Chapter 2, we have been working to define tools that support school change and that are based on the Learner-Centered Principles and Learner-Centered Model. We described results with the Assessment of Learner-Centered Practice surveys that have been validated and used at all levels of schooling (grades K–3, 4–8, 9–12, and college) to examine classroom practices and their alignment with the Learner-Centered Principles and Learner-Centered Model. In Chapter 3, we introduced you to the School–Level Assessment of Learner-Centered Practices and how this self-assessment and reflection tool works in conjunction with the classroom level Assessment of Learner-Centered Practices surveys to determine if practices are systemically "learner-centered." You also had an opportunity to look at some sample items and the types of feedback available to school leaders and staff from the School-Level Assessment of Learner-Centered Practices surveys.

To fully understand how this school–level tool can be used, it is important to understand the self-assessment and reflection process that engages individuals and groups in understanding and dialoguing about the results.

Why Self-Assessment?

In our research (cf. McCombs & Miller, 2007) with a variety of K–12 school systems and higher-education institutions, including community colleges, we learned that it is vital to have the right tool that identifies basic beliefs, values, and assumptions about learners, learning, teaching, and the elements that support these. The right tool needs to provide an effective and efficient way to identify personal and group discrepancies. As we saw earlier, discrepancies in values and perceptions of reality give rise to a recognition of the need and will to change. As you saw in Table 3.2 on page 61 in Chapter 3, it is possible for school leaders to look at various discrepancies among staff perceptions in the eight areas assessed by the School-Level Assessment of Learner-Centered Practices surveys. As a reminder, these eight areas are:

- Expectations for Students
- Instruction and Management Practices
- Curriculum Structures
- Assessment and Grading Practices
- Professional Development Practices
- Parent and Community Involvement Strategies
- Leadership Style and Practices
- Policies and Regulations

Figure 4.3 shows an example of how different groups of staff in one school district hold different learner-centered goals (beliefs and values).

Using the information in Figure 4.3, the school leader can begin a dialogue about why the beliefs and values about these eight learner-centered areas of practice differ and how well they reflect the desired learner-centered approach. Following this dialogue, these results are then compared to these same staff members' perceptions of the degree to which these practices are actually in place. Figure 4.4 shows an example of how staff in one district differed in their perceptions of the degree to which learner-centered practices were actually in place.

The leadership role in this process is to help all staff reflect, at length and in depth, on why their perceptions differ and what approaches they recommend for better aligning all staff into communities of learners and practice. Of particular interest in this example is that, in seven of the eight school practices, the three administrators perceived the practices to be in place to a greater degree than all the other staff, which would provide a natural starting point for the dialogue about why their perceptions differ from the other groups.

Which Process of Reflection Is Recommended?

Our experience has been that reflection must begin at an individual level and then be shared in small groups. The individual reflection must be guided

Figure 4.3   District Goals by Various School Staff

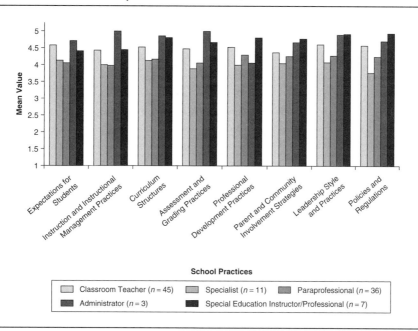

Figure 4.4   District Perceptions of Actual Practices by Various School Staff

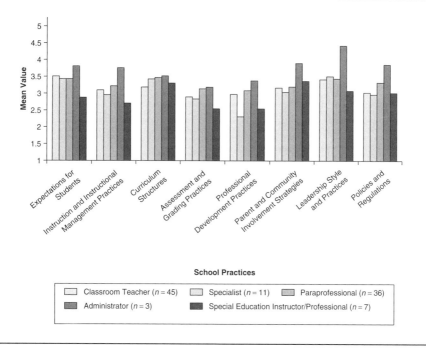

Table 4.1   Guided Individual Reflection Process for Interpreting School-Level ALCP Results

Part 1: Results for the School-Level ALCP Goals Portion

1. Look at the results for what people in your school, district, or college described as their goals for the system.

2. Identify the areas in which the group you identify with (e.g., classroom teacher) had HIGHER goals than other groups. Write down the school practice areas where this occurred.

3. Identify the areas in which the group you identify with had LOWER goals than other groups. Write down the areas where this occurred.

4. Identify which groups' goals were most different from the group you identify with, either higher or lower. Write these areas down and indicate whether they were higher or lower.

5. Reflect on possible reasons for the results you have written down. Try to put yourself in the position of the other groups as compared to your own group. List the reasons you think might account for the differences.

Part 2: Results for the School-Level ALCP Actual Practices Portion

1. Compare the results for the goals of people in your school, district, or college with the results for what people perceived to be actual practices.

2. Note any similarities or differences in patterns between the two graphs. Write down your observations.

3. Look more closely at the results for what people described as the actual practices in your school, district, or college.

4. Identify the areas in which the group you identify with (e.g., classroom teacher) had HIGHER perceptions of actual practice than other groups. Write down the school practice areas where this occurred.

5. Identify the areas in which the group you identify with had LOWER perceptions of actual practice than other groups. Write down the areas where this occurred.

6. Identify which groups' perceptions of actual practice were most different from the group you identify with, either higher or lower. Write these areas down and indicate whether they were higher or lower.

7. Reflect on possible reasons for the results you have written down. Try to put yourself in the position of the other groups as compared to your own group. List the reasons you think might account for the differences.

so that people can ask common questions and derive individual answers to these questions. Table 4.1 provides a list of steps in the reflection process that can generate the types of questions that trigger meaningful inquiries into potential reasons for why various groups of people may hold different goals for the district or school. This reflection process helps individuals think about other people's or the group's perspective as compared with theirs.

After sufficient time for individual reflection, perhaps over a period of days or weeks, the leader asks the participants how they would like to share their reflections. In some cases people feel more comfortable beginning with the group they identify with and then sharing out to the larger group. Often an expert facilitator can be helpful in further guiding these sharing-out sessions that are aimed at the goal of further connecting the group, resolving differences, and moving into learning groups that can further study the issues raised.

As the larger group discussion emerges, we have found it helpful to discuss questions such as the following:

- Is there consensus on the areas of our goals that we most want to start working on?
- Which strategies are most likely to move us closer together in our beliefs and values?
- What do we think are the main reasons for discrepancies between our goals and our perceptions of actual practice?
- What are the areas of school-level practice that we need to work on to bring more groups into alignment, as well as bring these areas into alignment with our goals?
- How do we want to proceed in working together to resolve our discrepancies in goals and perceptions of actual practice?

At this point we invite you to complete the following exercise in Box 4.6 as a way of reflecting on what you've been reading so far in this chapter, and to think about how to apply some of the ideas we are presenting.

The next step in this chapter is to explore further implications of implementing learner-centered tools in your leadership role and to raise some important implications from the current research literature as reported below.

IMPLICATIONS OF IMPLEMENTING LEARNER-CENTERED LEADERSHIP TOOLS

As we indicated earlier, implementing learner-centered leadership tools is a powerful way to support everyone in a system in discovering their purpose, beliefs, and values. These tools also help them learn their assumptions about their roles and the characteristics they believe should define learning and systems of schooling. The creation of new paradigms and designs for education require a thorough understanding of what these models should include, which learning and instructional practices should be in place, and the kinds of curriculum structures needed to support authentic, natural, and lifelong learning. The central question is: What defines positive, inclusive, diverse, and equitable school climates and cultures of continuous learning, improvement, and change?

Defining New Models of Education

A recent report of a special National Study Group for the Affirmative Development of Academic Ability (2004) crafted a vision for affirming academic ability, nurturing intellective [sic—see below] competence, and moving all students to high levels of academic achievement. A particular focus was minority and low-income students and the development of competencies that

Box 4.6   My Perceptions of My District's Learner-Centered Goals

1. How committed is your school, district, or institution to learner-centered goals? Rank them on the scale below.

	Strongly Disagree						Strongly Agree		
	1.0	1.5	2.0	2.5	3.0	3.5	4.0	4.5	5.0

Expectations for Students

Instruction and Instructional Management Practices

Curriculum Structures

Assessment and Grading Practices

Practices

Professional Development

Parent and Community

Strategies

Leadership Styles and Involvement

Policies and Regulations Practices

2. How do you think the perceptions of other leaders about the goals in your school, district, or institution differ from yours?

3. How do you think the perceptions of these goals held by other groups—i.e., teachers, specialists, paraprofessionals, and special education personnel—differ from yours?

4. To what degree are these practices actually in use in your school, district, or institution? Use the scale below to rank them.

	Strongly Disagree						Strongly Agree		
	1.0	1.5	2.0	2.5	3.0	3.5	4.0	4.5	5.0

Expectations for Students

Instruction and Instructional Management Practices

Curriculum Structures

Assessment and Grading Practices

Practices

Professional Development

Parent and Community

Strategies

Leadership Styles and Involvement

Policies and Regulations Practices

5. How do you think the perceptions of other leaders about the actual practices in your school, district, or institution differ from yours?

6. How do you think the perceptions of these actual practices held by other groups—i.e., teachers, specialists, paraprofessionals, and special education person- nel—differ from yours?

7. Of the metacognitive strategies we've described in this chapter, which ones do you think will be the most appropriate and effective for the people in your school, dis- trict, or agency to begin learning?

could eliminate the academic achievement gaps among various groups of chil- dren. Specific competencies the report addressed included

- literacy and numeracy;
- mathematical and verbal reasoning;
- problem solving;
- sensitivity to multiple contexts and perspectives;
- relationship skills;
- self-regulation;
- resource recognition and help-seeking; and
- skill in accessing and managing information.

The Study Group began with the argument that "Affirmative development of academic ability is nurtured and developed through (1) high-quality teaching and instruction in the classroom, (2) trusting relationships in school, and (3) supports for pro-academic behavior in the school and community" (p. 1).

The Study Group defined intellective competence as a holistic set of affec- tive, cognitive, and situative mental processes that help learners make sense of their experiences and solve problems, and they recommended a systemic approach that addresses classroom, school, and community. At the classroom level, they recommended inquiry-based approaches for helping all students acquire knowledge, followed by learning techniques and practice of basic skills and concepts until they become automatic. The group recommended authentic, naturalistic situations with a focus on collaborative learning and social inter- action. Further, they proposed that students should be taught strategies for transferring what is learned from one task to another through problem-based approaches that emphasize metacognitive strategies which help students gain insights into strategic knowledge and monitoring of their learning processes.

At the school level, the group emphasized relationships that aim to build relational diversity and trust among the students in their institution/school.

At the family and community levels, the group stated that supports must be in place to promote the economic, health, and personal welfare of all, and they recommended community service projects, as well as strategies to provide education supports to families.

Overall, the recommendation of the Study Group (2004) is that academic environments be "learner-centered." However, school leaders are finding that creating learner-centered academic environments is becoming an increasingly challenging goal. One of the big issues facing our nation's schools is that as many as 33 percent of new teachers leave within three years and another 46 percent leave in the first five years (Rubalcava, 2005). The reasons given for leaving revolve around a mismatch of goals versus realities. Many teachers go into teaching because they want to connect with students as individuals, create a sense of community, and help students develop their personal creativity and talents—goals which, according to Rubalcava, are very different from current teaching realities. When Rubalcava asked new teachers to indicate which of the following four goals of education are most important to them—citizenship, socialization, economic efficiency, and self-actualization—they picked self-actualization and socialization. In contrast, the goals of the school agenda currently in place focus on economic efficiency with their emphasis on testing, accountability, and predetermined content objectives.

With an emphasis on learner-centered environments, however, Rubalcava (2005) has found teachers are able to balance current policies and focus on nurturing students' emotional health and creativity. The learner-centered teachers engage students in critical thinking and creative expression, using strategies such as cultural exchanges, role playing, environmental projects, story writing, literature-based learning, integrated physical education, and inquiry-based collaborative learning. Rubalcava believes that helping new teachers connect meaningfully with their students is the primary ingredient in the success of any of these strategies.

Preparing Students for Citizenship in a Global World

In addition to the importance of leaders responding to teachers' moral concerns and convictions about their roles, they also need to prepare students for their places in a rapidly expanding and increasingly global world.

Fuhrman and Lazerson (2005) report that, given the critical role public schools play in shaping our understanding of ourselves and our national aspirations, most Americans believe that education should be about citizenship. In addition to academic content, people cite democratic deliberation as a critical component, with teachers having the greatest potential influence on what students as future citizens think. The respondents in Fuhrman and Lazerson's study believe that, without these deliberations in school settings, students fall victim to influences of the media, which reflects a continuing deterioration in public discourse. These respondents advocate a more pervasive role for civic education, in which students learn to argue and appreciate, understand and criticize, persuade and collectively decide, in moral terms, how to deal with ongoing disagreements that are part of the American democracy.

Joining those who argue that a traditional liberal education contributes to the development of citizenship in a democratic society, Vanhuysse (2006) contends that a general education contributes to the development of creativity and students' future roles in a global society. He points out that Albert Einstein defended generalism in schools over a half-century ago on the basis that it promotes better adaptability to change when it is the foundation of cultural life, including specialized knowledge. Those who study creativity in artistic and scientific endeavors, such as Csikszentmihalyi (1996), have also argued that breakthroughs depend on linking information that is usually not thought of as related by having a breadth of general knowledge beyond the limits of a specific knowledge domain. A learner-centered approach, with its focus on expanding students' individual abilities to understand and link information, processes, and ideas, offers a powerful way to develop the capacity to participate in the democratic deliberations essential to successful citizenry.

A New Direction for Curriculum

Among those suggesting that our current curriculum structures need to be completely rethought and revamped, Vanhuysse (2006) points to general or classic education as a way to ensure that the scientific and intuitive orientations of the human mind are not kept separate because their cross-fertilizing results in the creation and production of knowledge. He argues that knowing about and critically debating our past allows students to learn a flexible openness to and ability to cope with what is new. He states,

> A related and more positive argument in favor of a generalist or classic education is that because it captures better and more recognizably the essence of human life, and perhaps because it is mediated via aesthetic or other emotions, the classics simply are conducive to *better learning*. (2006, p. 12)

As shown by Simon (1983), traditional liberal arts curricula help students learn better and remember longer. They can attend to issues longer and think harder about them, leading to deeper impressions that last longer, particularly when this curriculum is taught in the context of critical dialogue.

Brady (2008) suggests even more innovative and "out-of-the-box" curriculum models. A long-time advocate that curriculum needs to be about life and to ask the deep personal questions that lead to genuine understanding of ourselves and our world, he contends that the basic reason for educating people in any society is survival, which means making sense of our experiences of life. This need is what Brady maintains gave rise to the academic disciplines and the school subjects based on them. He believes that continuing to protect those subjects has become more important than solving the problems which led to their creation. He also believes that our curriculum and discipline structures need to be continuously re-keyed to real-world problems, which isn't happening at present.

For Brady (2008), the key to focusing on real-world problems that are part of life and that are facing humanity at this moment is a curriculum based on personal inquiry. Such a curriculum would have the ability to solve what he lists as twenty problems that need urgent solutions, shown in Table 4.2 (Brady, 2008, pp. 2–4).

Table 4.2   20 Essential Problems With Today's School Curriculum

1. An acceptable curriculum will be guided by a clear, overarching aim shared by students, parents, educators, and the larger society. No such aim is presently in place.

2. Reality is systemically integrated, and the brain perceives it seamlessly. The curriculum—which is supposed to model reality—ignores its holistic nature.

3. Knowledge is exploding, but no criteria establish what new knowledge is important, or what old knowledge to exclude to make room for the new.

4. Recent years have brought new and useful insights into how the brain processes information, but the discoveries are largely ignored.

5. Research confirms a relationship between intellectual development and physical activity, art, music, varied experience, and so on, but the curriculum treats these as "frills."

6. The present curriculum is shaped primarily by expert opinion in a handful of disciplines. Intellectually, there's little students can do with this secondhand information except try to remember it. Thought processes other than recall—classifying, hypothesizing, generalizing, synthesizing, valuing, and so on—are largely neglected.

7. The curriculum is inefficient. Lip service is given to student differences, but general education requirements are so time-consuming there's little opportunity to develop individual abilities and interests.

8. The traditional curriculum casts students in passive roles, as absorbers of existing knowledge rather than as active creators of new knowledge. The future, unknowable, demands a curriculum that teaches students how to construct knowledge.

9. No convincing case is being made for the relevance of the content of the traditional curriculum. "You'll need to know this next year," "It's in the book," and "This will be on the test," aren't arguments likely to convince students that school work merits their time, effort, and emotional commitment. Problems with boredom, disengagement, classroom discipline, attendance, dropouts, and so on, are inevitable consequences of a dysfunctional curriculum.

10. All humans have and use a system for organizing knowledge shaped by their society. To make sense, to be remembered, and to be useful, everything taught must fit into this system. If it doesn't, it goes into short-term memory and soon disappears. This knowledge-organizing framework isn't "surfaced" so students can examine, refine, and make deliberate use of it.

11. The traditional curriculum neglects vast areas of knowledge of critical importance in making personal decisions and in drafting wise public policy.

12. Change is a fact of life and is everywhere apparent in the natural and human-made worlds. The traditional curriculum has no built-in mechanisms forcing it to adapt to current reality, anticipate probable and possible futures, and shape preferable ones.

13. The desire to learn is one of the deepest of all human drives. However, instead of cultivating and encouraging this intrinsic love of learning, present curriculum-based instruction relies primarily on extrinsic motivators—the threat of failure, fear of censure or the law, or the promise of praise, gold stars, grades, certificates, diplomas, or future success.

14. Complex technology and pressure from business and industry have elevated in the public mind the importance of specialized studies, particularly in mathematics and science. As a consequence, students considered "best" are channeled into narrow fields without adequate exposure to other dimensions of life, particularly the complex moral and ethical issues raised by developments in technical fields and their potentially devastating impact on society.

15. Curricular emphasis on merely distributing information has given rise to simplistic, superficial, destructive notions—instruction that confuses "harder" with "better"—to standards that merely standardize, and to machine-gradable tests incapable of evaluating the quality of complex thought processes.

16. The traditional curriculum fails to lead students in a systematic way through ever-increasing levels of intellectual sophistication. To the extent there's concern for coordinating what's taught, it's limited to efforts within fields of study without concern for the whole.

17. The transition from the static, insular nature of school to the dynamic, exposed nature of adult life is so abrupt many students are unable to adequately cope. The curriculum should so thoroughly integrate education and life there's little or no sense of transition.

18. How little most adults can recall of what they once "learned" in school testifies to the inadequacy of the theory that "if you throw enough mud on the wall some of it is bound to stick." The brain's ability to cope with large amounts of unorganized information dispensed at fire-hose velocity is extremely limited, a fact routinely disregarded by the traditional curriculum.

19. The young learn at a phenomenal rate. Long before they start to school, most can acquire more than one language, internalize the complex rules governing myriad social situations, master many technological devices, learn the rules of any number of games, and much, much else. All this without being able to read or compute. In school, however, the abilities which make such learning possible are smothered by the assumption that learning comes primarily from interpreting and manipulating symbols—literacy and numeracy.

20. Finally, and perhaps most importantly, learning isn't primarily a matter of transferring information from those who know to those who don't know, but of discovering relationships between parts of reality not previously thought to be related. Because the present curriculum erects awkward, arbitrary, artificial walls between the study of various aspects of reality, fragmenting it into disciplines, subjects, courses, themes, and so on, the basic process by means of which individual and collective knowledge expands is blocked. Only if students have in place and know how to use a framework of ideas that includes and logically relates everything they know is it possible for them to generate a full range of hypotheses about possible relationships. Because humankind's very survival hinges on the ability to create new knowledge, it's impossible to exaggerate the societal costs of a curriculum which fails to provide students with the basic intellectual tool by means of which knowledge is constructed.

Source: Brady, 2008

To address the problems in Table 4.2, Brady (2008) suggests a powerful conceptual tool—stories—that educators can use to help students learn what they need to know in today's world. This tool is one that helps students develop skills for understanding the systemic relationships between specific things they already know, and for predicting or anticipating the consequences of the interactions of those things. It helps turn information into knowledge and knowledge into wisdom through making sense of specific past, present, anticipated, and imagined experience by means of stories.

Brady (2008) has shown that using stories helps, not only students, but all of us, to elaborate and integrate five kinds of information. What we are thinking about related to the problem to be solved is pulled from the individual's consciousness based on their prior experiences with similar problems. For structure, the problem is organized around common story elements: (1) a setting, (2) time dimensions, (3) the actors or participants, (4) action, and (5) the states of mind (beliefs, values, assumptions) that explain the action. Brady believes that, woven together systemically, these aspects of stories are the building blocks of meaning. The five structures, with their vast, supporting conceptual substructures drawn from everyday language and the specialized vocabularies of the disciplines, are a society's "model of reality," and its "master sense-making system." Individuals adopt and adapt the model as a guide to everyday behavior. In Brady's view, the five building blocks are tools which, because of the integrated nature of the reality they model, are best used simultaneously. He has found that when students are helped to raise this five-element knowledge-organizing model of reality into consciousness and use it to guide thought, they will perform at intellectual levels beyond present expectations, including in the specialized studies that make up the traditional curriculum. In short, Brady has found that the best way to teach the young to think is to teach them to think about thinking through the process of developing stories related to real life problems.

Extending the impact of this curriculum tool into the broader world, Brady (2008) believes that societies helped to raise this implicitly known knowledge-organizing model into consciousness. As they use it to understand themselves and those societies with which they interact, they will experience significantly fewer intra- and inter-societal frictions and miscommunications. He further believes that when individuals make formal use of the brain's "master" approach (that is, finding the whole through constructing stories) to selecting, organizing, integrating, and creating knowledge, the result will be an elimination or radical reduction in severity of every one of the twenty problems with the general education curriculum earlier identified.

Tackling Diversity and Equity Issues

Fullan (2006) has recently argued that in today's global world, education has a need to more actively, constructively, and responsibly play a role in developing an equitable society. The transformation he writes about is one that goes beyond changing schools and works toward reducing income and education gaps in literacy, numeracy, and students' mental and physical well-being. This means that leaders will have to gain an increased understanding of the larger social context and what it means to be accountable in a larger sense. Fullan also argues that capacity-building means that leaders also understand how people and systems change as they work on continuous improvement and reform of schools. He states that capacity-building is crucial and that "to secure new beliefs and higher expectations—critical to a turnaround situation—people first need new experiences that lead them to different beliefs" (p. 60). Systems must first work on internal accountability that focuses on aligning individual responsibility with collective expectations and accountability data. This can then lead to external accountability, where visionary leadership integrates top-down and bottom-up approaches in ongoing and dynamic ways, creating and mobilizing many change agents to achieve greater equality and prosperity in their largest and most diverse senses.

TOOLS FOR ANSWERING THE TRULY IMPORTANT QUESTIONS

In this section we want to increase your understanding and provide some additional tools and insights into the leadership role as a personal journey of learning and change. Here we address tools for creating positive school climate, understanding the reciprocal relationships between learning and change, empowering others to share leadership capacity throughout an organization, and fostering meaningful learning partnerships and communities of learning. We also discuss how emerging and existing technologies can play a role in these efforts.

Foundational Principles as Tools for Creating Positive School Climate

Recent work by Mills (2005, 2007) makes clear that there are basic underlying principles that determine school climate, student behavior, and the ability of students to learn. As we discussed earlier in this chapter, his research with fundamental principles that underlie all human behavior has shown that, in the field of human sciences or human behavior, most models of leadership and learning are not built upon such principles. He believes that this confusion or proliferation of different models and methods comes from a misuse or misunderstanding of the most basic principles behind who we are, and how we all work, as human beings. From his work in schools and communities for over twenty five years, he has discovered that we are all using the same basic elements to produce the reality we see and live at each moment in our lives, whether we realize that fact or not. Mills (in press) states that just as all substances in the physical world are built from atoms and their elementary particles, all psychological emotional states are built from the same elements. These elements are

1. thought, as the most basic human capacity or psychological function;
2. consciousness, the capacity for awareness; and
3. mind, the power and intelligence behind psychological functioning.

Mills (in press) has found that knowing how each of these three elements works, and the nature of how their foundational principles work, gives us an understanding of why anyone engages in particular behaviors and actions. In Mills' framework, one begins by understanding about the people involved:

- *how they are thinking* about their situation at any given moment; and
- *how real and compelling* those thoughts appear to them.

Mills states:

> *Consciousness* is the function or capacity we have to experience the world around us, period. It is the ability to simply be aware. However, it is our thoughts that come into our awareness, not the external world! The only way we can know the world is through the seamless meld of *thought* and *consciousness*.
>
> In other words, *consciousness* is the capacity to channel our thoughts through our senses, and turn them into how we see life as a reality. *Consciousness* is the medium which brings thought to life. It translates our thoughts into the language of the body, creating the "realness" of our perception: sensation, feeling, and emotion.
>
> Additionally, *mind* as a principle or function is much more than the brain. The brain is the mechanism, or the "biological computer" that stores information and memories and conducts business in our physical body. The *mind* is the power behind the brain, behind all of our psychological functioning. Without a power source, no computer would work. Without the intelligence and energy of *mind*, neither our thinking nor our consciousness would come alive. This life force or energy brings life to *thought* and *consciousness* but cannot tell us how to use these capacities, so we still have free will, the ability to use thought either for or against ourselves.
>
> How do these basic principles relate to state of mind and school climate? When we grasp the fundamental nature and function of thought, we see the inside-out nature of life. This understanding allows us to drop our attachment to personal, memory-based "ego-" related thoughts. We become less attached to our separate reality. When we are less gripped by our habitual thinking, we have relaxed enough to allow wisdom to come through. This occurs naturally, just like the sun shines through when a cloud cover starts to dissipate. The source of wisdom is not the brain or the intellect. The source of wisdom is the intelligence behind life itself that we are calling Mind. This fact is why everyone has direct and immediate access to wisdom as soon as their mind clears. (Mills, in press)

What this means is that even before school leaders begin the task of understanding the basic principles of learning and change, they must develop an understanding of the principles of thought, consciousness, and mind. They must be open to looking closely at their higher purposes, and step outside the realm of conditioned thinking to more greatly appreciate themselves and others. The exercises you completed in Boxes 4.1 and 4.2 provide the first step toward seeing how you habitually think about problem situations and how your thinking may be interfering with your ability to understand the situation—"problem"—in a completely different way. As you learn how to better observe and change your own thinking, you will be much better able to empower others in your educational system to discover their agency over their thinking and their purpose in creating a new vision of learner-centered schooling.

Tools for Understanding the Principles of Learning and Change

In our work with schools, school districts, and a variety of community and other colleges over the past twelve years, we have learned that there are a number of tools that help leaders and their faculty and staff to see the connections between principles of learning and principles of change. An additional tool has come from our work in understanding the states of change that individuals and systems undergo as they strive to create systems that contribute to ongoing learning and continuous improvement. Taken together, these tools contribute to a sharing in the ownership of learning and the development of partnerships between students and school staff members at all levels. These groups learn to share the responsibility for achieving valued learning outcomes and contribute to the development of professional lifelong learning communities. They strive for increasingly more effective learner-centered practices that prepare students for their global futures and the development of their unique talents and potentials.

Principles of Learning and Change

As with the development of the Learner-Centered Psychological Principles (APA, 1993, 1997), we undertook an extensive review and summary of the literature in 1995 and 1996 to identify and describe principles of change based on research evidence (cf. McCombs & Whisler, 1997; McCombs, 1999b; McCombs & Miller, 2007). These principles came from a variety of sources describing how individuals and systems successfully change and sustain these changes and are shown in Figure 4.5.

We invite you to try a mind experiment with the statements in Figure 4.5: Replace the word "change" with the word "learning" for each of these principles. In spite of some awkward wording, you will discover that the principles apply either to "learning" or to "change." Learning and change are, in fact, flip sides of the same psychological process—each is about "changing your mind." This is quite literally true.

If you are a school leader, you know only too well that people naturally resist change, particularly when they are feeling fearful or insecure. As leaders it is important to trust that people will come along when they are ready. The same is true in learning situations. We all know of situations where students weren't ready to learn what we wanted to teach them. Reminding ourselves that learning and change are reciprocal processes—flip sides of the same basic psychological and neurological process—helps leaders and those they lead to

Figure 4.5   Principles of Learning and Change©

In Living Systems, change and learning are flip sides of the same psychological processes. Each is characterized by a transformation in thinking, each is engaged in at a personal level, and each is based on research-validated principles of human learning, motivation, and development. The following principles represent what we know about personal and organizational change. They are grouped into the three domains in all Living Systems: Personal, Technical, and Organizational.

Personal Domain
- Change is a new way of thinking—it starts in the hearts and mind of individuals, and results in seeing learning and learners differently.
- Change is seen differently by different people—to be successful, it must be built on areas of agreement.
- Focusing on learners and learning creates a common vision and direction for change.
- Change begins with hope—believing it is possible.
- Change requires permission to make mistakes and engage in conflict resolution and negotiation skills.

Technical Domain
- Substantive change seeks answers to perplexing issues and must be supported by opportunities for inquiry, dialogue, learning, reflection, and practice.
- Honoring the learner's ability to make choices about and control his or her own learning facilitates change.
- Change occurs when each person sees him- or herself as a learner and sees change as basically a learning process.
- Like learning, change is a lifelong and continuous process.
- A critical outcome of the change process is the creation of learning communities that enhance, support, and sustain the motivation for ongoing learning and change.

Organizational Domain
- Change is facilitated when individuals feel personally empowered by feelings of ownership, respect, personal support, and trust.
- Key stakeholders must be involved in the change and know precisely what is to be changed.
- Like learning, change occurs best when it is invitational and not mandated.
- Change requires commitment of resources, including time, knowledge, and leadership skills.
- Change is facilitated by leaders who share power, facilitate communication, and are inclusive of all learners.

© Copyright 1999 Barbara L. McCombs, PhD., Senior Research Scientist, University of Denver Research Institute, 2050 E. Iliff Avenue, Boettcher East—Room 224, Denver, CO 80208.

show the compassion and patience needed. It is also helpful to understand the stages individuals go through to arrive at sustainable change.

Understanding the Stages of Change

Our review of the change literature also revealed that there are stages of change that individuals and organizations go through. We have shown these in Figure 4.6 as a set of phases indicating that change never proceeds in orderly,

Figure 4.6   Stages of Change

- *Phase I—Developing Awareness, Will to Change, and Ownership of the Need to Change—Leadership Role:* Showing the need for change, explaining that change is possible, inspiring hope and the will to change.
- *Phase II—Observing Models and Building Understanding of Personal Domain Practices—Leadership Role:* Demonstrating and observing different models, discussing "what and how."
- *Phase III—Adapting Strategies, Building Skills, and Developing Personal and Shared Responsibility for Continuous Learning, Change, and Improvement—Leadership Role:* Encouraging the tailoring of different approaches and strategies, coaching, trying out, revising in learner-centered support groups and learning communities.
- *Phase IV—Adopting and Sustaining Attitudes and Practices that Contribute to Continuous Learning, Change, and Improvement—Leadership Role:* Support for ongoing self-assessment, reflection, networking, and lifelong learning activities.

linear steps. Rather, it is more of a spiraling process, like learning, in which individuals and organizations may proceed through the phases only to find themselves returning to an earlier phase when new situations arise. Figure 4.6 also indicates the primary leadership role that is most facilitative of positive change at each phase.

During each of the phases or stages in the process of change, effective leaders are able to see the systemic nature of the process and the "big picture" vision of how, in living systems, as the change process proceeds, solutions not initially seen may suddenly emerge, among which will be the emergence of leaders at other levels of the system. These are people who respond to the personal call to be change agents and facilitate the change process at their levels of influence. From this emergence of new leaders, ever-wider networks and possibilities are formed that, in turn, generate new leaders so that wider networks and possibilities emerge. And so on. The networks of new leaders thus form even wider networks of possibilities for leadership and change. At its most basic level, change is about changing our minds, individually and collectively, and proceeding with an intentional willingness to continue the process.

What transformational leaders know from their own experiences is that what needs to be sustained is an *attitude of ongoing learning, change, and improvement.* Unlike traditional models of schooling, in the learner-centered educational models needed for the future, it is *not* particular programs or practices that are sustained. In fact, sustaining particular programs or practices may be ineffective because in most educational contexts, the rapidly changing nature of our world and the changing needs of students dictate that the system be flexible, evolving, and changing in response to these realities.

As we mentioned earlier, all change begins with a perceived crisis that instills a sense of the need to change. At this initial stage, leaders can support people in recognizing the crisis, as it helps develop an awareness that change is needed. In turn, this awareness helps generate a will to change and to take ownership of the need to change for the benefit of all in the system, individuals, and the collective group.

Figure 4.7   An Example of Using the Stages of Change to Facilitate Personal Change

Instructions to Individuals: Relate a profound change in your own life to illustrate the four stages of change.

For example:

- *Phase I—Developing Awareness...* I realized after seventeen years in the same school that I needed to refresh my understanding by studying new theories of teaching and learning.

- *Phase II—Observing Models...* I began to talk with friends and colleagues about what books and articles I should read. I talked with and watched other younger teachers in my building as they taught.

- *Phase III—Adapting strategies...* I collected a list of new teaching strategies from my reading and observations. I modified these in ways that I knew would be authentic for me, and I asked one of my innovative teacher friends to be a coach and mentor as I tried out the new strategies.

- *Phase IV—Adopting and Sustaining Attitudes and Practices...* When I began achieving more success with my students using the new approaches and strategies, I began talking to other colleagues in the building about the value of changing what they were doing. We talked with the administration and were supported in forming learner-centered support groups and ongoing learning communities. I assumed a leadership role in organizing these groups, and we now have a commitment by all in my building to keep these going.

Leader's Role:

- Relate to participants that there is a large overlap between personal change and organizational change.

- Ask volunteers in small groups to relate a significant change they have made and to organize the narrative of the change according to the four stages of change.

- Before the volunteers "tell their story," the rest of the members of the small groups peruse the *Principles of Learning and Change* that you provide as a handout.

- When the volunteers are telling their stories, the rest of the small group members are attempting to find examples within the stories that reflect particular principles of learning and change found on their handout.

- When a volunteer is finished, the rest of the small group offers feedback based on their analysis of the story using the *Principles of Learning and Change* (e.g., "Once you tailored your teaching strategies to what you believed you could authentically do and got some coaching from a teacher you admired, you believed it was possible for you as well.")

- Conclude with a large group discussion of insights about the change process that have been made as a result of this activity (e.g., "Hope seems to almost always be a requirement for positive change to occur. It now seems clear that relationships are a big part of making the changes we need to make personally and in our school system.")

- Record these insights and generalizations on a flip chart and post them for the group.

To help you better understand how the stages of change can be a tool you can use in your leadership journey, look at the example in Figure 4.7, which shows how the change process can be used as an exercise in helping people within a school organization personally understand how the process works. Figure 4.7 also explains how you could use this exercise in groups to facilitate the development of communities of learners in your system.

Finally, we have learned that there is a learner-centered process that best facilitates change in an organization. It is comprised of the elements shown in Figure 4.8, which is a summary of what is involved in applying

Figure 4.8   Learner-Centered Processes That Best Facilitate
Transformational School Change

- Invite people into the change process. Remember, change can't be mandated!
- Begin with the people who are most interested. Build numbers from that core group. Remember that change in living systems occurs because of critical relationships—not because of critical mass!
- Include people with divergent and diverse viewpoints to enliven the discussions and build authentic consensus. Remember that we learn the most from people whose views differ the most from our own. Engaging in respectful dialogue is the most likely way to build consensus.
- Trust that people will come to the change process when they are ready. Trying to hurry their process will likely produce more resistance, not less. Address resistance openly as a natural human process. Examine what is producing the resistance as a group. Remember that learning and change are flip sides of the same psychological process; sometimes people just have to feel free of fear before they can take that first step. They may need to see others go first before they can get on board.
- Build opportunities for people to make connections to what they are being asked to do and what they already understand and value. They also need to make deeper connections and relationships with others in the group in order to provide support for each other. Remember that both learning and change are facilitated by positive relationships and learning support systems.
- Use the LCPs to align instructional practices across the domains of learning. Remember that the LCPs are the foundation for holistic and systemic change across domains of human learning and across domains of living systems functioning, beginning with the personal and moving to the technical and organizational changes that emerge from dialogue. Remember, too, that the LCPs apply to all of us as learners in designing new practices for ongoing professional development as well as new practices for student learning.

learner-centered principles to the change process. We invite you to refer to this as a support to your own voyage as a leader of change.

Expanding the Learning and Change Network Through Technology

We have a nation and world of school-age children who are experts with technology. On the other hand, we have a nation and world of educators who are often feeling left behind by the technology revolution, and most schools still lack sufficient technology to use it effectively in the teaching and learning process (Hannum & McCombs, 2008). Many educators and scholars are arguing that this technology divide between adults and youth is a serious issue in engaging students in the school learning process. For example, Caine and Caine (2006) contend that education could be compatible with a world steeped in technology, innovation, global communication, and cultural diversity. They also assert that we could create new paradigms of schooling that educate all citizens to live successfully in a society governed by healthy relationships and high academic knowledge—and that part of that education could include instant messaging and instantaneous access to information through the World Wide Web.

As most of us are well aware, today's youth are experts in technology and also aware that schools do not provide them with the type of education they find motivating. For example, recent research confirms that the context for learning must start with what we know about today's youth (e.g., Swanson, 2004). For many high school students, there is a lack of motivation toward academic activities which Legault, Green-Demers, and Pelletier (2006) describe as amotivation (the absence of motivation). This class of behaviors can be attributed to low beliefs in one's abilities to be successful, beliefs that the activity isn't worth the effort or energy required, and/or the low value students place on a task in terms of importance or relevance and features of the task that are perceived as boring or tedious. Given the prominence of this problem, Legualt et al. (2006) argue that academic attitudes and behaviors are strongly influenced by the social context of schools and particularly by the perceived support for autonomy, competence, and relatedness. In a series of studies, these authors looked at the different conditions that give rise to academic motivation, verifying the need for a positive social context and support for autonomy, competence, and relatedness. The study also confirmed that if students believe they are neither smart nor capable of exerting effort, they are the most detached from school. Most important was teacher support of student competence by providing students with information and feedback about their academic abilities.

These motivational findings are related to findings that youth are becoming increasingly competent and knowledgeable about technology in all its various forms. Middle school students are flocking to the Web by the millions to build networks beyond classroom walls and to form communities around their passions and talents (Richardson, 2006; Wallis & Steptoe, 2006). They are displaying a range of creative and problem-solving skills in their use of technology tools. Clem and Simpson (2007) report that today's digital learners are different in many ways, requiring teachers and other educators to design new kinds of lessons that engage students with new technologies, including simulation-style games. Some of the important differences in digital learners include

- they are proactive, autonomous learners who seek needed information from the environment to meet their own self-determined goals;
- they process information very quickly, deciding almost immediately whether or not something is relevant and useful;
- they relate first to graphics, then to text;
- they solve complex problems in collaborative learning groups;
- they are active participants in their own learning, doing first and asking questions later;
- they learn best through trial and error; and
- they are undeterred by failure and see it as a necessary learning experience that simply leads to a "restart."

We can see the power of creative capacity in students' responses to and interactions with technology, which is clearly a tool of innovation that is underutilized and inequitably distributed in public schools. In spite of these inequities, most educators and many parents are aware of the gap between students' use and understanding of the latest digital technologies and how these technologies are used/not used in the schools. Prensky (2006) contends that schools are stuck in the 20th century, while students have rushed into the 21st century. Today's students were born into the digital age and are fluent in the digital language of computers, video games, and the Internet. Many even report learning to read from games rather than teachers and school. Because students are empowered by technology in so many ways outside their schools, more than ever they need a meaningful voice in their own digital-age education (McCombs & Vakili, 2005).

March (2006) makes the point that in this era of instant gratification, schools must provide education that is real, rich, and relevant. With this challenge comes the opportunity to shift students from consumption to action and creativity, which makes it more imperative than ever that teachers stay on top of innovative ways to use technology in learning. Most promising are collaborative partnership models shown to be highly effective, such as Dennis Harper's Gen Y program (Harper, 2002). What makes this program so innovative is that teachers and students are partners in using technology in learning. Students are taught to work with teachers to use technology in ways that are interesting and relevant, while teachers are taught to work with students to design the lessons in ways that promote learning. Together, both teachers and students learn the best ways to learn with technology.

It is a significant leadership challenge to understand and become familiar with who students are, which technologies they know and use frequently, and how they would like to see these technologies used in their education. Including students as partners in school transformation is an essential empowerment strategy that contributes to the success of new learning and to the creation of new educational models.

Tools for Empowering Others to Share Leadership Capacity

Wheatley (2007) describes the qualities of leaders who empower and evoke the best qualities in others as qualities that "…affirm life's capacities to self-organize in creative, sustainable, and generous ways" (p. 1). Specifically, Wheatley describes these qualities as

- knowing one cannot lead alone;
- having more faith in people than they do in themselves;
- recognizing human diversity as a gift, and the human spirit as a blessing;
- acting on the fact that people only support what they create;
- solving unsolvable problems by bringing new voices into the room;
- using learning as the fundamental process for resiliency, change, and growth; and
- offering purposeful work as the necessary condition for people to engage fully. (p. 1)

A respected writer in the area of leadership, Linda Lambert has argued for constructivist leadership that focuses on the major concepts of reciprocity, learning, community, and purpose (Lambert, 2000, 2002, 2003). Lambert broadens the concept of leadership so that it is a shared responsibility for a shared community purpose (Lambert, 2002). This constructivist approach to leadership means that it is guided by inquiry, dialogue, reflection, and action. Its reciprocity lies in staff interactions and dialogue that identifies and articulates current practices, assumptions, and beliefs. People make sense of what they are learning and frame new actions and practices based on new understandings (Lambert, 2000) Lambert (2003) also sees leadership as a process that takes people to higher levels of development through sharing of knowing, learning, and leading, all of which lead to a community with shared purpose.

Stilger (2007) discusses what he sees as the four things needed to create the conditions for a transformation: leadership, conversation, local action, and emergence. From his work at the Berkana Institute, Stilger believes that the leaders we need are already present and that the nature of leadership that can take us to transformed systems consists of the following:

- Its **intent** and its essence is that it *affirms life*. Embracing mystery and awe, life affirming leadership begins with a wild embrace of a universe of possibilities present when life is lived fully.
- Its **source** is deeply *enspirited*. It lives inside each of us and it can be cultivated. Particular landmarks in the terrain of our lives make this source of leadership accessible to each of us.
- Its **practice** is *servant leadership*. Certain practices and awareness of leadership allow us to step forward as leaders in service to the whole. These practices and awareness are easily accessible to each of us. They are, in fact, the practices we have seen regularly from those leaders who arise when called to do the work that needs to be done. (p. 1)

In sum, the leadership role is one that moves from self (the inner journey) to influencing the others in our systems (the outward manifestation).

Tools for Fostering Learning Partnerships and Learning Communities

Our approach to fostering learning partnerships and building communities of learning grows out of the descriptions of empowering leaders we have presented thus far. We believe it is important for school leaders to understand that empowerment is a natural response to the inner work we have been describing throughout this chapter. Part of that inner work requires a clear understanding of what many see as the "big picture" of our human condition and the need for fundamental changes in how our organizations and our entire world are run.

David Korten, co-founder and board chair of the Positive Futures Network (www.yesmagazine.org), has recently written about the need for a global change in the way we run our world. He argues that there are two generic names for the way this organizing can be done: One is Empire, in which domination is the organizing principle, whether it be among nations or family members. The other, Earth Community, organizes through partnership. Korten (2006), citing evidence from quantum physics, evolutionary biology, developmental psychology, anthropology, archaeology, and religious mysticism, believes this second organizing principle unleashes human potential for creativity, cooperation, and sharing of resources and surpluses for the good of all.

Historically, Koren tells us, the earth was once ruled by Earth Community principles but turned to Empire principles about 5,000 years ago. Although this Empire domination has changed in form over the centuries, it has survived even in democratic reforms. From Korten's (2006) perspective, the domination of a few on the top and many on the bottom has led to sexism, racism, economic injustice, violence, and environmental destruction that may be leading us to the point of destruction.

Korten's (2006) advice to leaders is that, in order to move toward an Earth Community of partnership cultures and institutions, people need to work together from the bottom up in inclusive communities and using inclusive dialogues that cut across racial, religious, and class lines to create a world that works for everyone. As commitment and engagement grow, they create a growing potential to merge into ever-larger dialogues. Korten (2006) believes that a global awakening to higher levels of human consciousness is already underway with the growing leadership of women, communities of color, and indigenous people. Korten contends that, once the process starts, it progresses through three "turnings" from dominator ethos to a partnership ethos in which relationships predominate:

- **Cultural Turning**—The Great Turning begins with a cultural and spiritual awakening—a turning in cultural values from money and material excess to life and spiritual fulfillment, from a belief in our limitations to a belief in our possibilities, and from fearing our differences to rejoicing in our diversity. It requires reframing the cultural stories by which we define our human nature, purpose, and possibilities.
- **Economic Turning**—The values shift of the cultural turning leads us to redefine wealth—to measure it by the health of our families, communities, and natural environment. It leads us from policies that raise those at the top to policies that raise those at the bottom, from hoarding to sharing, from concentrated to distributed ownership, and from the rights of ownership to the responsibilities of stewardship.
- **Political Turning**—The economic turning creates the necessary conditions for a turn from a one-dollar, one-vote democracy to a one-person, one-vote democracy, from passive to active citizenship, from competition for individual advantage to cooperation for mutual advantage, from retributive justice to restorative justice, and from social order by coercion to social order by mutual responsibility and accountability." (p. 16)

Stories are a powerful way to both keep various principles in place as well as to change them. We all need to be involved in creating and disseminating our stories of success with partnership cultures and institutions. Korten (2006) maintains the time is now and people are ready.

Now take a few moments to reflect and complete the exercise in Box 4.7.

In our discussion of the Learner-Centered Model in Chapter 2, we provided short descriptions of learner-centered self-assessment and reflection tools, and in Chapter 3 we described them in a bit more depth. In the next section, we describe these tools in greater detail in order to show you how they can be used in the process of leading change to learner-centered schooling in your school, district, or agency. We also want to show you how these learner-centered tools can promote lifelong learning skills in students.

SELF-ASSESSMENT AND REFLECTION TOOLS TO CHART THE JOURNEY

The Assessment of Learner-Centered Practices School and Classroom Surveys as Part of a Change Process

In our earlier book for teachers—*Learner-Centered Classroom Practices and Assessments: Maximizing Student Motivation, Learning, and Achievement*—we described the set of self-assessment and reflection tools that teachers can use in their own journey to learner-centered schooling (McCombs & Miller, 2007). Here we describe how school leaders can use these tools to support their own self-assessment and reflection.

The Assessment of Learner-Centered Practices System of Self-Assessment and Reflection

As we pointed out in Chapter 3, the school-level Assessment of Learner-Centered Practices (Assessment of Learner-Centered Practices) survey comprises the first step a leader takes in aligning learner-centered beliefs and values with perceptions of actual learner-centered practices. Through using the Assessment of Learner-Centered Practices system, discrepancies identified at the personal and system levels provide the impetus for change. Identifying these discrepancies between what people in the system perceive are the learner-centered goals and what they perceive are the actual learner-centered practices creates a personal and organizational crisis, which then engenders an individual and collective recognition of the need to change.

The Assessment of Learner-Centered Practices process is designed to be nonevaluative and nonthreatening. It is a personal and collective process that respects the confidentiality of individual and group responses. No information is shared with others without the explicit permission of those involved.

The Assessment of Learner-Centered Practices self-assessment and reflection system was designed to be

- nonthreatening;
- a set of tools for learning and change; and
- a series of opportunities to share expertise.

Box 4.7   Building Innate Health

Jot down your thoughts and reflections about the questions below. If possible, talk these over with a colleague or learning partner.

1. Describe your perception of how committed your school, district, or agency is to the innate health of its students, teachers, families, and administrators.

2. If your school, district, or agency is not very committed to the innate health of those in the system, what do you believe you can do to change the situation? Describe what you believe you could do over the course of the next year.

3. If your school, district, or agency has a commitment to the innate health of those in the system, what do you see is your next step in furthering that commitment? Describe what you believe you could do over the course of the next year.

It was designed specifically **not** to be

- a set of evaluations of competence;
- a compilation of one-size-fits-all strategies; and
- a set of "cookbook" teaching and learning procedures (McCombs, 2003a; McCombs & Miller, 2007).

The Assessment of Learner-Centered Practices system uses a guided reflection process to identify and facilitate the individual interpretation and identification of areas that need to change at the personal or systems level. Basically, the process involves a trusted person within the system—or an outside consultant—who has been trained to do the guided reflection process providing feedback to individuals about the meaning of their responses. This process provides

- individual and confidential feedback on an individual's scores relative to the Learner-Centered Rubric, a validated range of scores from the most effective leaders and teachers;
- time for reflection on areas of beliefs or practices that could shift in more learner-centered directions; and
- encouragement for individuals to take personal responsibility for ongoing learning and continuous assessment and improvement of practice.

The main purpose of the guided reflection process is to help individuals feel comfortable with and excited about changes they identify themselves following an explanation of their personal results on the school or classroom Assessment of Learner-Centered Practices surveys. The process shows individuals how to identify the discrepancies they want to work on and to find their own answers to questions about how their practices can change for the better relative to the shared vision for their system.

This learner-centered system is a set of tools that *can render the process of change a process of learning,* particularly at the classroom level, where the Assessment of Learner-Centered Practices teacher and student surveys described in Chapter 3 can provide insights and suggest areas of change in the following:

1. *Teacher Assessment of Learner-Centered Practices Surveys:* Teachers self-assess their
   a. beliefs and assumptions about learners, learning, and teaching;
   b. most important characteristics related to effective teaching as supported in the research literature; and
   c. perceptions of the frequency of the practices in the domains of the learner-centered practices for grades K–3, 4–8, 9–12, and college level which we described in Chapter 3.
2. *Student Assessment of Learner-Centered Practices Survey:* Students self-assess their
   a. perceptions of the frequency of the practices in the same domains of learner-centered practice for grades K–3, 4–8, 9–12, and college level;
   b. motivation in areas shown by the research to be most related to a variety of positive academic, social, and behavioral outcomes.

We will present you with an opportunity to look at these surveys in more detail in Chapter 5, where we will share with you our experience using these surveys in research spanning the past fifteen years as a way to reinvigorate teachers and students alike and help bring back the joy of teaching and learning for everyone in the system.

The Personal and Systems Change Process

The principles of learning and change we have described, combined with the Assessment of Learner-Centered Practices assessment system, yield a change process that functions at both the personal and the systems level. Our hope is that you will also choose to incorporate some or all of the other tools we described earlier in this chapter that support people in embarking on their inner journey and aligning their own deepest purposes with the changes needed in the educational system of which they are a part.

One of the ways the Assessment of Learner-Centered Practices self-assessment and reflection system supports the systems change process is that it identifies areas of ongoing professional development and learning for those in your system. As we suggested in our book for teachers (McCombs & Miller, 2007), these professional development needs can be identified as follows:

- School Level
  First, identify common areas of discrepancy from the School-Level Assessment of Learner-Centered Practices surveys in either goals or

perceptions of actual practice, disaggregated by categories of personnel, departments, courses, or other breakdowns relevant to the system.

Next, prioritize in the process of group dialogue those areas with the largest discrepancies that could benefit from further learning and professional development.

Then, identify the types of learning and content needed and the best sources for these.

Finally, identify the resources available and/or needed. Be sure to tap first those resources that exist within the organization—those individuals who emerge as leaders and experts in the areas of discrepancy that are identified.

- Classroom Level

  Begin by identifying common areas of discrepancy between teacher and student perceptions of the frequency of practice in the domains assessed by the Classroom-Level Assessment of Learner-Centered Practices surveys. At a group level, and with the permission of teachers participating in the survey process, disaggregate the data by departments, courses, grade levels, or other relevant breakdowns.

  In group meetings with teachers, next identify those areas where teachers agree to some common areas of practice where groups of individuals could benefit from professional development, field trips to see other school models, or self-studies in certain areas where a number of teachers are struggling to identify new practices to reach their students. Also examine common areas in teacher beliefs and other characteristics where teachers agree they could benefit from further learning and study of the latest theories and research on learning and teaching. Again, remember to identify individuals who are already experts in particular domains of learner-centered practice. They can be the ones to model, coach, and mentor others in your system.

  Our work with systems in facilitating these personal and systems change processes has shown us that they work, as we described in our case study story in Chapter 3 of a struggling middle school.

A Tool for Assessing and Monitoring Lifelong Learning

One of the most important consequences of learner-centered schooling is that it creates a community of learners dedicated to learning throughout their lives, in contexts both inside and outside of schools. As this outcome became clear, we began working with colleagues in Bristol, England, to discover what defines lifelong learning and to examine relationships between the development of lifelong learning outcomes in students and the presence of learner-centered practices at the school and classroom levels. Our colleague, Dr. Ruth Deakin Crick, created an instrument, described in her new book, *Learning Power* (Deakin Crick, 2006), to measure various aspects of lifelong learning and its relationship to learner-centered practices. We describe the instrument here as a tool you can use to assess the effectiveness of changes you make toward a learner-centered educational system.

Deakin Crick (2006) argues that, if our goal is to encourage the development of lifelong learners who are capable of active agency and participation in their own learning process and goals, then it is important to understand their personal qualities and characteristics, as well as to understand how those qualities might be encouraged and nurtured. Deakin Crick defines lifelong learning as "learning to learn" and considers it, as do we, an essential 21st-century skill that supports active agency, citizenship, and positive character formation, all desirable characteristics of fully-participating global citizens.

Learning power is a term Deakin Crick (2006) uses to describe that complex mix of dispositions, values, and attitudes that characterize effective learners. It is a form of self-awareness that includes feelings, thoughts, and actions. From a series of empirical studies Deakin Crick conducted, seven dimensions of learning power emerged. Six of the seven dimensions are positive, and one is negative, but all are seen as related to each other and as part of the same "energy source," as opposed to being separate entities. All are incorporated in the instrument she and her colleagues developed to assess lifelong learning.

An Instrument for Assessing Lifelong Learning

The Assessment of Effective Lifelong Learning survey for students in upper elementary through secondary school years is described by Deakin Crick, Broadfoot, and Claxton (2004). The seven dimensions of learning power assessed by the Assessment of Learner-Centered Practices are

- *Changing and learning*—the learner's sense of her- or himself as changing and learning over time;
- *Meaning-making*—the learner's capacity to integrate information and to engage with what really matters personally;
- *Critical curiosity*—the inclination to want to get beneath the surface of things;
- *Creativity*—risk taking, playfulness, lateral thinking, and intuition;
- *Learning relationships*—interdependence in the past and present, rather than dependence or isolation in learning;
- *Strategic awareness*—awareness of one's own learning thoughts, feelings, and processes and the capacity to manage them;
- *Fragility and dependence*—a learner who is stuck, static, and passively dependent.

In addition to creating an individual learning power profile, the Assessment of Learner-Centered Practices system can calculate the average scores for a whole class of students and present the information to the teacher in a way that shows how many students in the class fit within the low, medium, and high category in each dimension (Deakin Crick, 2006). This information gives teachers an indication of the whole class's "personality" in terms of learning power, suggesting what areas the teacher might focus on to meet the learning needs of most students. At the level of the class group, Assessment of Learner-Centered Practices feedback provides graphs for each of the learning dimensions.

Relationships Between Learner-Centered Practices and Lifelong Learning

Deakin Crick, McCombs, Hadden, Broadfoot, & Tew (2005) examined the relationships among the seven dimensions of learning power as measured by the Assessment of Learner-Centered Practices survey and the "learner-centered-ness" of teachers as assessed by the grades 4–8 and 9–12 student and teacher Assessment of Learner-Centered Practices surveys. The studies were conducted in four upper primary schools and one secondary school in Bristol, England. All the schools were participants in a values and learning network and saw the project as congruent with and building on the values consultation work they were currently undertaking. The four primary schools were from middle class suburban areas and an urban working class area. The secondary school was a city centre comprehensive school that drew students from all over the city. A total of forty-three teachers and 851 students took both the Assessment of Learner-Centered Practices and Assessment of Learner-Centered Practices surveys.

The research was a cross-sectional case study designed to explore the relationships among a range of learner-centered variables in order to develop hypotheses about learner-centered cultures (Deakin Crick et al., 2005). Data were collected from students and their teachers in three schools during the academic year 2002–2003. The four variables were

1. students' self-report on seven dimensions of learning power as assessed by Assessment of Learner-Centered Practices;
2. students' perceptions of their teacher's learner-centered practices on four dimensions and student motivational variables as assessed by Assessment of Learner-Centered Practices;
3. students' perceptions of their school's emotional climate as assessed by an Emotional Literacy Audit, a tool developed for use in achieving emotional literacy goals in England that is comparable to our School-Level Assessment of Learner-Centered Practices survey in that it looks at the alignment of basic person-centered school climate goals and practices; and
4. student attainment data based on teacher assessment of national curriculum levels in English, math, and science.

The major findings in this study were

- As expected, all domains of learner-centered practice were positively correlated (correlations ranged from .2 to .5) with all the positive Assessment of Learner-Centered Practices variables and negatively correlated (correlations ranged from -.2 to -.4) with the Fragility and Dependence variable. The Assessment of Learner-Centered Practices student motivation variables were correlated in expected ways with the Assessment of Learner-Centered Practices variables, thereby demonstrating additional construct validity for the Assessment of Learner-Centered Practices variables.

- Also as expected, there was a positive relationship between student self-efficacy and all standardized attainment scores (correlations ranged from .13 to .15) and negative correlations between effort-avoidance strategies, performance-oriented goals, work-avoidance goals, and all standardized attainment scores (correlations ranged from -.14 to -.29).
- In terms of predictive relationships among both Assessment of Learner-Centered Practices and Assessment of Learner-Centered Practices variables and student motivation (self-efficacy, the strongest predictor of student attainment), results showed that student self-efficacy is primarily predicted by student learner-centered variables and three learning power variables. No teacher learner-centered variables met the $p < .05$ significance level, replicating U.S. findings. With student learner-centered variables alone, fifty-one percent of the variance was accounted for; with Assessment of Learner-Centered Practices variables only, thirty-three percent of the variance was accounted for, while the complete model accounted for fifty-four percent of the variance in student self-efficacy. This finding is most critical in showing the importance of both sets of variables.
- High learner-centered groups were found to demonstrate higher attainment than medium or low learner-centered groups. Thus, if learner-centered is defined as a complex combination of student perceptions of learner-centered practices and high self-efficacy, the expected relationships with attainment are significant.

More simply, these findings show that learner-centered practices are highly related to dimensions of learning power or lifelong learning. Although further research is necessary to replicate these relationships in U.S. schools, we have a high degree of confidence that such relationships will be found. Those wishing to learn more information about Assessment of Learner-Centered Practices and Deakin Crick's (2006) work can secure her book listed in our Resources section at the end of this book.

Understanding the Role of Dialogue in Leading for Learning

We have seen that one essential practice of effective leaders is they make their beliefs and opinions visible. According to Wheatley (2001a), leaders should be "disturbed" to be able to consciously choose whether their basic beliefs and assumptions need to be challenged and changed. Wheatley also claims that there is healing in moments where we are willing to sit and listen. Listening creates relationships, and Wheatley contends that our natural state is to be together and move toward wholeness.

As we mentioned earlier, Wheatley and others at the Berkana Institute have revealed that change occurs when networks of relationships form. People in these networks share a common cause and vision of what is possible (Stilger, 2007). When separate local efforts connect and strengthen as communities of practice, it is possible for a new system to emerge suddenly and surprisingly. The emerging system becomes a system of influence that creates radical change, with emergence taking things to scale.

Stilger (2007), whose ideas we referred to in our introduction to Chapter 3, believes what is needed is for leaders to recreate the forms and practices that give rise to meaningful conversations in which the following things are developed: *clarity* about what needs to be done; *courage* to take the next steps; *commitments* to support each other in these steps; and *capacity* needed to get the job done. Change begins at the local level within a community that is committed to this change. Leaders can help communities (a group of committed people) to be resilient, whole, and sustainable through focusing on what Stilger defines as basic human needs around the world:

- having a sustainable food supply, exploring a blend of traditional wisdom and modern solutions to health and healing;
- discovering the essential role of learning in our cultures that moves us beyond traditional definitions of schooling and education;
- reconceptualizing waste as an asset for ecobuilding and upcycling;
- reclaiming our creativity through expression and dialogue in media, art, and culture; and
- creating and sustaining businesses that we believe in and that honor workers, communities, and the environment.

Imperative Questions We Must Ask Ourselves to Begin the Dialogue

In June 2007, one of us, Barbara McCombs, joined with other nationally and internationally recognized educational scholars and visionaries to help define the questions we *must* ask ourselves as leaders of a movement to transform education. The group, led by Bill Spady and called the New Possibilities Network (we will say more about this in Chapter 7), summarized our intention:

> As Americans seek to define what they mean by 21st-Century learning, it's common to think of it as the "new things" that should be added to today's politically-driven, standards-based curriculum and testing mandates. That approach assumes that our familiar curriculum structure, adopted in the 1890s, adequately addresses the conditions, opportunities, and challenges our young people will face in their 21st-Century family, career, community, and personal lives. It does not and cannot—no matter how many desirable things we attempt to pile on top of this deeply flawed structure. (pp. 1–2)

Implicit in the group's statement is a series of questions that we believe each of us needs to—is required to—ask ourselves and those in the organizations we serve. The questions and our responses constitute the beginning of a personal and public dialogue that can begin the process of school transformation. Take a few minutes to review these questions in Table 4.3.

Table 4.3   Questions for a Public Dialogue

Why leave in place and reinforce an Industrial Age curriculum structure that...

1. ignores the intrinsic talents, interests, motivations, and identity of the individual learner?
2. ignores the inherent systemic, integrated nature of life experience and knowledge?
3. has no clear, overarching, life-enhancing aim?
4. does not respect the brain's need for meaning, order, and organization?
5. neglects important bodies of knowledge, aspects of life experience, and avenues of study?
6. fails to move students smoothly through ever-increasing levels of learning complexity?
7. does not provide criteria for discerning the importance or ultimate significance of content?
8. neglects higher-order thought processes and complex life-performance abilities?
9. unduly emphasizes symbol-manipulation skills over other kinds of competence?
10. encourages simplistic, one-dimensional, paper-pencil methods of evaluation?
11. penalizes, rather than capitalizes on, differences among students?
12. makes unreasonable demands on memory while downplaying interpretation and application?
13. ignores deeply significant ethical and moral issues and ways to address them?
14. assigns students unnaturally passive roles in the learning process?
15. fails to put specialized content in a broader or holistic perspective?
16. does not encourage novel, creative thought, problem framing, or problem solving?
17. is overly dependent on extrinsic motivation, grades, and credentialing?
18. has no built-in self-renewing capability or capacity to evolve as new discoveries emerge?
19. neglects the basic knowledge-creating benefits of collaborative exploration and work?
20. lacks a comprehensive, unifying vocabulary shared by all educators and learners?

Clearly, the first step in engaging in the dialogue necessary to respond to these questions is to build trust among all constituencies in your system. In our experience, we have found that this trust starts with openness and transparency—a willingness for each leader to be him- or herself and to share their personal stories, purpose, and vision. Conversant with the tools we have shared with you thus far, you can demonstrate and model who you are, relying on the courage and enthusiasm that comes from within. You can also model what we believe is the most important thing of all—the genuine and clear understanding of what it takes to move from complexity to simplicity in knowing principles of self, of learning, of leading, and of living systems.

Returning to Our Moral Purpose as Leaders

Addressing the topic of moral leadership, Pellicer (2007) describes leadership as a reflective journey into oneself. He poses a set of critical questions he believes moral leaders should consider, devoting a chapter to each (pp. xx-xxi). We highly recommend this book, which you will find referenced in our Resources section at the end of this book. In his book, ten of the important questions he urges school leaders to consider are:

1. Why is it better to know some of the questions rather than all the answers?
2. What is a leader?
3. Why should leaders care about caring?
4. What do I care about?
5. What do I believe about people?
6. Am I willing to share power?
7. Do I care enough to do the little things?
8. What does it mean to be responsible?
9. Can I care enough to be my own best friend?
10. How can a school be transformed by my leadership?

We believe the questions raised by Pellicer (2007) are tools for beginning your own inner dialogue.

SELF-REFLECTIONS

We invite you to review the questions in Table 4.3, as they can help guide dialogue in schools and communities across our country. To be effective, these dialogues must be inclusive and involve multiple segments of our society in addition to the students, administrators, teachers, and parents who are most concerned about our current educational paradigm. We will be saying more in the remaining chapters about what we believe it will take to get the public dialogue going and about the role of school leaders in this process. For now, we invite you to consider the next reflection on our journey.

We designed the exercise in Box 4.8 to help you assimilate the ideas we've been presenting so far. The questions are those raised by Pellicer (2007); they are designed to help you integrate the ideas presented in this chapter and reflect on any changes in your own thinking about your leadership role.

WHAT'S NEXT

In Chapter 5, we will explore further what learner-centered assessment tools can accomplish and provide a thorough description of and examples from the Assessment of Learner-Centered Practices assessment system. You will be invited to see how all the tools described in this chapter can contribute to taking learner-centeredness to a systems level. You will have an opportunity to try out parts of the ALCP surveys for yourself. Following our pattern in each of the previous chapters, Chapter 5 includes exercises designed to help you think about and reflect on the ideas and explore how you might use these tools in your own leadership role.

Box 4.8   More Reflections

Directions: Think about and write down your responses to the following questions. As you reflect about your answers, integrate what you have learned in this chapter.

1. Why is it better to know some of the questions rather than all the answers?

2. What is a leader?

3. Why should leaders care about caring?

4. What do I care about?

5. What do I believe about people?

6. Am I willing to share power?

7. Do I care enough to do the little things?

8. What does it mean to be responsible?

9. Can I care enough to be my own best friend?

10. How can a school be transformed by my leadership?

5

What the Learner-Centered Assessment Tools Can Accomplish

We can no longer tinker with a broken and inhuman paradigm of schooling. We must stop schooling our children as if they were products and reclaim our schools as sacred places for human beings. We must rethink our classrooms as vibrant spaces that awaken consciousness to the world, open minds to the problems of our human condition, inspire wonder, and help people to lead personally fulfilling lives. If our democracy is to thrive, our schools must change into these exciting spaces.

—Steven Wolk (2007, p. 658)

By now we are hoping you are ready to actually experience what the Assessment of Learner-Centered Practices self-assessment and reflection tools can accomplish along your path to creating learner-centered educational classrooms and schools. In this chapter, after providing the context for why learner-centered assessment tools are needed and what they can accomplish in a systemic change process, we then describe more detail and examples from the school- and classroom-level Assessment of Learner-Centered Practices surveys that you can use to track progress toward becoming learner-centered at all system levels. We will show you how these assessment tools can be used to support learning and reflection while also maximizing student motivation, learning, and achievement. At the end of this chapter, you will have an opportunity to use these tools and determine their value for yourself.

As background and introduction to what learner-centered assessment tools can accomplish, we invite you to consider several perspectives that provide the context for using the Assessment of Learner-Centered Practices assessment tools and the tools we described in Chapter 4:

- what parents, educators, and community members want education to accomplish;
- what school leaders need to do to give others what they want;
- what the big issues are facing most school leaders; and
- what leaders need to know to encourage a new model of staff development and continuous learning.

WHAT IS EXPECTED OF OUR EDUCATIONAL SYSTEM?

Current public polls indicate that people are becoming increasingly aware of problems with our current educational policies and practices. For example, a recently released Gallup Poll by Phi Delta Kappa (Rose & Gallup, 2007), the 39th Annual PDK/Gallup Poll of the Public's Attitudes Toward the Public Schools, found that

- the public's view of NCLB is becoming less and less favorable (down from thirteen percent to forty percent who see the implementation of the law as somewhat to very unfavorable);
- forty-nine percent of those polled indicate the NCLB law has focused on the wrong standard of school success, which indicates showing that the NCLB is trending toward being seen as unfavorable to the public;
- growing familiarity with NCLB has led to growing disapproval, indicating a shift from blaming the schools to blaming the law for large numbers of failures;
- the public believes that NCLB's emphasis on English and math is reducing the attention to other subjects and that this is a matter of concern;
- the public, despite its desire for high standards and accountability, does not approve of the strategies used in NCLB;
- the increase since 2002 in the percentage who say there is too much testing, particularly the twenty percent increase among parents, indicates that the public's view of standardized testing is becoming less favorable;
- the public is growing disenchanted with the increasing reliance on standardized testing;
- almost three-fourths of the public wants to see improvement come about through reforming the existing public schools, and only about one-fourth wants to find an alternative;
- if charter schools are considered as an alternative, they are the most popular of the alternatives currently being considered or implemented;

- the importance of a good education has become self-evident, with K–12 schools moving toward the top of the policy agenda, causing the public to take an increasing interest in its local schools; and
- the public looks to the schools as the one place where diverse needs of all students can be addressed, making schools the logical place to address behavioral, social, and emotional needs.

These poll results make it clear that parents and educators are increasingly concerned about our current educational paradigm. For example, Wolk (2007), who is both the parent of a seven-year-old son and an associate professor of teacher education, is highly concerned about the number of worksheets that are profoundly affecting his son's love of learning and schooling. This "fill-in-the-blank" form of schooling is little different from his own school experience and part of what he thinks is a delusion about what schools are really accomplishing today (p. 649). Wolk argues that schools need to be inspiring children to be thoughtful, use their imagination, learn to be empathetic, and develop a sense of social responsibility.

Moving Beyond Content to Learner-Driven Inquiry

The model currently in place, with its emphasis on content-driven learning of endless pages of textbook facts, is not helping students love to read or learn, but, rather, is only leading many students to hate learning. Schools are presently characterized by boredom rather than places that foster imagination. Wolk (2007) insists that they should be places that foster creative thinking rather than perpetuating "intellectual, moral, and creative mediocrity" (p. 649). He believes schools should be places that prepare children for life, the world, and thinking for themselves. To do this requires intense and ongoing dialogue committed to discerning what we believe to be the purposes of schools and how they can be remade "into vibrant workshops for personal, social, and global transformation" (p. 650).

Wolk (2007) also confronts the issue that the sole focus of our current paradigm is an economic one—one of preparing students to be productive workers who fulfill their role as consumers, thereby improving the status and prosperity of our nation. And, in spite of much that is written claiming schools should prepare students to be active citizens in a democracy, Wolk claims schools are now doing just the opposite. Their focus is on content delivery rather than authentic and vibrant daily discussions of what it means to live and be part of a democracy. If schools were educating people rather than preparing workers, Wolk argues that they would be

- teaching students how to understand who they are and their identities in a cultural, political, and moral sense by learning through knowledge to master themselves;
- teaching students how to develop their love of learning by exploring their own questions and interests in context where they can choose and

take control over their own learning by reading the best children's and young adult literature;

- showing teachers how to teach and model the caring and empathy required for a healthy democracy, undertaken with a rigor and a perusal of history that asks students to consider the tough issues we need to address as a community in order to improve our chances of survival;

- helping teachers acquire an environmental literacy that engages children in a critique of how we live, the amount of energy we consume per capita, and how they can be part of a citizenry that corrects our environmentally unsound lifestyles by taking meaningful field trips to witness and experience the ecosystems that support life;

- teaching students and teachers how to heal our cultural divides and develop the appreciation needed to live in a multicultural community;

- teaching teachers how to develop social responsibility, and to understand how to live for the common good over individual gain by inspiring children to work for a better world;

- showing teachers how to teach for peace and nonviolence, and to help children make more peaceful decisions and develop compassion for victims of violence and war;

- supporting teachers in creating curriculum that lets children participate in an in-depth study of media to develop the literacy to critique the media they see and hear;

- teaching students how to develop global awareness and knowledge about the decisions we make that impact the health and well-being of others on the planet; and

- teaching students how to investigate an in-depth understanding—from a moral perspective—of issues related to their daily lives, such as money, family, food, and happiness to help children articulate the meanings of these concepts in their lives.

Overall, Wolk (2007) believes that present-day schools are an insult to children by not honoring them as unique people. He concludes that schools today are not willing to make the dramatic, personal, and social transformative changes to the curricula and practices that would provide for content to be taught as inquiry-based units rather than as a standardized curriculum.

Seeing Schools as Part of a Larger Life System

In Chapter 4 we emphasized the importance of stories as a way for learners to elaborate and integrate new information. Brady (2008) believes that the fundamental focus of schooling should be on helping students to think in an intense and focused way about life. Like Wolk, he urges educators to construct curriculum around the questions of life and how our existing systems function. In the process of inquiry that Brady suggests, students are led to personal discoveries of how to think systemically and how to consider all the elements of a system through constructing stories of what doesn't work and what possibilities exist. Through this process of asking questions about life and constructing stories about how various systems work (and don't), students—as well as their teachers—come to a greater understanding of everyone's roles in the transformation of ourselves, our systems, and our global society.

Caine & Caine (2006) confirm the value of such an approach to natural learning. They contend that if we want to combine academic and natural learning, the best way is to create environments in which students can pursue the questions they are most interested in. While keeping curriculum goals and outcomes in sight, the teaching process is one that responds to student choices and integrates students' interests into a curriculum focused on high standards of learning. Caine and Caine's research shows that, when teachers use such a process, teaching automatically becomes differentiated, and the personalized instruction students experience leads to improved test scores. This sort of teaching process supports students in activating their brains—they make decisions based on authentic questions that engage the executive functions of the prefrontal cortex. The process produces a cycle of perception, thought, and action in which students engage all their senses and emotions, make associations with prior knowledge and experience, articulate questions that lead to planning their inquiry, and take action in creating products that help them integrate new information. Sometimes students engage in this process individually, while at other times, they share the process with others. All students work at an appropriate level of complexity, where they have multiple opportunities for self-assessment and space to negotiate with and help one another.

For teachers to operate in such an inquiry-based and life-driven process, they must hold students to rigorous standards of thinking and acting (Caine & Caine, 2006). The role of teaching changes to one of

- maintaining a class atmosphere of relaxed alertness that helps students feel motivated, competent, and confident;
- immersing students in complex life experiences in which standards are embedded; and
- allowing students to actively process their experiences by using well-formed questions that guide them to reach intended skills and competences while using their authentic voices and choices.

Overall, the teaching process helps teachers deal with student differences, draw out student strengths, and sustain high standards while learning from life.

Williams and Imam (2007) point out that the same systems concepts needed to understand, design, and transform a system such as education are also needed to evaluate such systems. Applied to evaluation, the most effective systems concepts to use are self-assessment and reflection. Both are thoughtful, inquiry-driven processes that lead to community building, dialogue, and openness among all stakeholders. Those involved develop a willingness to see the big picture, develop more profound meanings tied to real life, and explore—as well as challenge—existing judgments and perceived boundaries and constraints. People in the system begin to think differently and find more effective ways to deal with uncertainty and complexity, and they develop new methodologies to deal with dynamic changes and the evolutionary nature of change (Williams and Imam, 2007). The group becomes able to deal with the phenomena of emergence and interdependence. Williams and Imam conclude that the process is one that can be helpful to leaders with a shared responsibility for evaluating the process as they embark on transformation projects.

Given that the public is increasingly discontented with how schools are functioning, we believe it is vital that school leaders know what they can do to begin effecting the sorts of changes that our students and their families want and deserve.

HOW SCHOOL LEADERS CAN PROVIDE WHAT IS WANTED

Fullan (2003) sees that the challenge for today's school leaders is to lead system transformation by resolving the top-down/bottom-up dilemma that is part of systemic change. That is, leaders need to learn to balance the details of the functioning of the system with the overall vision of what the system is about and how it must be nurtured in order to function to the benefit of all its constituents.

One way leaders can retain an overall picture of the system is to provoke the sorts of cultural changes that result in professional learning communities that can sustain capacity for leadership and learning. Principals have to go beyond being instructional leaders to create a hierarchy of moral purpose that starts with the individual, moves out to the school, then to the region and society. To do these things, school leaders must understand

- what it takes to expand the learning agenda beyond testing;
- how to meet diverse student needs including those living in poverty;
- how to focus on improving the quality of student-teacher relationships; and
- which approaches are most effective for students from impoverished backgrounds.

Expanding the Agenda Beyond Testing

A number of researchers are providing evidence that high-stakes testing will not improve schools (Amrein & Berliner, 2003; Berliner, 2005; Nichols & Berliner, 2007). On the contrary, research is consistently showing that a focus on high-stakes testing narrows curriculum and "dumbs down" instruction. As a result, students disengage, and many drop out mentally, emotionally, or physically. Beyond these negative outcomes, many schools are induced to push students out, increase grade retention, force many teachers to leave, and impede real and needed improvements. The bottom line is that those students most in need of quality schools are those the most hurt.

In the past decade, and more, of research, we have learned that those states without high-stakes tests had

- more improvement in average scores on the National Assessment of Educational Progress (NAEP) than states with such tests;
- improvement at a faster rate on a variety of standardized tests; and
- higher motivation and lower dropout rates.

In fact, researchers have found that the stakes attached to performance on these tests lead to less intrinsic motivation to learn and lower levels of critical thinking (Amrein & Berliner, 2003; Neill, 2003). In environments where the focus is on student performance on high-stakes tests, teachers are less inclined to encourage students to explore concepts and subjects of interest to them—obstructing students' path to becoming lifelong, self-directed learners. High-stakes testing does not adequately deal with issues such as educating low-income and non-English-speaking students, and it can lead to teaching to the test and inflated and/or misleading test scores. More effective approaches include engaging students in self-evaluation and meaningful feedback in the form of formative assessment, which particularly benefits low achievers.

Among the many pointing out how NCLB places high-poverty and racially diverse schools at a disadvantage, Kim and Sunderman (2005) examine student achievement data from six states. Their findings indicate that using mean proficiency scores that require all subgroups to meet the same accountability goals highlight the selection bias inherent in these practices. They suggest alternative accountability system designs as better and more valid ways to improve student achievement. These include those that use multiple measures of student achievement, factor in student improvement on reading and mathematics achievement tests, and incorporate state accountability ratings of school performance. We go further to suggest that these assessment systems measure more holistic student outcomes that include improvements in motivation, complex thinking, and social and emotional skills.

Reaching Diverse Students

Among the ideals of the *Brown v. Board of Education* decision was to define as one of the important functions of public education that of educating enlightened citizens. Wraga (2006) argues that recent reform efforts, and notably the NCLB Act, have replaced this ideal with exalted academic achievement and the training of productive workers. Further, instead of schools achieving the ideal of being publicly supported, current policies to privatize public education are flourishing, which has created a sense of urgency to educate for democracy in an era of accountability. As we indicated earlier, this sense of urgency is also fueled by the widening achievement gap for students of color and students from impoverished backgrounds.

Many states are also taking a stand against state tests and other standardized tests because of their socioeconomic bias. One example is the Colorado Coalition for Better Education, which has consistently opposed the Colorado Student Assessment Program (CSAP) because of its strong correlation between family income and test performance (Babbidge, 2006). This group has studied CSAP scores and reports that, as the percentage of students receiving free and reduced lunches in a school goes up, test scores go down.

Increasing the Quality of Student-Teacher Relationships

We contend that, to reach diverse students, a learner-centered educational model as we have been describing throughout this book is needed. We have already explored many of the features of this model. Our research, and that of numerous others, shows that a major focus of any educational process, including a learner-centered one, must be on the quality of student-teacher relationships.

Decades of research have confirmed the importance of student-teacher relationships in student motivation, social outcomes, and classroom learning (cf. McCombs & Miller, 2007). Further benefits of having a good relationship with teachers are that students experience their academic work as meaningful, personal, complementing their other goals, and promoting their understanding. In contrast, students who have poor relationships with teachers see their academic work as coercive, repetitive, isolated, irrelevant, and contrary to their social and academic goals (Davis, 2006). Good relationships are defined by low levels of conflict and high levels of closeness and support. Through these relationships, children learn how to regulate their behavior and affect, and develop social competence.

In a qualitative case study that analyzed features of a fifth grade classroom, Hadjioannou (2007) found that there were seven aspects of the classroom that appear essential for promoting quality teacher-student relationships and authentic discussions.

- First, the physical environment of the classroom community needs to be comfortable, support needs for belonging, and be socially demanding so that individuals are required to be vulnerable by offering opinions, reflecting, and sharing personal experiences.
- Second, the curricular demands need to be shaped around negative policies such as testing to allow quality discussions.
- Third, teacher beliefs need to be consistent with how learning occurs and with the nature of knowledge; in addition, teachers need to know what is involved in learning the discipline, have respect for students' intellects and background knowledge, and understand that teaching is a facilitation process.
- Fourth, students' beliefs about discussions need to include a willingness to actively participate and to appreciate the importance of active contributions to their own understanding.

- Fifth, the relationships among members need to be positive and of high quality, demonstrating mutual respect, caring, collaboration, humor and playfulness, and friendliness.
- Sixth, classroom procedures need to foster respect through explicit rules, shared responsibility for classroom management, and efforts to maintain student dignity for any disruptions.
- Seventh, norms of class participation need to encourage participating, listening attentively and respectfully, supporting diverse opinions, and bringing personal examples to the discussions.

Hadjioannou (2007) claims that students will not participate honestly in authentic discussions if teachers claim indisputable authority or fail to foster amiable relations that provide opportunities for students to express themselves and interact and collaborate with others. Leaders cannot prescribe these qualities for teachers. Rather, guided by Hadjioannou's findings, teachers can create classroom communities that develop their own rituals, norms, and balances.

We believe that what is required of all leaders in educational systems is to authentically address diverse student needs and prepare them for the future, as summarized three decades ago by Wass & Combs (1974) in their description of the qualities that characterized effective teachers:

- they know the world and their subject areas;
- they are sensitive to people and have the capacity for empathy;
- they possess accurate and appropriate beliefs about other people and their behavior;
- they have positive beliefs about their own self;
- they hold appropriate and congruent beliefs about their goals for teaching, the classroom, schools, and society; and
- they have discovered their own unique, appropriate, and authentic ways of teaching.

We believe these same characteristics define the people in a learner-centered system and particularly the new leaders needed to address today's schooling challenges and issues.

As a way to pause and digest what you have been reading, take a few moments to continue your discoveries of your characteristics as a learner and leader by completing the exercises in Box 5.1 and 5.2.

THE BIG ISSUES FACING TODAY'S SCHOOL LEADERS

Some of the biggest issues facing school leaders in today's policy environment include (1) student disengagement and dropout, (2) urban school inequities, and (3) relying on research evidence. In this section, we discuss what leaders need to know in order address these issues effectively.

Box 5.1   How Do I Prefer to Learn: 4

Answer the questions below[1]. Remember that you can choose as many responses as you wish for each item. Mark your responses to the items here, and then tally your learner profile as described below.

50. Before I start the day, I like to:
    a. do something with someone else. (er)
    b. read a newspaper. (li)
    c. plan the day. (lo)
    d. do something physical like stretch or exercise. (p)
    e. prepare my appearance. (ra)

51. Before I go to bed, I like to:
    a. stretch. (p)
    b. read. (li)
    c. think about the things I need to do for tomorrow. (lo)
    d. listen to music. (mu)
    e. communicate with someone else. (er)

52. When I am upset, the surest thing to make me feel better is:
    a. talking to someone. (er)
    b. playing or listening to my favorite music. (mu)
    c. vigorous exercise. (p)
    d. contemplating the problem until I feel better. (ra)
    e. writing in my journal. (li)

53. When I am in a grocery store, I notice:
    a. a change in prices. (qu)
    b. a change in the product displays. (s)
    c. an employee who used to wait on me is no longer there. (er)
    d. a change in the location of my products. (lo)
    e. free samples of food. (p)

54. Which of these would I most like to learn?
    a. statistics. (qu)
    b. a new language. (li)
    c. playing an instrument. (mu)
    d. a racquet sport. (p)
    e. drawing or painting. (s)

55. When I have a doctor's appointment, what do I notice about the waiting room?
    a. the comfort of the furniture. (p)
    b. the reading material. (li)
    c. how I feel. (ra)
    d. the music. (mu)
    e. the other patients. (er)

56. On my vacation, I like to:
    a. spend time thinking. (ra)
    b. learn a new physical activity. (p)
    c. keep a travel diary. (li)
    d. listen to music. (mu)
    e. look at scenery. (s)

57. I really like to:
   a. go to the music store. (mu)
   b. write in my journal. (li)
   c. move my body. (p)
   d. organize closets or drawers. (lo)
   e. play number games (e.g., dominoes, Monopoly®, blackjack). (qu)

58. When I am in the mall, I remember where my car is by:
   a. telling myself where it is. (li)
   b. using deduction. (lo)
   c. counting the number of rows. (qu)
   d. letting my body take me back to it. (p)
   e. visualizing the parking lot. (s)

59. When I read the news in a paper or online, I first look at:
   a. the gossip column or blogs. (er)
   b. sports statistics. (qu)
   c. the listing of contents. (lo)
   d. the music section. (mu)
   e. the layout and design. (s)

60. When I am driving, I notice:
   a. the appearance of other cars. (s)
   b. gas mileage and/or distances. (qu)
   c. my own thoughts. (ra)
   d. music on the radio or music player. (mu)
   e. legroom and seat comfort. (p)

61. When moving furniture into a room, I:
   a. measure the space and the furniture to make sure everything fits. (qu)
   b. describe to someone else how and where to place it. (li)
   c. visualize it and use my sense of proportion to judge whether or not it will fit. (s)
   d. sit in it to see if it is comfortable. (p)
   e. ask someone else to place it. (er)

62. If all these items had to be replaced, I would first choose:
   a. my calculator. (qu)
   b. my books. (li)
   c. my cell phone. (er)
   d. my reclining chair. (p)
   e. my music player or music collection. (mu)

63. If I were to paint a room in my house, I would first:
   a. measure the dimensions and calculate how much paint to purchase. (qu)
   b. decide which color would look best. (s)
   c. call a friend for help. (er)
   d. think about it for a while. (ra)
   e. plan what I need to do. (lo)

(Continued)

Box 5.1   (Continued)

64.   I like to play games (e.g., cards, board games, sports) because:
   a. I enjoy playing with other people. (er)
   b. I enjoy how I feel. (ra)
   c. I like to be the score keeper. (qu)
   d. I enjoy describing the action. (li)
   e. I like thinking of possible strategies. (lo)

Tally Your Learner Profile

To tally your learner profile, you'll need your responses to all 64 items, which are included in Boxes 1.1, 2.1, 3.1, and 5.1. Using the tally boxes below, enter the total number of responses you made in each of the eight categories. Use the codes in parentheses following each response, which correspond to the eight tally boxes. For example, if on item 1 you chose responses b, d, and e, you would tally one mark each for spatial (s), musical (mu), and quantitative (qu). Enter the total for each category in the total boxes.

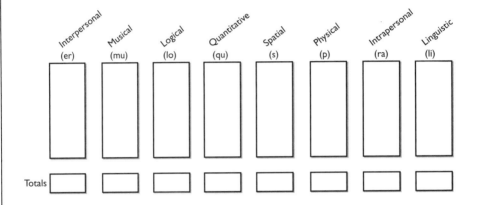

Key to the Eight Patterns of Attending and Learning

You will undoubtedly notice that these eight patterns partially reflect Howard Gardner's model of Multiple Intelligences (MI). Miller and Miller's research, which resulted in *The Smart Profile* (1994), began as a way of identifying patterns of attending and learning. Their approach involved interviewing hundreds of people of various ages. At the end of the interview process, the authors concluded that, for most ordinary people, the logical and the mathematical were two separate categories, which is reflected in their instrument. In addition, the definitions of the patterns used here reflect the authors' interview results rather than Gardner's original descriptions.

Each of us naturally attends and learns more easily and fluidly in some ways than in others, using a unique blend of patterns in combination with our individual and unique characteristics within each pattern. We have included a more complete description of these eight patterns in the Appendix on page 236.

Interpersonal your orientation toward other peoples' feelings, desires, and ideas; your ability to empathize. Examples include mediation, diplomacy, collaboration, group process, leading others through facilitation, and friendship.

Musical your understanding and use of melodic and harmonic sounds as they unfold across time, including songs and musical rhythms, styles, and themes.

Logical how you organize and reason. Examples are your organization of drawers, office, closets, activities and events, systems of knowledge; your reasoning toward logical games and puzzles, computer hardware and software, and in science.

Quantitative your orientation toward numeracy, numbers, and the symbolic representational systems of quantity. Examples include calculation, using mathematical rule systems such as algebra, and familiarity with such relations as proportions (as in cooking, calculating gratuities, or figuring out a sales price), ratios, and equivalencies, and the use of proofs as a way to solve problems.

Spatial your orientation toward the physical world of observable things, including geography and landscape, maps, color and line, textures, composition, design, photographs, paintings and sculpture, graphs, movies, video and computer games, fashion, interior design, how machines work, and spatial games.

Physical using your body to understand and express emotions, ideas, and experiences in such ways as acting and performing, dancing, playing sports or physical games, body work, miming, and working out.

Intrapersonal your understanding and expression of yourself through such means as self-reflection, solitude, working alone, leading others through example, following personal convictions, and pursuit of personal growth.

Linguistic your orientation to verbal language(s), including stories, words, sounds, meaning, grammar, and spelling. Examples include making verbal notes, playing with language, telling or writing stories, reading, making speeches, and focusing on conversation.

---

[1] The questions and scoring system used in this book are from Miller, L. and Miller, L. C. (1994). *The Quick Smart Profile*. Austin, TX: Smart Alternatives, Inc. Used by permission.

Promoting Resiliency to Address Student Dropout

Most of us intuitively understand that students drop out or disengage from school learning because they see it as boring, irrelevant to their needs and interests, or at the worst extreme, fearful and disenfranchising. It is important to understand what we know about the dropout problem and about how to prevent it through promoting resiliency in both students and school staff. In these times of changing educational policies, we need to develop strategies to navigate through them while we construct something new.

Understanding the Dropout Problem

Azzam (2007) describes recent statistics showing the five major reasons students leave school:

- they are bored (forty-seven percent);
- they missed too many days and couldn't catch up (forty-three percent);
- they spent most of their time with people who were not interested in school (forty-two percent);
- they had too much freedom and not enough rules (thirty-eight percent); and
- they were failing (thirty-five percent). (p. 91)

Box 5.2   How Do I Naturally Attend and Learn?

Using the tallies you generated and the "Key to the Eight Patterns of Attending and Learning" in Box 5.1, journal your responses to the following questions.

1.   Rank the eight patterns from most responses to least.

2.   Which pattern(s) received the greatest number of scores?

Take a few minutes to compare your strongest pattern(s) with the "Key to the Eight Patterns of Attending and Learning" in Box 5.1. Then describe your particular characteristics that reflect this pattern (or patterns).

Now describe how the characteristics you just described affect your abilities as a leader.

3.   Which pattern(s) received the second greatest number of responses?

Using the "Key to the Eight Patterns of Attending and Learning" in Box 5.1, describe your particular characteristics that reflect this pattern (or patterns).

4.   Which pattern(s) received the least number of responses?

How would you describe your attentional/learning characteristics within this pattern?

Describe how you compensate for attending/learning less naturally and/or fluidly using this pattern/these patterns.

Now describe how this being your least natural way to attend and learn affects your ability as a leader.

Seventy percent of these students felt they could have graduated if they had tried and worked harder, and if their teachers had demanded more. Seventy-one percent of students who dropped out said they started losing interest in school by the ninth grade or earlier. Azzam (2007) concludes that the issues these students identified are problems that can be solved by transformation in schools and in the way dropouts are viewed.

Barton (2006) reports that high school dropout rates have increased in the last decade. Depending on what sources are studied, these rates vary from a low of 12.9 percent in some states to a high of forty-five percent in other states. According to Barton's research, minorities have higher dropout rates; black males fare the worst, with a high of sixty-one percent in some urban schools, compared with forty-nine percent for Latino males and forty-two percent for white males. Dropout rates in these same schools for girls were forty-three percent for black females, thirty-five percent for Latino females, and twenty-nine percent for white females.

These dropout rates are linked to students' deteriorating economic position and earning power. Barton's (2006) research on factors that affect dropout rates indicates that those factors include coming from low-income or single-parent families, getting low grades in school, being absent frequently, and changing schools. For Barton, these factors make it imperative for schools to both make high school more rigorous and to keep more students in high school through graduation.

Models That Promote Psychosocial Processes and Resiliency

A national study of low socio-economic status SES and minority elementary students indicated that the most powerful school characteristics for promoting resiliency (academic success) included a supportive school environment model that was safe and orderly and that promoted positive student-teacher relationships (Bolman, 2002). Phillips (1997) has shown that students in these environments displayed greater engagement in academic activities, a stronger sense of math efficacy, higher self-esteem, and a more positive outlook toward school. These models are particularly needed in today's culture that has fewer and less stable family and social institutions that promote resilience. Schools can help meet these needs to the extent they are focused on learner needs that go beyond academic competence.

Williams (2003) argues persuasively that decades of research into human resilience document the power of caring teachers and schools to develop young people who can successfully overcome risks and challenges. When teachers convey high expectations, they provide opportunities for students to be active participants in their own learning process. Caring teachers can make the difference between risk and resilience, providing not only opportunities for students to achieve academic skills, but also providing a confident and positive model for character development. These teachers are compassionate, interested in, actively listen to, and get to know the gifts and talents of individual students (Williams). They hold strong beliefs in all students' innate resilience and capacity to learn.

According to Williams (2003), caring teachers are student-centered and understand that successful learning means engaging the whole child. They connect learning to students' lives, culture, and strengths. They give students a voice and opportunities to make choices, as well as opportunities to work with and help others through strategies such as reciprocal peer tutoring and service-learning. The fundamental characteristic of schools that can make the difference between risk and resilience is the quality of relationships between teachers and students—a hallmark and foundation of the Learner-Centered Principles and its manifestation in learner-centered classrooms and schools.

With a focus on relationships, teachers can build small learning communities where the need to belong is met. Corbett, Wilson, and Williams (2005) argue that, in urban schools in particular, great teachers believe it is their job to make sure that all students succeed. These teachers use a variety of best practices—cooperative groups, checking for understanding, hands-on activities, connecting new content to prior knowledge, and other strategies consistent with the Learner-Centered Principles. Moreover, according to the results of a three-year study of teachers in two urban school districts, Corbett et al. (2005) found that teachers' attitudes were the primary factor that made the difference in helping students succeed. When kids were asked about these teachers, they responded that they like the strict approaches and high expectations because they know their teachers care and want them to have a good education. Great teachers also give students responsibility to make choices and participate in meaningful activities. Thus, this study supports what we consistently find with learner-centered practices—the practices alone are not enough to bring about student success; teachers also must possess the beliefs, attitudes, and characteristics that support their students' learning and grown.

Addressing the Challenges in Urban Schools

One of the major needs of students in urban high schools is learning to appreciate diversity and respect multiple viewpoints (Boaler, 2006). Meeting these needs contributes to producing citizens who are active participants in a democratic society. But is this something that urban schools can accomplish in this era of accountability? Boaler (2006) thinks so and reports the results of a four-year longitudinal study conducted in three high schools, where approximately seven hundred students were followed between 2000 and 2004 as they progressed through their mathematics classrooms. Of the three high schools, one was urban with all the problems associated with students coming from homes with few financial resources and being linguistically diverse. Students in this high school were compared with students in two suburban high schools. Through the use of a variety of methods, students in the urban school outperformed their suburban peers in mathematics and were consistently more positive about mathematics from their sophomore year on.

What were these methods? They included creating student-teacher collaboration teams to design curriculum and teaching methods, encouraging a shared commitment to equity, a commitment to heterogeneous classes, and a teaching approach in which students worked in groups on complex conceptual problems that were grounded in real world experiences (Boaler, 2006). In addition to their high mathematics achievement, students learned to respect people from different cultures and backgrounds and to open their minds to different ways of thinking. Undergirding the methods were three premises: commitment to the learning of others, respect for the ideas of others, and learning to communicate. One of the positive benefits was that students learned that with persistence and collaboration, they could solve complex problems—a result that contributes to better schooling outcomes as well as to students' lives after they leave the school environment.

Understanding and Being Critical of Current Educational Research

It is interesting to note that—as important as it is to engage in practices that are research-based—one can't always believe research findings and their interpretations. For example, Davis (2007) makes the case that not everything research has to say about schools should be trusted because the quality of educational research is very much a function of where it is generated and by whom. Davis warns about research from academics who have lost touch with the day-to-day complexities of human interactions in schools. Many of this "ivory tower" research is written for other academics, not for practitioners. Even the language used creates a communication gap.

Davis (2007) raises an additional concern about studies that report on events that occurred at a single point in time and make big press because of startling findings but can't be—or aren't—replicated. He advises that practitioners read research published in reputable refereed journals. He recommends reading all research critically and looking for common threads from diverse studies and research reviews. In the end, Davis tells practitioners to "trust their gut" in matching research findings with their own situation and experience.

There is some debate regarding the validity of qualitative research. The current policy context places a premium on deriving evidence-based practices from the traditional quantitative approach of conducting randomized control experiments. Some researchers, however, are arguing that, while in need of standards, qualitative research provides a richer source of evidence (e.g., Freeman, deMarrais, Preissle, Roulston, & St. Pierre, 2007). According to Freeman et al., one strength of qualitative research is that it is open and incorporates diverse philosophies, theories, and research designs that match the complexities of school-based contexts.

Although they agree with the principles of rigorous science employed in quantitative research, Freeman et al. (2007) argue for a balance in setting standards of evidence that pertain to the descriptive accounts of practice, which are the hallmark of qualitative research. They maintain that qualitative research should be judged by the significance of its results in the context of its own methodological requirements (Freeman et al.). That is, qualitative research must subject all forms of data (e.g., from interviews, observations, case studies) to systematic analysis as well as thorough (1) descriptions of the design and methods and (2) considerations of the strengths and limitations of the study. Freeman et al. conclude that researchers in any tradition—quantitative or qualitative—should resist political pressures to impose restrictive standards and inhibit the creation of new methodologies that capture the richness and complexities of educational systems. Expert judgment is required to understand and interpret the theoretical frameworks and assumptions underlying any educational research, quantitative or qualitative.

In our view, school leaders must judge all research and its findings from their own wisdom and experience. There will always be debates about research methodologies, what defines the nature of "truth," and the role of science in defining practice in all kinds of human systems. We believe that basing judgments on learner-centered principles that have stood the test of time are the soundest ways to ensure that we produce the educational systems we want and need for the future. From this premise, we next turn to what we see as the new role of school leaders in helping to ensure that they and their staff develop and sustain an attitude of ongoing learning, change, and development. You will see that our recommendations align with Learner-Centered Principles and conform to what we know about the natural learning principles we have discussed thus far.

THE LEADER'S NEW ROLE IN STAFF DEVELOPMENT

To align existing or new models of learner-centered education with what we know about learning and learners requires a thorough understanding of the role of human purposes and values in living systems and how ecological approaches function. This understanding is central to knowing what learner-centered self-assessment and reflection tools can accomplish in your leadership role in helping your staff learn and develop new learning approaches.

Using Ecological Models of Human Development to Establish Leaders

Among those promoting the use of ecological models of development for teachers in alternative certification and preparation programs, Chin and Young (2007) report on the results of a large-scale study of this approach for individuals in California's teacher internship program. They define an ecological approach as one that "...focuses on persons and situates their desires and attitudes toward teaching as shaped by their particular life circumstances and personal histories" (p. 74). Such approaches consider the person as a whole and examine the interactions between individual characteristics of those in the program and the environments that influence their choices. In this approach it is possible to look at developmental processes within the cultural and historical environments from which they unfold. Examining these developmental processes provides a fuller picture of how socialization into a profession is tied to personal life histories and emotional commitments of the novices that enter teaching (Chin & Young, 2007).

Using ecological principles, the alternative certification program in California employs teachers who are concurrently enrolled in a teacher preparation program and provides them with mentors who support them throughout their internship experiences. This ecological approach uses:

- persons as the unit of analysis;
- a dialectical process to analyze how people's thinking is transformed through human activities; and
- agency as the microsystem that is situated in the larger settings and macrosystems that define key cultural aspects of the individuals and the educational system. (Chin & Young, 2007)

Personal background data are collected that describe individual life courses, along with data on the timing of when individuals chose teaching as a career and historical trends in how society views public schools. With this person-centered approach, relevant characteristics are combined to develop typological profiles, which we describe in more detail in the following section.

Focusing on Deeper Human Values and Purposes

Understanding the reasons why individuals choose to go into education can provide valuable insights for school leaders. Chin and Young's (2007) study found that service was a primary reason for entering teaching, but race/ethnicity and gender were associated with different profiles. All teachers in the program fit the profile that said they were motivated to enter teaching because it was compatible with their lifestyles. Latino teachers, on the other hand, were more represented as working class activists who entered teaching with a strong sense of service to certain communities so they could reform schools to better serve these communities. African Americans were underrepresented in the romantic idealists typology in which the primary motivation to enter teaching by primarily young females was not only to serve, but also to seek personal and intellectual fulfillment from their jobs. Conversely, African Americans were overrepresented in the typology of following in the family tradition, in which their motivations for choosing teaching were aligned with both a strong desire to serve and a positive view of teaching derived from having parents who worked extensively with young people.

Chin and Young (2007) also found that the second-career seekers had a higher percentage of white men who were seeking to change careers. Finally, the career explorer category was more likely to include males seeking secondary credentials; these males were not motivated by the desire to serve or to find a fulfilling career but by finding an efficient way to obtain a credential. Chin and Young conclude that those who design teacher education programs need to consider how best to support people with these differences.

From our perspective, this research supports the view that school leaders need to understand why people enter the teaching profession. They also need to understand their own and other's underlying beliefs and assumptions about

Figure 5.1   Beliefs and the Change Process

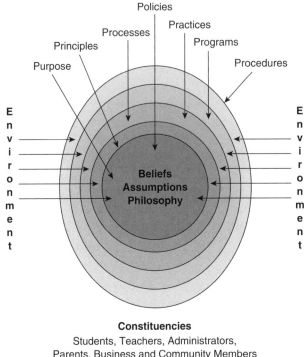

Policies

Practices

Processes

Principles

Programs

Purpose

Procedures

Environment

Environment

Beliefs
Assumptions
Philosophy

Constituencies
Students, Teachers, Administrators,
Parents, Business and Community Members

learning, learners, and teaching. Our beliefs and values guide the decisions we make that support teaching and learning throughout all aspects of the educational process and system. This living-systems perspective is illustrated in Figures 5.1 and 5.2.

These figures remind us that the shared beliefs, assumptions, values, and philosophies of those in the educational system result in the purpose, principles, processes, policies, practices, programs, and procedures that are developed and implemented in the system (McCombs & Miller, 2007). The "environment" refers to the overall educational context—the school, classrooms, and family influences. The overall vision and processes needed in their system arise from everyone, beginning with an exploration of beliefs, values, and so on—reflected in all the "P" words in Figure 5.1.

Figure 5.2 illustrates the central role of people in establishing the personal and system climate for schooling, along with a visualization of the reciprocal role of learning and change in living systems (McCombs & Miller, 2007). As people explore their fundamental beliefs, assumptions, values, attitudes, behavior, and learning together, they are inspired to make both personal and systemic changes by creating new meanings, learning relationships, and ways of interacting that, in turn, influence each individual learner in the system.

To give you an opportunity to reflect on what you've been reading in this chapter, the exercise in Box 5.3 is designed to help you think about and reflect

Figure 5.2   Elements of Living Systems

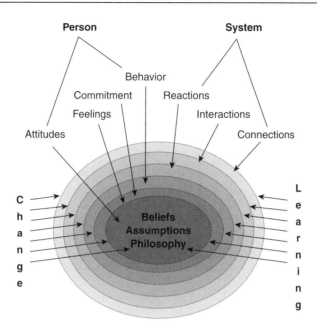

Constituencies
Students, Teachers, Administrators,
Parents, Business and Community Members

on what you as a leader have encountered as you have tried to deal with the issues and challenges we have discussed so far in this chapter. As you engage in this exercise, share with a learning partner or colleague, if possible.

You are now ready to learn our rationale for creating the Assessment of Learner-Centered Practices surveys and the change process these surveys support. We begin by summarizing the background for developing these surveys and their supporting research.

BACKGROUND AND SUPPORTING RESEARCH FOR THE ASSESSMENT OF LEARNER-CENTERED PRACTICES SURVEYS

Our impetus for developing the Assessment of Learner-Centered Practices school- and classroom-level surveys and the change process tools we described in Chapter 4 was simple: We wanted to help educators at all levels of the educational system understand how the *Learner-Centered Psychological Principles*

Box 5.3   Identifying the Context for Using the ALCP Assessment Tools

---

1. Describe what the parents, educators, and community members in your school and community want education to accomplish.

2. Describe what you need to do in order to provide what you described in #1.

3. List the biggest issues facing you as a school leader. Describe how you plan to address these big issues (see pp. 139).

4. Describe how you can incorporate the principles of ecological (living) systems into your role in staff development.

(Learner-Centered Principles; APA, 1997) translated into practice and educational transformation. We began with the development of classroom level surveys for teachers and students because this was the level our feedback from educators told us was most needed when the APA *Principles* were first released in 1993. Teachers at all levels from kindergarten through college told us that they needed ways to know if the practices they were engaging in were "learner-centered." That began our journey into the development of, first, the classroom and then the school-level Assessment of Learner-Centered Practices surveys.

The Development and Validation of the Classroom-Level Assessment of Learner-Centered Practices Surveys

In our study into what more simply defined "learner-centeredness" at the classroom level, we discovered a list of ten "nonnegotiables" in terms of practice. We also discovered that these were elements that students must perceive in order for any practices at the classroom level to be considered learner-centered.

The "Nonnegotiables" of Learner-Centered Classroom Practice

Our identification of the following core elements of learner-centered classroom practice began with reducing the fourteen Learner-Centered Principles to what they implied for practice. We went to the research literature and confirmed that these were essential components for maximizing student motivation and achievement. As described by McCombs & Miller (2007, pp. 103–105), these ten elements are:

1. *Choice:* opportunities for students to choose what they learn, and/or how and when they learn it, and/or under what conditions. Students

understand they may have limited choice about content, but they appreciate having choices about how they can learn it, the time frame in which they have to learn it, and whether they work individually, in groups, under headphones, sitting on the floor, or slumped at a table. They regard these processes as positive indicators that their teacher is taking them into account and valuing them as learners.

2. *Responsibility:* opportunities for students to take responsibility for their own learning. Students tell us they are much more motivated to learn when their teachers assume they (the students) are responsible for their own learning. When teachers assume the responsibility for their students' learning, students tell us they feel the learning they are expected to do has little if anything to do with them, their interests, or their learning needs.

3. *Relevance:* learning skills, processes, and information that are relevant to students' lives. The relevance of what students are learning is closely related to their taking responsibility for their own learning. Students say they are more motivated to learn when their teachers take the time to learn what is relevant to them and to structure their classrooms around that relevance.

4. *Challenge:* learning that is challenging, yet not impossible. Students want to be challenged and appreciate teachers who can challenge them to perform at their highest levels, while at the same time not intimidating them. Learner-centered teachers understand the importance of optimal challenge and how to provide this for each individual student. As one of our learner-centered teachers explained, it is important that students also learn to accept their own mistakes while challenging themselves. As this teacher put it, "I want my students to know that mistakes are great moments! One of my students showed he got the message as he told me, 'I just had a great moment—I got a B instead of the A I expected in science. Guess I need to focus more, huh?'" (personal communication, March, 1999)

5. *Control:* opportunities for students to control aspects of the learning environment, especially how the classroom functions. These functions include classroom rules for how students interact with each other and their teacher, how tardies and absences are handled, what to do about disruptive students, how to handle assignments turned in late, and how homework is assigned. Students report that when they have a say in classroom functioning, they feel engaged, treated fairly, and respected. Even more important, when students have a voice, they "own" the rules and classroom procedures—making the job of classroom management much easier for teachers.

6. *Connection:* experiences that contribute to students feeling connected to their peers, their teacher(s), their school, and their community. Students must feel connected to the content and perceive its relevance to their interests and lives. To achieve maximum learning and motivation to learn and stay in school, they must also feel positive social and

emotional connections throughout their experiences of being in school. Students from elementary through high school report that teachers who get them involved in school governance, extracurricular school activities, and community service learning projects feel more a part of their school community and connected to their classmates and teachers

7. *Respect:* an atmosphere of mutual respect. Students say that the best teachers are those who both command from and show respect for individual students and their diverse needs and backgrounds in their classrooms. They also teach students to appreciate that others have a right to their views—views that might be important to know. These teachers take individual learners and their learning seriously. They also model a respectful attitude toward others.

8. *Competence:* opportunities for each student to show competence. Students report that they learn better in classrooms in which the teacher builds activities and processes through which they can feel they are learning, can be successful learners in a variety of content areas, and are accomplishing something important. Learner-centered teachers know how to structure classroom activities so that students can be successful in mastering their own quality standards of achievement.

9. *Cooperation:* an atmosphere of mutual cooperation and collaboration. Students say that the best teachers are those who model what it means to cooperate—that is, to be co-learners and collaborators in learning. These learner-centered teachers understand that competition may sometimes be helpful to introduce a spirit of fun into potentially boring classroom activities, but that competition can also give some students the message that they will not be as successful as other students. This can hamper these students' intrinsic motivation and their understanding of the value of cooperation as a strategy to achieve shared academic and social classroom goals.

10. *Relationships:* opportunities for students to build relationships with peers and teachers. Students say they learn better in classrooms in which they develop meaningful and positive relationships with their teacher and their classmates. They feel safe to make mistakes and not be ridiculed. They also learn to respect diverse perspectives and ways of teaching and learning. From students' perspectives, teacher practices that promote positive relationships are the most important contributors to motivating them to learn and do their best.

With an understanding of these basic elements and what they meant in classroom practice, we were ready to begin the development of the classroom Assessment of Learner-Centered Practices teacher and student surveys. We started with the development of items for the middle and high school levels in 1995, as these were the areas educators were most concerned about. Our validation process and findings evolved to the development and validation of Assessment of Learner-Centered Practices surveys for lower elementary, upper elementary, and college level students.

Validation Process and General Findings With the
Classroom–Level Assessment of Learner–Centered Practices Surveys

Our validation process was one of beginning with local area middle and high schools in Colorado. These samples provided initial data to reduce the size of the surveys and define subscales of items in terms of practices that clustered together from factor analyses. The details of this validation process are described by McCombs and Lauer (1997). The resulting surveys were field tested in large national samples with students and teachers in diverse rural, suburban, and urban schools. The result was a refined set of items for both the student and teacher Assessment of Learner-Centered Practices surveys.

We subsequently further refined the initial set of surveys by subjecting them to more extensive field testing in middle and high schools in the late 1990s and early 2000s (McCombs & Quiat, 2002; McCombs & Weinberger, 2001, 2002; Meece, Hermans, & McCombs, 2003). This field testing resulted in validating separate high school and middle school versions. Although the domains of practice remained the same, we were able to differentiate developmental differences in specific practices that were most effective for students at these two stages of development. We were also able to confirm that the same pyramid of importance for these domains of practice existed at both the middle and high school levels, as shown in Figure 5.3.

As this figure illustrates, our evidence showed the most important domain of practice for middle and high schools students is Creating Positive Relationships, followed by practices for Honoring Student Voice, Encouraging Higher Order Thinking, and Adapting to Individual Difference. In other words, being learner-centered starts not with adapting to individual differences, but with establishing positive student-teacher relationships—an important finding that helps educators relax! If teachers first establish those relationships, listen to student voices, and support their thinking and learning skills, their students feel listened to and respected. In the absence of first addressing practices in the first three domains shown in Figure 5.3, however, students will not perceive their teachers as "learner-centered," and the importance of adapting to individual differences increases.

We found similar results at the lower elementary and college levels. As at the middle and high school levels, the most important domains of practice at both levels began with establishing positive student-teacher relationships. In fact at the college level, beginning with this domain of practice was perceived to be even more important by students (McCombs, 2003b, 2004b; McCombs & Pierce, 1999; Pierce, Holt, Kolar, & McCombs, 2004) than for students at the lower elementary level (Daniels, Kalkman, & McCombs, 2001; Daniels & Perry, 2003; McCombs, Daniels, & Perry, in press, 2008). The pyramids of domains of practice for the grades K–3 and college levels are shown in Figures 5.4 and 5.5.

Again, as with all our validation findings, student perceptions of practices predict the outcomes we value, such as high achievement and motivation, and low absenteeism and disruptive behaviors. In addition, across the developmental span from kindergarten through college, learner-centeredness is defined by

Figure 5.3 Practices Aligned With the *Learner-Centered Psychological Principles* (APA, 1997) for Middle and High School Levels[1]

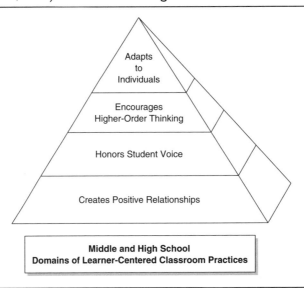

Figure 5.4 Practices Aligned With the *Learner-Centered Psychological Principles* (APA, 1997) for the Elementary School Level[1]

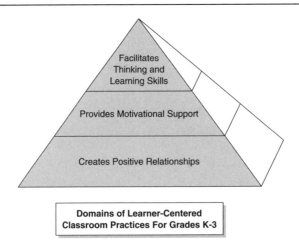

Figure 5.5   Practices Aligned With the *Learner-Centered Psychological Principles* (APA, 1997) for the College Level[1]

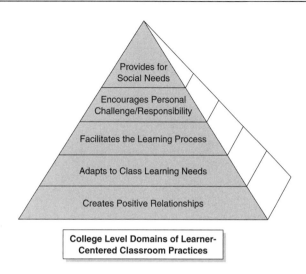

Provides for
Social Needs

Encourages Personal
Challenge/Responsibility

Facilitates the Learning Process

Adapts to Class Learning Needs

Creates Positive Relationships

College Level Domains of Learner-
Centered Classroom Practices

[1] © Copyright 1999 by Barbara L. McCombs, PhD. Not to be used without prior written permission from Dr. Barbara L. McCombs, Senior Research Scientist and Director, Human Motivation, Learning, and Development Center, University of Denver Research Institute, 250 E. Iliff Avenue, Room 224, Denver, CO 80208-2616. The ALCP surveys were based on the *Learner-Centered Psychological Principles* distributed by the American Psychological Association (APA, 1997).

students as those practices that begin with establishing positive student-teacher relationships and end with practices that adapt to individual differences. The specific variables measured in the grades K–3, 4–8, 9–12, and college level surveys and the validated Learner-Centered Rubric—the score teachers should ideally reach—are shown in Tables 5.1 through 5.3. As we explained in Chapter 4, we use a guided reflection process to help teachers interpret these scores and change their practices in more learner-centered directions.

You can use the classroom level surveys to accomplish your goals of increasing student learning and motivation, while also decreasing negative outcomes, such as low attendance and disruptive behavior. This tool is one that benefits everyone in the system, beginning with students and their classroom teachers.

The Development and Validation of the School-Level Assessment of Learner-Centered Practices Surveys

At the school, or systems level, learner-centeredness involves the relations among teacher beliefs, teacher practices, and student outcomes, shown in Figure 5.6, which you first saw as Figure 3.1 in Chapter 3.

Table 5.4 describes the system of Assessment of Learner-Centered Practices surveys we developed for the school and classroom levels. The overall system allows people at various system levels to self-assess and reflect on their beliefs and the degree to which their own and others' practices are consistent with the

Table 5.1   Variables Measured in the Assessment of the K–3
Learner-Centered Practices (ALCP Surveys)*

Teacher Variables	Grades K–3 LC Rubric**
Teacher Beliefs:	
Learner-centered beliefs about learners, learning, and teaching	High ≥ 3.4
Non-learner-centered beliefs about learners	Low ≤ 2.3
Teacher Perceptions of Classroom Practices:	
Creates positive interpersonal relationships/climate	High ≥ 3.5
Adapts to individual developmental differences	High ≥ 3.2
Facilitates learning and teaching	High ≥ 3.4
Teacher Self-Efficacy:	High ≥ 3.1
Teacher Beliefs About Early Childhood:	
Teachers can influence these difficult stages	High ≥ 3.1
Difficult stage	Low ≤ 1.9
Reflective Self-Awareness:	High ≥ 3.0
Autonomy Support:	
Moderately controlling	High ≥ 3.0
Highly controlling	Low ≤ 2.7
Moderately autonomy-supportive	Low ≤ 3.1
Highly autonomy-supportive	High ≥ 3.0

Student Variables	Grades K–3 LC Rubric**
Student Perception of Classroom Practices:	
Creates positive interpersonal relationships	High ≥ 3.7
Adapts to individual developmental differences	High ≥ 3.5
Facilitates learning and teaching	High ≥ 3.6
Differences Between Student and Teacher:	Low ≥ 0, or ≤ -.2
Perceptions of Classroom Practice:	
Creates positive interpersonal relationships/climate	Low ≥ -.2
Adapts to individual developmental differences	Low ≥ -.3
Facilitates learning and thinking	Low ≥ -.3
Student Learning and Motivation Variables:	
Self-efficacy	High ≥ 3.8
State epistemic curiosity	High ≥ 3.8

*All scores have a range from 1 to 4.
**Learner-centered rubric based on scores from classrooms in prior validation studies
(McCombs & Lauer, 1997; McCombs & Weinberger, 2001) that had the highest student achievement and motivation.

Table 5.2 Variables Measured in the Assessment of the 4–8 and 9–12 Learner-Centered Practices (ALCP Surveys)*

Teacher Variables	Grades 4–8 and 9–12 LC Rubric**
Teacher Beliefs: (Items 1–35)	
Learner-centered beliefs about learners, learning, and teaching	High ≥ 3.2 and 3.2
Non-learner-centered beliefs about learners	Low ≤ 2.2 and 2.4
Non-learner-centered beliefs about learning and teaching	Low ≤ 2.5 and 2.4
Teacher Perceptions of Classroom Practices: (Items 36–60)	
Creates positive interpersonal relationships/climate	High ≥ 3.6 and 3.6
Honors student voice, provides individual learning challenges	High ≥ 3.5 and 3.4
Encourages higher-order thinking and self-regulation	High ≥ 3.4 and 3.2
Adapts to individual developmental differences	High ≥ 3.0 and 2.7
Teacher Self-Efficacy: (Items 61–66)	High ≥ 3.1 and 3.2
Teacher Beliefs About Adolescence/Middle Childhood: (Items 67–76)	
Teachers can influence difficult stages	High ≥ 3.4 and 3.5
Difficult stage	Low ≤ 2.8 and 2.0
Reflective Self-Awareness: (Items 77–91)	High ≥ 3.0
Autonomy Support: (Items 92–111)	
Moderately controlling	High ≥ 2.8 and 3.0
Highly controlling	Low ≤ 2.4 and 2.5
Moderately autonomy supportive	Low ≤ 3.3 and 3.0
Highly autonomy supportive	High ≥ 3.3 and 2.9

Student Variables	Grades 4–8 and 9–12 LC Rubric
Student Perceptions of Classroom Practices: (Items 1–25)	
Creates positive interpersonal relationships/climate	High ≥ 3.1 and 3.3
Honors student voice, provides individual learning challenges	High ≥ 3.0 and 3.2
Encourages higher-order thinking and self-regulation	High ≥ 3.2 and 3.1
Adapts to individual developmental differences	High ≥ 2.8 and 2.2
Differences Between Student and Teacher:	
Perceptions of Classroom Practices:	
Creates positive interpersonal relationships/climate	Low ≥ -.2
Honors student voice, provides individual learning challenges	Low ≥ -.1
Encourages higher-order thinking and self-regulation	Low ≥ 0
Adapts to individual developmental differences	Low ≥ -1
Student Learning and Motivation Variables: (Items 26–72)	
Self-efficacy (Items 26, 33, 40, 47, 54, 61)	High ≥ 3.6 and 3.4
State epistemic curiosity (Items 32, 39, 46, 53, 60, 67, 70)	High ≥ 3.1 and 2.9
Active-learning strategies (Items 27, 34, 41, 48, 55, 62, 68, 71)	High ≥ 3.1 and 3.0
Effort-avoidance strategies (Items 28, 35, 42, 49, 56, 63, 69, 72)	Low ≤ 1.8 and 2.0
Task-mastery goals (Items 29, 36, 43, 50, 57, 64)	High ≥ 3.4 and 3.1
Performance-oriented goals (Items 30, 37, 44, 51, 58, 65)	Low ≤ 2.6 and 2.6
Work-avoidance goals (Items 31, 38, 45, 52, 59, 66)	Low ≤ 2.0 and ≤ 2.1

*All scores have a range from 1 to 4.
**Learner-centered rubric based on scores from classrooms in prior validation studies (McCombs & Lauer, 1997; McCombs & Weinberger, 2001) that had the highest student achievement and motivation.

Table 5.3   Variables Measured in the College Level ALCP Surveys[*]

Teacher Measures	Learner-Centered Rubric
Teacher Beliefs:	
Learner-centered beliefs about learners, learning, and teaching.	High ≥ 3.1
Non-learner-centered beliefs about learners	Low ≤ 2.1
Non-learner-centered beliefs about learning and teaching	Low ≤ 2.3
Teacher Classroom Practices:	
Establishes positive interpersonal relationships	High ≥ 3.4
Facilitates the learning process	High ≥ 3.5
Adapts to class learning needs	High ≥ 3.3
Encourages personal challenge and responsibility	High ≥ 3.0
Provides for individual and social learning needs	High ≥ 3.6
Teacher Self-Efficacy:	High ≥ 3.1
Reflective Self-Awareness:	High ≥ 3.1

Student Measures	Learner-Centered Rubric[**]
Student Perceptions of Classroom Practices:	
Establishes positive interpersonal relationships	High ≥ 3.3
Adapts to class learning needs	High ≥ 3.4
Facilitates the learning process	High ≥ 3.3
Provides for individual and social learning needs	High ≥ 3.5
Encourages personal challenge and responsibility	High ≥ 2.6
Differences Between Student and Teacher:	Low ≥ 0 to -.7
Perceptions of Classroom Practices:	
Establishes positive interpersonal relationships	Low ≥ -.2
Adapts to class learning needs	Low ≥ -.1
Facilitates the learning process	Low ≥ -.1
Provides for individual and social learning needs	Low ≥ .1
Encourages personal challenge and responsibility	Low ≥ -.1
Student Learning and Motivation Variables:	
Self-efficacy	High ≥ 3.4
Active-learning strategies	High ≥ 3.2
Effort-avoidance strategies	Low ≤ 1.7
State epistemic curiosity	High ≥ 3.2
Task-mastery goals	High ≥ 3.3
Performance-oriented goals	Low ≤ 2.0
Work-avoidance goals	Low ≤ 1.8
Achievement Scores	High ≥ 87.6

[*]Scores range from 1 to 4 except Achievement Scores which range from 0 to 100.

[**]Learner-Centered Rubric based on scores from classrooms in prior validation studies (McCombs & Lauer, 1997; McCombs & Weinberger, 2001) that had the highest student achievement and motivation.

Figure 5.6 A Learner-Centered Model of Relations Between Teacher Beliefs, Teacher Practices, and Student Outcomes

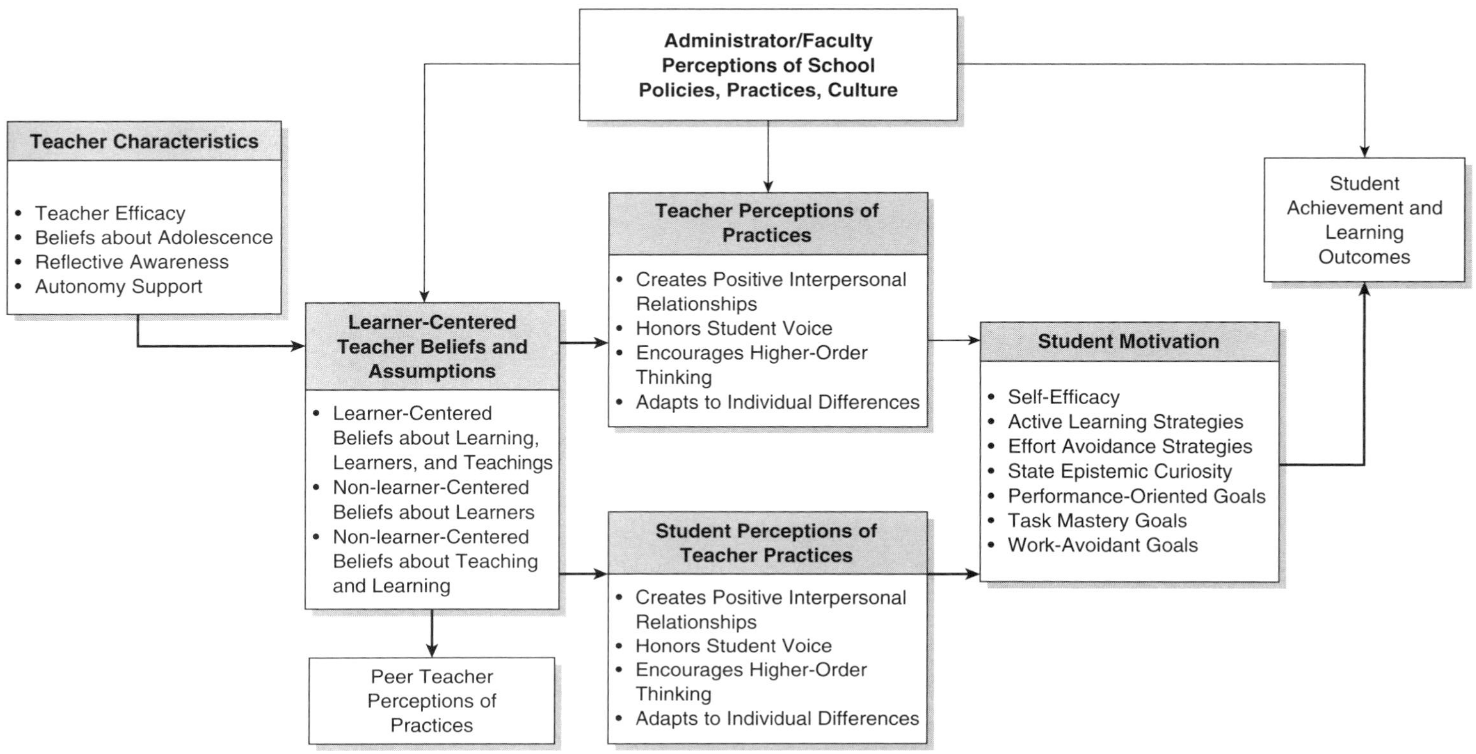

Teacher Characteristics

- Teacher Efficacy
- Beliefs about Adolescence
- Reflective Awareness
- Autonomy Support

Learner-Centered Teacher Beliefs and Assumptions

- Learner-Centered Beliefs about Learning, Learners, and Teachings
- Non-learner-Centered Beliefs about Learners
- Non-learner-Centered Beliefs about Teaching and Learning

Administrator/Faculty Perceptions of School Policies, Practices, Culture

Teacher Perceptions of Practices

- Creates Positive Interpersonal Relationships
- Honors Student Voice
- Encourages Higher-Order Thinking
- Adapts to Individual Differences

Student Perceptions of Teacher Practices

- Creates Positive Interpersonal Relationships
- Honors Student Voice
- Encourages Higher-Order Thinking
- Adapts to Individual Differences

Peer Teacher Perceptions of Practices

Student Motivation

- Self-Efficacy
- Active Learning Strategies
- Effort Avoidance Strategies
- State Epistemic Curiosity
- Performance-Oriented Goals
- Task Mastery Goals
- Work-Avoidant Goals

Student Achievement and Learning Outcomes

161

Learner-Centered Principles. As we discussed in Chapters 3 and 4, the survey results provide the school leader with the opportunity to identify discrepancies between beliefs and practices for him- or herself and for various groups within the school system. The school-level assessment is the initial tool that starts the process of moving to a learner-centered educational system. It also provides the basis for initial dialogues essential to the process of change in thinking and in practices.

Description of the Development of the School-Level Assessment of Learner-Centered Practices Survey

Our motivation in developing the School-Level Assessment of Learner-Centered Practices Survey came from the research showing how change occurs in living systems. We began our work on this school-level survey in the late 1990s (McCombs, 1999b) and have continued to the present. We began by compiling a list of what research showed to be the primary elements of school functioning from a systems perspective. You will remember our discussion of these elements on pages 61–62 in Chapter 3 and on page 98 in Chapter 4:

- Expectations for Students
- Instruction and Management Practices
- Curriculum Structures
- Assessment and Grading Practices
- Professional Development Practices
- Parent and Community Involvement Strategies
- Leadership Style and Practices
- Policies and Regulations

The format for the survey responses was inspired by those working in the field of perceptual and developmental psychology (e.g., Harter, 2006) who believe that asking individuals to identify their values or goals, in conjunction with their perceptions of actual practices, provides an effective way to identify discrepancies that can motivate changes in behavior and practices. As we explained earlier, the discrepancies yielded by this approach can be provided as individual- and group-level feedback and which you can then use to begin the dialogues leading to change.

Although you had a chance to see examples of the School-Level Assessment of Learner-Centered Practices feedback in Chapters 3 and 4, we want to share two more examples of what the feedback can tell you. First, there is a table that can provide actual means and standard deviations for each of the eight areas by the group breakdowns chosen. In the example in Table 5.5, the data from a small school with one administrator (hence no standard deviation data) and twenty-three teachers are shown.

For those who prefer looking at the data in a chart form, Figures 5.7 and 5.8 provides a different example of how the data for three groups (parents, teachers, administrators) can be plotted to show discrepancies in the eight areas of school functioning.

Table 5.4   The System of Assessment of Learner-Centered Practices (ALCP) Surveys©

Purpose: To support a research-validated personal change process in which teachers, students, parents, and administrators use self-assessment tools from the Assessment of Learner-Centered Practices (ALCP)© to reflect on (1) discrepancies between their own and their students' or faculty's perceptions of practices and (2) construct areas of needed change and strategies for achieving desired changes.

Rationale: New models of professional development for teachers are focusing on empower-ment, teacher responsibility for their own growth and professionalism, teachers as leaders, as well as teacher development of higher order thinking and personal reflection skills. A key to teachers' abilities to accept and implement these new models is support in their development in the form of self-assessment tools for becoming more aware of their beliefs, practices, and the impact of these practices on students. Information from teachers' self-assessments can then be used by teachers to identify—in a non-threatening and non-judgmental context—the kinds of changes in practice that are needed to better serve the learning needs of all students. In this way, teachers can begin to take responsibility, from the very beginning, in developing their own professional development plan.

Teacher Surveys for K–12 and College Levels—Includes validated measures at the K–3, 4–8, 9–12, and college levels for increasing teacher awareness of the impact on student motiva-tion and achievement of the degree to which their beliefs and classroom practices are learner-centered or non-learner-centered.

- *Teacher Beliefs and Assumptions*—Measures teachers' self-assessments of their beliefs about learners, learning, and teaching.

- *Teacher Assessment of Classroom Practices*—Measures teachers' own perceptions of practices in the domains most related to student motivation and achievement.

- *Peer Teacher Assessment of Classroom Practices*—Measures another teacher's assessment of a peer teacher's practices that can create comparisons of the discrepancies between that teacher and his/her peer perceptions of classroom practices in the same domains as assessed by the teacher.

Student Surveys for K–12 and College Levels—Includes separate validated surveys for K–3, 4–8, 9–12, and college levels that identify students not being reached and the alignment of teacher and student perceptions regarding the frequency of learner-centered classroom practices.

- *Student Assessment of Classroom Practices*—Measures students' perceptions of their teach-ers' practices in the same domains as in teacher measures; allows for comparisons of the discrepancies between each student and their teacher's perceptions of classroom practices in each domain of classroom practice.

- *Student Motivation*—Measures students' self-reports of motivation in terms of self-efficacy, learning goals, learning strategies, and intrinsic motivation (interest) or knowledge-seeking (epistemic) curiosity.

Administrator/Staff/Parent Survey for K–12 Level—Provides validated survey for identi-fying individual goals and actual perceptions of leadership and school climate factors related to school-level learner-centered practice domains.

- *Assessment of K–12 School-Level Practices*—Measures administrator, faculty, other school staff, and parents' perceptions of school practices in the areas of instructional practices, expectations, staff "voice," and policy that can create discrepancies between each adminis-trator, staff, and parent beliefs and perceptions of practice in the preceding areas.

Table 5.5   Assessment of Learner-Centered Practices: School-Level Survey

School Practice Area	Administrator		Teachers		Total Sample		Validation Sample	
	Mean n = 1	Sd	Mean n = 23	Sd	Mean n = 24	Sd	Mean n = 565	Sd
Expectations for Students								
Goal	4.71		4.55	0.59	4.56	0.58	4.83	0.25
Actual	4.71		3.96	0.68	3.99	0.68	3.37	0.68
Instruction and Instructional Management Practices								
Goal	5.00		4.17	0.94	4.21	0.93	4.55	0.43
Actual	5.00		3.96	0.60	4.01	0.62	2.75	0.62
Curriculum Structures								
Goal	5.00		4.39	0.94	4.41	0.93	4.60	0.44
Actual	5.00		4.18	0.65	4.21	0.66	2.93	0.61
Assessment and Grading Practices								
Goal	5.00		4.41	0.75	4.43	0.74	4.38	0.60
Actual	5.00		4.08	0.80	4.12	0.81	2.56	0.80
Professional Development Practices								
Goal	5.00		4.36	0.92	4.39	0.91	4.70	0.42
Actual	5.00		4.11	0.70	4.15	0.71	2.88	0.78
Parent and Community Involvement Strategies								
Goal	5.00		4.41	0.74	4.43	0.73	4.73	0.60
Actual	5.00		3.88	0.65	3.93	0.67	3.21	0.64
Leadership Style and Practices								
Goal	5.00		4.48	0.81	4.50	0.8	4.52	0.50
Actual	5.00		4.04	0.88	4.08	0.88	2.96	0.76
Policies and Regulations								
Goal	5.00		4.60	0.65	4.61	0.64	4.52	0.50
Actual	5.00		4.21	0.77	4.25	0.77	2.96	0.76

And now—the moment we hope you have been waiting for—a chance for you to experience taking a shortened version of the School-Level Assessment of Learner-Centered Practices yourself!

EXPERIENCING THE SCHOOL-LEVEL ASSESSMENT OF LEARNER-CENTERED PRACTICES SURVEY FOR YOURSELF

We have created a version of the school-level survey that you can use to experience what can be learned from this Assessment of Learner-Centered Practices

Figure 5.7   Goals of an Elementary School

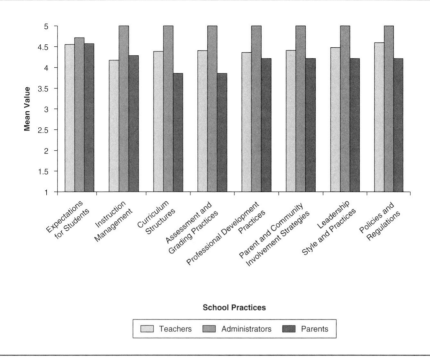

Figure 5.8   Actuals of an Elementary School

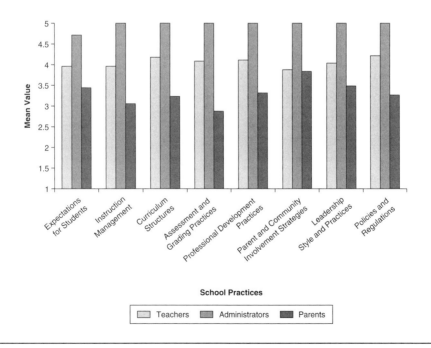

Survey. You will also have a chance to score your results and compare them to our validation learner-centered rubric for both your goals and perceptions of actual practice.

Taking the Short Form of the School-Level Assessment of Learner-Centered Practices Survey

The short form of the school-level survey is presented in Box 5.4. Follow the instructions, being sure to answer each item twice—once for your goals and once for your perceptions of actual practices in the system you serve.

As you could tell from the sample School-Level Assessment of Learner-Centered Practices Survey, there is a longer actual survey that provides more complete information about goals and perceptions of actual practices in each of the eight areas assessed. To learn more about how you can get involved in taking this longer survey, please contact Barbara McCombs at bmccombs@du.edu. The survey is part of a comprehensive, online system of learner-centered assessments developed with colleagues in Bristol, England. This comprehensive system includes all classroom-level surveys as well as the school-level survey. The system provides feedback through consultation and training-of-trainer materials.

Experiencing the Assessment of Learner-Centered Practices Individual Feedback Process

Once you have finished taking the short version of the sample School-Level Assessment of Learner-Centered Practices Survey, you can score your results and receive feedback, which allows you to identify discrepancies between your values and the reality you perceive in your school context. You can then—if you choose—identify changes you may want to make in either your goals or your perceptions of actual practices.

Take a look at how to score and interpret your results using Table 5.6.

Think about your results and whether there were any surprises. Many school leaders are surprised that their perceptions of actual practices are higher than the LC Rubric. If yours were, that's great—it means you are already leading a school that is more learner-centered than our national validation sample.

In our work with a variety of school systems using the school-level ALCP surveys as a starting place, we have seen some remarkable changes in the development of a more positive school culture. When the staff feels it has a voice and that leadership is interested in working on areas where either values or perceptions of practices differ, a stronger community and commitment to change occurs. This example is from a high school district in Illinois where we worked with them to become more learner-centered:

> The staff in this high school district was generally excited about becoming "learner-centered." There were, however, some faculty who didn't think the leadership team sufficiently recognized their efforts to improve

Box 5.4   The Assessment of Learner-Centered Practices (ALCP): School-Level Survey (K–12)©

SAMPLE ITEMS

DIRECTIONS: Each item below has two parts: (1) what practices and policies you believe your school or district **should have** in six key areas of school operation; and (2) what practices and policies your school or district **already has in place**. For each item, please think about and respond to **both parts**. Indicate the degree to which you agree with each statement as a **practice goal** and the degree to which you think it **already exists**. Blacken the responses for each item on your answer sheet that best indicates your choice on **both parts** according to the following scale:

Strongly Disagree -------------------- **Strongly Agree**

A	B	C	D	E
SD				**SA**

Remember that each statement has two parts. Mark BOTH your parts for each item.

EXAMPLE ITEM:

Practice Goal   **Already Exists**

A B C D E		A B C D E
SD SA	Classrooms that are bright and cheery.	SD SA

This survey asks you to assess your goals for school-level practices and your perceptions of what already exists in eight areas: Expectations for Students, Instruction and Instructional Management Practices, Curriculum Structures, Assessment and Grading Practices, Professional Development Practices, Parent and Community Involvement Strategies, Leadership Style and Practices, and Policies and Regulations.

YOU MAY NOW BEGIN!

PLEASE TURN THE PAGE

Box 5.4   (Continued)

Sample Items

<u>**Practice Goal**</u>   <u>**Already Exists**</u>

1. Expectations for Students

I. **A B C D E**   Students are expected to be   **2. A B C D E**
    <u>SD</u>   <u>SA</u>   responsible for their own learning.   <u>SD</u>   <u>SA</u>

5. **A B C D E**   Each student's abilities are respected   **6. A B C D E**
    <u>SD</u>   <u>SA</u>   and valued.   <u>SD</u>   <u>SA</u>

11. **A B C D E**   Students are expected to excel in   **12. A B C D E**
    <u>SD</u>   <u>SA</u>   their areas of highest interest.   <u>SD</u>   <u>SA</u>

2. Instruction and Instructional Management Practices

15. **A B C D E**   Students are given choices in how,   **16. A B C D E**
    <u>SD</u>   <u>SA</u>   when, and with whom they want to learn.   <u>SD</u>   <u>SA</u>

17. **A B C D E**   Students are involved in creating their   **18. A B C D E**
    <u>SD</u>   <u>SA</u>   own learning plans and goals.   <u>SD</u>   <u>SA</u>

23. **A B C D E**   Instruction is presented in flexible   **24. A B C D E**
    <u>SD</u>   <u>SA</u>   blocks of time to meet student   <u>SD</u>   <u>SA</u>
                         learning.

3. Curriculum Structures

29. **A B C D E**   Curricula is thematic and integrated   **30. A B C D E**
    <u>SD</u>   <u>SA</u>   across disciplines and content areas.   <u>SD</u>   <u>SA</u>

33. **A B C D E**   Curricula builds in learning strategies   **34. A B C D E**
    <u>SD</u>   <u>SA</u>   and helps students to reflect on their   <u>SD</u>   <u>SA</u>
                         learning.

41. **A B C D E**   Curricula gives students the   **42. A B C D E**
    <u>SD</u>   <u>SA</u>   opportunity to learn about other   <u>SD</u>   <u>SA</u>
                         cultures and perspectives.

4. Assessment and Grading Practices

43. **A B C D E**   Assessment practices foster student   **44. A B C D E**
    <u>SD</u>   <u>SA</u>   responsibility for learning (e.g., self-   <u>SD</u>   <u>SA</u>
                         evaluation.)

51. **A B C D E**   Assessment practices provide multiple   **52. A B C D E**
    <u>SD</u>   <u>SA</u>   ways for students to demonstrate   <u>SD</u>   <u>SA</u>
                         knowledge and skills.

43. **A B C D E**   Assessment practices provide students   **44. A B C D E**
    <u>SD</u>   <u>SA</u>   with feedback of progress toward   <u>SD</u>   <u>SA</u>
                         learning goals.

5. Professional Development Practices

57. **A B C D E**   Teachers are given training in adapting   **58. A B C D E**

SD	SA	to individual differences in student learning needs.		SD	SA	

59. A B C D E   SD   SA   Staff is helped to develop learning communities where they are co-learners with students.   **60.** A B C D E   SD   SA

65. A B C D E   SD   SA   Staff is shown how to use tools for self-assessing their own and their students' views of classroom practices.   **66.** A B C D E   SD   SA

6. Parent and Community Involvement Strategies

71. A B C D E   SD   SA   Mentoring programs are available for parents and community members to work with students.   **72.** A B C D E   SD   SA

75. A B C D E   SD   SA   Learning opportunities are available for parents and community members in the school.   **76.** A B C D E   SD   SA

83. A B C D E   SD   SA   Service-learning experiences are provided to connect school and community.   **84.** A B C D E   SD   SA

7. Leadership Style and Practices

85. A B C D E   SD   SA   Leadership provides learning environments that allow students and individual or group learning.   **86.** A B C D E   SD   SA

89. A B C D E   SD   SA   Leadership establishes a school climate that is supportive and inclusive.   **90.** A B C D E   SD   SA

95. A B C D E   SD   SA   Leadership provides time for teacher study and ongoing discussions to improve learning.   **96.** A B C D E   SD   SA

8. Policies and Regulations

99. A B C D E   SD   SA   Policies promote the integration of technology into curriculum, instruction, and staff development.   **100.** A B C D E   SD   SA

107. A B C D E   SD   SA   Policies provide options for students to develop academic and nonacademic talents.   **108.** A B C D E   SD   SA

109. A B C D E   SD   SA   Policies provide alternatives to grades and test scores for rewarding student learning.   **100.** A B C D E   SD   SA

Table 5.6   Understanding Feedback from the Asssessment of Learner-Centered Practices (ALCP): School-Level Practices Survey

The ALCP School-Level Survey is based on the *Learner-Centered Psychological Principles* (ASPAS 1993, 1997) developed and distributed by the American Psychological Association. The Principles address the comprehensive needs of the learner and are consistent with the research on teaching and learning. The complete ALCP School-Level Practices Survey (SLPS) is a 112-item self-assessment measure that asks administrators, faculty, involved parents, and other school and district personnel to indicate the degree to which various learner-centered practices—categorized in the areas of Expectations for Students, Instruction and Instructional Management Practices, Curriculum Structures, Assessment and Grading Practices, Professional Development Practices, Parent and Community Involvement Strategies, Leadership Style and Practices, and Policies and Regulations—are held as Practice Goals Already Exist in their buildings.

Items are rated on a five-point Likert-type scale for both the practice goals and perceived actual practice for each item in each of the eight categories. Mean ratings of goals versus practice for the eight school practice areas can be compared for different groups of respondents within a school and also with the validation sample of teachers and school administrators from diverse rural, suburban, and urban school districts. SLPS results indicate differences in beliefs about the value of different educational practices as well as differences in perceptions concerning the existence of these practices in respondents' current school settings. School leaders can use feedback from the SLPS to help plan for school restructuring and improvement and design staff development. Sample items from the SLPS are shown below.

Instructions for Scoring and Interpreting Your Results: The short form SLPS survey you took contains a total of 24 items, with 3 items per each of the eight areas of school functioning. *Give yourself a 5 for all E responses, a 4 for all D responses, a 3 for all C responses, a 2 for all B responses, and a 1 for all A responses.* You can use the table below to total your scores for each area and divide them by 3 for each area. *Compare your results to the LC Rubric for both your Goals and perceptions of Actual Practice. Circle areas where you may want to consider changes.*

Areas of Practice	Goals Score	Goals LC Rubric	Actuals Score	Actuals LC Rubric
Expectations for Students	Total = Divided by 3 =	4.83 or higher	Total = Divided by 3 =	3.37 or higher
Instruction and Instructional Management	Total = Divided by 3 =	4.55 or higher	Total = Divided by 3 =	2.75 or higher
Curriculum Structures	Total = Divided by 3 =	4.60 or higher	Total = Divided by 3 =	2.93 or higher
Assessment and Grading	Total = Divided by 3 =	4.38 or higher	Total = Divided by 3 =	2.56 or higher
Professional Developments	Total = Divided by 3 =	4.70 or higher	Total = Divided by 3 =	2.88 or higher
Parent and Community Involvement	Total = Divided by 3 =	5.51 or higher	Total = Divided by 3 =	2.76 or higher
Leadership Style and Practices	Total = Divided by 3 =	4.52 or higher	Total = Divided by 3 =	2.96 or higher
Policies and Regulations	Total = Divided by 3 =	4.52 or higher	Total = Divided by 3 =	2.96 or higher

Box 5.5   Reflections on the Learner-Centeredness of
My School, District, or Agency

1.   List the Areas of Practice in which your scores on the sample ALCP exceeded those
of the LC Rubric for the LC goals you believe should be in place in your school,
district, or agency:

2.   List the Areas of Practice in which your scores fell below the LC Rubric for the LC
goals you believe should be in place:

Why do you think your scores fell below the LC Rubric for these particular Areas
of Practice?

3.   List the Area(s) of Practice showing the greatest discrepancy between what your
score on the ALCP showed as being a goal and the actual practice in your school,
district, or agency.

Select the Area of Practice that showed the greatest discrepancy and describe specific steps you can take to resolve the discrepancy (i.e., what can you, as the leader,
do to bring this particular Area of Practice closer to your goal?).

student achievement in math and science. When the School-Level ALCP
results were shared, the faculty got the opportunity to present their
concerns and begin a dialogue about some new ideas and directions for
curriculum. This sharing became the beginning of an exciting initiative
that quickly spread and began to have an important impact on student
achievement. (personal correspondence, April, 2005)

SELF-REFLECTIONS

The exercise in Box 5.5 offers you an opportunity to begin integrating what you
are learning about the Assessment of Learner-Centered Practices Surveys with
your thinking about yourself as a learner and leader.

WHAT'S NEXT

In Chapter 6, we invite you to think about the student outcomes that will best
prepare them to be creative, innovative, lifelong learners, and productive citizens. We will explore the kinds of people we want our students to be, and we
will discuss how our rapidly changing world and technologies foster unique
leadership challenges for creating new kinds of learning partnerships and communities of practice so needed in this 21st century.

6

How We Can Move Toward New Student and System Outcomes

Students want a more interactive teaching style, a more relevant curriculum, school rules that are responsive to their living circumstances, and schools that give them a role and a voice in their own education.

—Pedro Noguera (2004, p. 31)

At the end of Chapter 5, you had a chance to experience a short version of the School-Level Assessment of Learner-Centered Practices and to complete some exercises that were aimed at helping you think through what you can accomplish in your new leadership role with learner-centered tools. In this chapter, we invite you to consider what outcomes you see as most crucial in designing new educational systems that prepare our students for the future world and their place in it. By all accounts, our students, as well as ourselves, will need to find their way to futures we can't even imagine or predict because of three interactive factors:

- the rapidly expanding and exploding technological capabilities;
- the large amount of information that will be available via the Internet alone; and
- the greater influence of various high-population global societies such as China and India.

In such a time of complexity and rapid evolution in the world as we know it, it becomes increasingly urgent that we prepare our students to achieve outcomes that go far beyond our current content and curriculum standards. We must also define outcomes that can take us forward in flexible and adaptable ways, on a scale not yet realized, for the future within the educational systems we create and transform.

As we have said previously, we think there is a way to navigate through this complexity. We have the freedom to craft an educational system, even given its unknowns, that is grounded on simple principles and truths about human capacities and learning potentials. To move toward this goal requires that our vision include the process of moving from complexity to simplicity. One way to achieve this is to visualize and define the student and system outcomes we want in the most future-oriented way possible.

To that end, in this chapter we challenge you to think about the student and system outcomes that will best prepare students to be creative, innovative, lifelong learners, and productive citizens. We will first set the context of present knowledge about the new directions needed and some of the innovative educational models beginning to emerge. Next, we will explore the kinds of people we want our students to be. In the context of these outcomes, we will discuss how our rapidly changing world and technologies create unique leadership challenges for creating new kinds of learning partnerships and communities of practice needed in this 21st century.

We'd like to invite you to begin the process by creating your own vision of the outcomes you think are needed by our students and by our educational systems. We'd like you to dream and think big, while at the same time keeping in mind the simple learner-centered principles and tools we have been discussing thus far. Take a look at the exercise in Box 6.1 as a way to start defining these outcomes.

We will ask you to return to this exercise at the end of this chapter after you have had a chance to consider what others are urging are the most important student and system outcomes. For now, we want you to consider a number of questions that help set the context for defining the student and system outcomes that follow from basic principles about human capacity and learning.

We begin by considering current imbalances and flaws that must be addressed in new designs. We move to a discussion of needed outcomes, and then to a discussion of how schools of the future can create lifelong learners and learning networks.

You will have the opportunity to reflect on these discussions and to take a detailed look at what these possibilities mean juxtaposed against your current state standards and outcomes. We suggest what we think are the best ways for building the learning partnerships and communities of learners that support ongoing learning, change, and improvement and that address the pressing issue of system inequities. We believe it is through the creation of these people- and learner-centered partnerships and communities that we will be able to most effectively reach the outcomes we value.

Box 6.1   Reflections on Myself as a Learner and Leader

> 1.   When you responded to the School-Level ACLP in the exercise in Box 5.4 on page 167, you were identifying your beliefs regarding the goals and actual practices in your school, district, or system along eight Areas of Practice. For each of the areas below, list the outcomes you would like to see in your school, district, or agency. Let yourself be creative and innovative!
>
> - Expectations for students
> - Instruction and instructional management practices
> - Curriculum structures
> - Assessment and grading practices
> - Professional development practices
> - Parent community involvement strategies
> - Leadership style and practices
> - Policies and regulations

UNDERSTANDING WHAT IS AND WHAT COULD BE

In this section, we explore the following questions:

1. What are the current imbalances and flaws that must be addressed?
2. What are the outcomes we need?
3. What is possible in schools of the future?

What Are the Current Imbalances and Flaws That Must Be Addressed?

One notable example of where the current educational paradigm is flawed is evident in U.S. high schools. According to Noguera (2004), the flaws at this level include

- the organization is fragmented and lacks coherence in mission;
- the curriculum is disconnected and lacks depth and intellectual rigor;
- the method of delivery continues to rely on lectures;
- students are increasingly bored and alienated and have created anti-intellectual peer cultures; and
- many high schools are too large and are overcrowded.

In spite of these flaws, many high schools produce high-achieving students. In an attempt to discover what characterized these schools, Noguera (2004) studied ten high schools where most students were from minority and low-income homes; he was able to identify those schools that were successful in fostering high student achievement. What characterized the successful schools as compared to those with medium or low achievement was that they had the common goal of personalizing the learning environment and improving student-teacher relationships.

The best schools also focused on developing their own school cultures and focused on teaching and learning. Noguera (2004) concluded that is was not what the schools did that set them apart but how they did it. They made sure that major stakeholders, particularly teachers, parents, and students, understood their reform strategy. Their reform efforts included school leaders seeking input and listening to what students wanted, which is an authentic role and voice in their own education—just what we believe are the defining features of a learner-centered education

In an analysis of how ready students are for a global citizenship, Stewart (2007) points out that we are headed for a multiethnic, multicultural, and multilingual world that is fundamentally different from the world most adults grew up in. She suggests that four new challenges face all of us:

1. economies are becoming more global;
2. science and technology are rapidly changing the world;
3. health and security issues will require more international cooperation; and
4. changing demographics are accelerating international migration.

Stewart (2007) concludes that radical changes are needed in education to help students become more knowledgeable about the world, learn how to communicate in multiple languages, and learn how to be informed and active citizens in a global community. That is, schools will need to be redesigned with an international focus, which will require new policy goals that address the issues that accompany such a focus. To be successful, schools must operate as effective systems, which we judge in terms of the outcomes we value most highly.

What Are the Outcomes We Need?

Suarez-Orozco and Sattin (2007) maintain that today's schools around the world are out of sync with what will be required of students in a global world. They contend that young people all over the world will need skills to be more innovative, culturally aware, and able to communicate and collaborate in sophisticated ways. The competitive model will no longer solve the global challenges; collaboration and the ability to communicate with an increasingly diverse population in the U.S. and world-wide are vitally important now and into the future. Suarez-Orozco and Sattin (2007) believe there are a number of things schools can do immediately, including placing student engagement at the center of learning, with a focus on central concepts arising from current events and issues relevant to students.

Suarez-Orozco and Sattin (2007) believe that the following is necessary to achieve these outcomes:

*   Teachers need to become partners with students and parents in tracking students' development and academic growth in the skills needed for productive lives in a global society.
*   Students need a more active role in defining a new global school mission and shared purpose, as well as in creating ways to work with partner schools in other nations on units that focus on global topics of mutual interest and relevance.

- Nourishing global sensitivity requires finding new ways for meaningful interactions, visits, and exchanges.
- Critical thinking and communication skills must be developed that build up interdisciplinary thinking and help students to use their new knowledge in an ethically and globally conscious manner. These skills will help students reflect on and understand their rights and responsibilities in a global society.
- Language, collaboration, and technology skills must be embedded across the curriculum to help students prepare for lifelong engagement with the world.
- Schools must provide for the education of the whole child for the whole world.

Levine (2007) approaches the question of outcomes by describing what he believes are the essentials needed for a successful journey to adulthood; these essentials are interpretation, instrumentation, interaction, and inner direction. From this perspective, students will need to

- know how to become in-depth analysts of concepts and interpreters of their own understanding, as well as critical, evaluative thinkers;
- know how to implement projects that have significant potential to solve important problems;
- know how to collaborate with others on projects that align with their interests and personal aspirations; and
- have opportunities to know themselves by posing and answering questions about themselves to prepare for needed career and leadership roles they will want to pursue in the future.

In Table 6.1, we have summarized the outcomes described in this section as a way to look at possibilities for the future.

What Is Possible in Schools of the Future

When we begin to expand our vision of what is possible in new educational systems designed with future unknowns in mind, we need to free ourselves of the "boxes" we have created that keep us stuck in the current paradigm. Knowing what those boxes are is a first step, along with knowing which student, teacher, and system outcomes are currently in place and driving the functioning of our system. Spady (2007) has summarized what he sees as the "boxes" we need to get out of to move our thinking forward, shown in Figure 6.1.

In addition to these constraints, the student, teacher, and system outcomes that are driving our current system include

- content standards in basic skills and core disciplines;
- student test scores that are based on the assessment of these content and curriculum standards;

Table 6.1   Outcomes We Are Being Urged to Pursue in
Our Schools for the Future

Students will need to be
- innovative;
- culturally aware;
- able to communicate and collaborate in sophisticated ways;
- in-depth analysts of concepts;
- interpreters of their own understanding; and
- critical, evaluative thinkers.

Students will need to be skilled in
- interpretation;
- instrumentation;
- interaction; and
- inner direction.

Students will need to know how to
- implement projects that have significant potentials to solve important problems; and
- collaborate with others on projects that align with their interests and personal aspirations.

Students will need to have opportunities to know themselves by
- posing and answering questions about themselves to prepare for needed career and leadership roles that they will want to pursue in the future.

Teachers will need to
- be partners with students and parents in tracking students' development and academic growth in the skills needed for productive lives in a global society;
- foster critical thinking and communication skills that develop interdisciplinary thinking;
- help students to use their new knowledge in an ethically and globally conscious manner;
- help students reflect on and understand their rights and responsibilities in a global society;
- help students prepare for lifelong engagement with the world; and
- have a more active role in defining a new global school mission and shared purpose, as well as defining ways to work with partner schools in other nations on units that focus on global topics of mutual interest and relevance.

School systems will need to
- place student engagement in key concepts that are grounded in current events and issues relevant to students at the center of learning;
- embed language, collaboration, and technology skills across the curriculum;
- find new ways for meaningful interactions, visits, and exchanges that should be a focus for nourishing global sensitivity; and
- educate the whole child for the whole world.

- teacher accountability for student test scores and content coverage on state standards; and
- system accountability for student and teacher achievement of minimum passing scores on state tests.

Figure 6.1   Natural Learning Isn't B☐xed In By Schooling!

- The Curriculum Subjects B☐X
- The Standards B☐X
- The Time B☐X
- The Grade Level B☐X
- The Test Sc☐re B☐X
- The Rep☐rt Card B☐X
- The Opp☐rtunity B☐X
- The R☐le B☐X
- The Classr☐☐m B☐X

Defining New Possibilities

Spady (2001) has argued that if schools were organized around competence rather than content, students would develop more skills than knowing, interpreting, understanding, recognizing, and remembering. Instead, they would learn to plan, design, organize, write, produce, perform, create, and engage using authentic life competencies. These life competencies have been summarized by Spady into five life performances that can be seen as applying to all learners in the system, shown in Figure 6.2.

To accomplish these kinds of outcomes, The New Possibilities Network was formed in the summer of 2007 by a group of forward-thinking educational researchers and international consultants. This network is comprised of seven individuals (one of us, Barbara McCombs, included) who have dedicated their careers to exploring and explaining the deeper nature of human capacity, learning, instructional systems, leadership, and educational transformation. Individually, each person has been recognized across the world as a leader in elevating educational thinking, policy, and practice to the direct benefit of students, educators, and the communities they serve. Members of this group include Bill Spady, Barbara McCombs, Renate and Geoffrey Caine, Marion Brady, Roger Mills, and Sid O'Connell. (References to work by each of these individuals are cited in the Resources section of this book.)

A primary unifying concept in our work in the New Possibilities Network is called "Natural Learning" (Spady et al., 2007). As its name implies, natural learning is not a 21st-century invention but as old as human existence itself. Most people understand that learning begins in the womb and continues uninterrupted throughout all of life. Moreover, learning happens every day as humans engage in life, and, like life, it has no artificial categories or boundaries. At its essence, natural learning, like the Learner-Centered Model we are advocating here, is

- purpose-driven
- life-grounded
- goal-directed
- action-based

Figure 6.2   Examples of Life Performance Outcomes[1]

1. **Learning and Living CONSCIOUSLY as:**

   Reflective, Self-Directed DEVELOPING PROFESSIONALS
   Prudent, Organized LIFE MANAGERS
   Self-Directed, Reflective INVESTIGATORS & LEARNERS
   Ethical, Spiritual BEINGS & ADVOCATES
   Informed, Reflective PERSONS
   Healthy, Confident LEARNERS & PLAYERS
   Ethical, Empowered HUMANS
   Unique, Loving SPIRITUAL BEINGS
   Aware, Reflective SPIRITUAL BEINGS
   Open, Growing LEARNERS

2. **Learning and Living CREATIVELY as:**

   Imaginative, Insightful OPPORTUNITY CREATORS
   Resourceful, Entrepreneurial OPPORTUNITY CREATORS
   Strategic, Resourceful PLANNERS & ORGANIZERS
   Visionary, Resilient EXPLORERS & PROBLEM SOLVERS
   Inquisitive, Visionary INNOVATORS
   Imaginative, Versatile EXPLORERS & INNOVATORS
   Eclectic, Visionary THINKERS & INNOVATORS
   Visionary, Innovative EXPLORERS & INVENTORS
   Visionary, Resourceful EXPLORERS & INNOVATORS
   Imaginative, Undaunted INNOVATORS

3. **Learning and Living COLLABORATIVELY as:**

   Reliable, Supportive TEAM MEMBERS
   Active, Collaborative CITIZENS
   Responsive, Effective LISTENERS & COMMUNICATORS
   Receptive, Collaborative PARTNERS & MENTORS
   Ethical, Responsive PARTNERS
   Respectful, Supportive COMMUNICATORS & PARTNERS
   Respectful, Responsive COMMUNICATORS & TEAM MEMBERS.
   Heartfelt, Trustworthy COMMUNICATORS & MENTORS
   Supportive, Trustworthy TEAM PLAYERS & MENTORS
   Honest, Affirming PARTNERS

4. **Learning and Living COMPETENTLY as:**

   Competent, Informed EMERGING PROFESSIONALS
   Skilled, Productive CONTRIBUTORS
   Creative, Adept PRODUCERS
   Adept, Productive PERFORMERS & IMPLEMENTERS
   Adept, Productive PERFORMERS
   Self-Directed, Resourceful CREATORS & PERFORMERS

(Continued)

Figure 6.2   (Continued)

Resourceful, Responsible IMPLEMENTERS & PERFORMERS
Joyful, Talented PERFORMERS & MANIFESTORS
Versatile, Productive PERFORMERS & IMPLEMENTERS
Reliable, Exemplary PRODUCERS

5. **Learning and Living COMPASSIONATELY as:**

Responsible, Contributing COMMUNITY PARTICIPANTS
Conscientious, Global STEWARDS
Caring, Global CONTRIBUTORS
Discerning, Compassionate STEWARDS & CONTRIBUTORS
Caring, Community CONTRIBUTORS
Caring, Responsible CONTRIBUTORS & STEWARDS
Discerning, Supportive ADVOCATES & CONTRIBUTORS
Forthright, Global LEADERS & STEWARDS
Active, Global CONTRIBUTORS & STEWARDS
Caring, Committed CONTRIBUTORS

---

[1] Compiled from projects and workshops facilitated by Dr. William Spady (2001).

- sense-making
- creative/generative

Using these six central defining concepts which underlie natural learning, school leaders can visualize the possibilities of what new system outcomes can be for all learners in the system.

New Possibilities on Truths About Human Capacity

A second major concept in the work of the New Possibilities Network emanates from a set of basic truths about human capacity—truths bolstered by human experience and a vast set of documented research (Spady et al., 2007). Among these, six stand out and serve as the foundation for our work:

1. Humans are born curious and naturally explore life and their world.
2. Humans vary greatly in their rates and ways of learning.
3. Humans are social and naturally learn with and from others.
4. Humans learn, create, and change throughout their lives.
5. Humans naturally use all their senses to learn.
6. Humans can take charge of their thoughts and emotions.

The members of the Network believe that now is the time for all of us to address these truths about both natural learning and human capacity and to explore with each other what these truths mean for how we learn, how we educate, and how we live as a species on this planet. As we proposed earlier, we believe that, through respectful and inclusive public dialogue involving concerned parents, community members, educators, and students, together we can create the kinds of educational models needed for all our children and youth as they enter a rapidly changing global world. As we have already pointed out, this open-dialogue approach is based on new findings from science that demonstrate the properties of living systems, which themselves acknowledge the need for individuals to create new systems in order to "own" them and take responsibility for their emergence and sustainability.

As a personal exercise, look at Box. 6.2, in which the six human capacities are listed, and you are asked to consider three questions. Reflecting on what you have learned about the principles of natural human learning, journal what comes to mind as "out-of-the-box" responses to these questions.

What Future Systems Could Look Like

Bottoms (2007) is among those who argue that high schools of the future will need to offer more student-centered, research-based instruction connected to a caring adult mentor. Instruction will need to focus on how knowledge and skills can be used in actual career settings and include opportunities to meet professionals in a variety of fields. Such schools help students finish their studies on time, continue their studies after high school, and better prepare students to succeed in college and work (Bottoms). Bottoms concludes, "But to achieve this goal, teachers and school leaders must accept responsibility for providing learning experiences that students see as important to their futures" (p. 37).

Coyote Ridge Elementary School in Broomfield, Colorado, is an example of a school that is well on its way to achieving the types of outcomes we have been describing. Coyote Ridge is described by the Hope Foundation (2007) as an example of a five-star school that is committed to educating the whole child. In spite of the current standards, content, accountability, and testing policies, this school is dedicated to teaching and rewarding students for demonstrating creativity, good citizenship, thoughtfulness, ethical behavior, and good health habits. Their approach has led to fewer disciplinary problems and increased enthusiasm from all students. The school has created sustainable and well-functioning learning communities driven by a common mission and vision. Students' behavior and academic success are recognized and celebrated, parents are highly involved, and everyone believes it is unacceptable for any child to fail.

Stookey (2003) provides another example of a school moving toward achieving desirable outcomes. Using new science principles that relate to living systems and chaos theory, he describes the approaches used at the Nova Scotia Sea School for teenagers where the program is designed to help young people discover their resilience through the skillful use of chaos. The techniques used are based on trust in the inherent wisdom of all people. Boats and the sea are used to help young people learn leadership, courage, responsibility, cooperation, generosity, and respect. A particularly unique feature is that students become skilled at resilience by learning to use obstacles to change directions and reveal new possibilities. Chaos is skillfully used to reveal a time of openness and creativity so that, during times of chaos and uncertainty, students discover how to rest in the chaos and allow it to resolve itself. This means letting things happen in their own time and allowing a greater solution or opportunity to emerge.

Box 6.2   Identifying Future Possibilities

SINCE ...	**What should Education look like?**

HUMANS are born curious and naturally explore life and their world...

HUMANS vary greatly in their rates and ways of learning...

HUMANS are social and naturally learn with and from others...

HUMANS can learn, create, and change throughout their lives...

HUMANS naturally use all their senses to learn...

HUMANS can take charge of their thoughts and emotions...

SINCE ...	**What should Educators do?**

HUMANS are born curious and naturally explore life and their world...

HUMANS vary greatly in their rates and ways of learning...

HUMANS are social and naturally learn with and from others...

HUMANS can learn, create, and change throughout their lives...

HUMANS naturally use all their senses to learn...

HUMANS can take charge of their thoughts and emotions...

SINCE ...	**What should Education Policy look like?**

HUMANS are born curious and naturally explore life and their world...

HUMANS vary greatly in their rates and ways of learning...

HUMANS are social and naturally learn with and from others...

HUMANS can learn, create, and change throughout their lives...

HUMANS naturally use all their senses to learn...

HUMANS can take charge of their thoughts and emotions...

Stookey (2003) explains that a chaotic situation requires courage because, in the short term, things may get worse before they get better. In the school experience, things are kept simple—students are in a close, inescapable environment (the boat, the river, the focus of the program). In this context of safety, students are offered a variety of interpersonal, environmental, skills-based, schedule-based complexities that they must solve as a team. Using the notion of a container, the students discover that the complexity of the situation reduces things to what matters the most. The instructor has the job of providing and manipulating the "container" but does not try to control how any of the participants experience the complexities or chaos. The wisdom of everyone is trusted, and each person is encouraged to come to her or his own conclusions about their experience as the chaos is allowed to resolve itself. Stookey attributes the success of this approach to the programmatic work that goes into creating a situation that has the potential for containment, friction, trust, and compassion. Some may see this as a harsh approach, but Stookey argues that using this technique in a universally applicable way allows ordinary chaos to become an ally that leads to resilience.

We chose to describe these two examples in particular because they are deliberately representative of out-of-the-box thinking. We intended them to help you see possibilities you may not have otherwise seen. With these in mind, we next invite you to apply what you have learned to a systems analysis problem.

Expanding the List of Possible Student, Teacher, and System Outcomes in Technology-Supported Models

The Association for Educational Communications and Technology (AECT, 2007) has recently released an initiative to transform American school systems. The initiative describes the association's mission, which is to work with state education agencies to help them break the cycle of failed education reforms. This initiative, called *Future Minds*, has the ultimate goal of working at the state education level to create quantum improvement through a transformational paradigm change. The paradigm shift they are advocating is one that moves from schooling that is suited to the Industrial Age to one that is suited to the Information Age and 21st-century needs.

The *Future Minds* initiative includes major shifts in desired outcomes (AECT, p. 6), categorized into the areas we outlined in Table 6.1.

System Outcomes

- Customized, tailored instruction
- Democratic classroom environment
- Students assumed to learn by doing
- Systems thinking

Teacher Practice Outcomes

- Teacher doing **with** students
- Self-directed student learning
- Multi-age grouping
- Interdisciplinary courses
- Teaching is process/performance-oriented
- Intrinsic motivation creates meaningful student engagement
- Student readiness and interest grouping
- Individual, small-group, and large-group activities
- Plentiful access to knowledge
- Multiple resources of various kinds

- Multimedia technologies
- Student progress customized in response to student's personal learning outcomes

Student Learning Outcomes

- Mastery-based assessments
- Authentic testing of student achievement of required standards
- Convergent and divergent learning
- Student motivated to learn
- Student independence/interdependence
- Engaged, lifelong learner

As with other visionary leadership groups emerging at this point in time, the *Future Minds* initiative emphasizes the belief that it is a moral imperative for the group to help state education officials and their primary stakeholders. The group sees the initiative as a way to help state-level people see the discrepancies between the models of schooling that currently exist and the models that are needed to make school systems compatible with our changing world.

Simplifying the Choices With a New Model: The Learner–Centered Educational System as an Intellectual Supply Chain

McCombs and a number of her colleagues have been working over the past two years to develop the Center for Innovation Science (CIS). Underlying this effort is the vision of creating and implementing a transformed educational systems model. To this end, we have developed a framework called the *intellectual supply chain* (ISC). The ISC, which supports the Learner-Centered Principles, is a system for integrating all major stakeholders in education and the workplace so that each has input at every level. It also discourages silos of isolated interest, allowing equitable access to the entire system by all learners. The major goal of the ISC is the alignment of all functions, content, and processes across the educational system and the workplace in order to nurture and further develop the natural human capacities of collaboration, learning, and creativity. Together, these capacities form the meta-competency needed for a positive and productive life in systems ranging from the personal, interpersonal, and life-work to the broader social-economic system levels. The goal of the ISC is an educational system that will be more responsive to technological changes and the need for innovation in the global economy.

Figure 6.3 shows a diagram of this system by illustrating how the concept of innovation science integrates the basic meta-competencies of collaboration, learning, and creativity as three sides of a triangle. Learning is the fundamental competency at the base, which supports the competencies of collaboration and creativity. To achieve the goal of innovative science from K through 20, participants engage in the processes of (1) constructive and respectful dialogue and (2) inquiry to find shared meaning. Both meta-competencies operate reciprocally, with each influencing and being influenced by the other. As

Figure 6.3   Innovation Science[1]

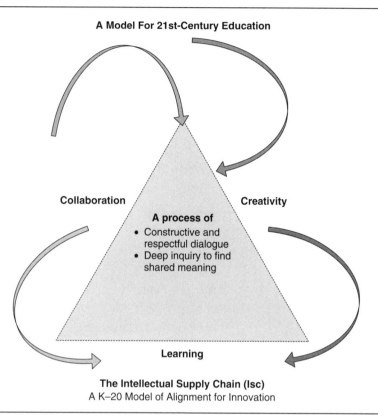

A Model For 21st-Century Education

Collaboration   Creativity

A process of
- Constructive and respectful dialogue
- Deep inquiry to find shared meaning

Learning

The Intellectual Supply Chain (Isc)
A K–20 Model of Alignment for Innovation

[1]This is the intellectual property of the Innovation Science team comprised of Drs. Beyerlein, Bink, McCombs, and Nemiro (2006). This is not to be used without written permission from Dr. Barbara McCombs, University of Denver Research Institute, 2050 E. Iliff Avenue, Boettcher East-Room 224, Denver, CO 80208.

school leaders and their staff engage in dialogue about what best promotes and develops these competencies in learners of all ages, the system becomes more integrated, which leads to the development of innovation capabilities in all learners.

Our vision for the Center for Innovation Science grew out of our shared understanding and concern over the flawed current public education system and the policies surrounding its operation. We observed that the public education system is presently incapable of developing the intellectual capital and innovation that will drive the economy in the 21st century. We reviewed empirical evidence showing that schools willing to step outside the narrow testing and accountability agenda and implement practices consistent with research-validated principles of human learning, motivation, development, and individual differences are achieving higher levels of student learning across academic and social-emotional domains. Thus, we verified that the balance of high achievement and positive personal development is possible.

The challenge is to capture these best practice principles in a new educational systems design that prepares all learners (students and adults alike) to be lifelong learners and innovators in the workplace and in life. The positive outcomes at an individual level can transfer to the ultimate establishment of new human social, economic, and political systems on a global scale. These new systems further promise to result in a more competent, more productive, more collaborative, and more creative world. The long-range goal of the CIS is to create a transformed view of educational systems that transfers to enlightened corporate settings using systems created through an understanding of nature's natural sorting system and principles of human learning, motivation, development, and individual differences.

ALIGNING THE NEW VISION WITH EXISTING REALITIES

We designed the exercise in Box 6.3 to provide you with an opportunity to begin linking your vision for your school, district, or other educational institution with the realities you face from local, state, and federal policies and legislation. As you engage in the exercise, let yourself think outside the "box"—i.e., the constraints that can hobble your creativity.

No doubt you have identified places where there are mismatches between what you would like to see in terms of outcomes and what exists in the reality of the system in which you serve. We hope, however, that you were able to see new ways in which these existing realities can be stretched and transformed to approach the simpler and more critical outcomes needed for students entering our global world. The next task is for you to consider how to produce the outcomes we need and value, create lifelong learners, and deal with some of the inequities that are in the current educational system design.

DEALING WITH CURRENT SYSTEM INEQUITIES IN NEW SYSTEMS DESIGNS

An overarching goal of designing systems for the future is to create lifelong learners. In earlier chapters we described how such systems share the practice of providing personally challenging and meaningful learning opportunities for all learners in the system. Further, in Chapter 4, we reported that learner-centered designs have been shown to produce higher levels of lifelong learning skills in students from varying backgrounds and educational experiences.

Given the increasing diversity in all our educational systems and at all system levels, it becomes a growing challenge for school leaders to ensure that the system is responsive to perceived problems in addressing diversity and current system inequities through establishing new learning partners and networks of learning communities dedicated to social justice goals and educating for democracy.

Box 6.3   Aligning Your Vision With the Realities of Policies and Legislation

Journal your responses to the prompts below.

1.   Describe how well the outcomes we described in the preceding section align with your state's learning standards.

2.   Describe how the outcomes you described in the exercise in Box 6.1 align with your state's learning standards.

3.   Describe the extent to which your state's learning standards reflect the Learner-Centered Principles.

4.   Describe how the outcomes you described in the exercise in Box 6.1 can be expanded to include those valued by your staff and community.

Addressing Diversity Issues

As students progress through the educational system from kindergarten through college, the current one-size-fits-all paradigm contributes in many cases to a widening of the achievement gap and a failure to meet the diverse needs of many cultural and ethnic groups. This becomes particularly evident at the college level. For example, Maldonado, Rhoads, and Buenavista (2005) argue that current integration and multicultural theories of student retention at the postsecondary level do not adequately address the academic needs of underrepresented students of color. Student-initiated retention projects (SIRPs), which are student organized, run, and funded, have been found to transform college structures, policies, and practices at several University of California campuses and the University of Wisconsin at Madison. In particular, SIRP programs designed to better address retention issues focus on (1) developing knowledge, skills, and social networks (tied conceptually to cultural and social capital); (2) building community ties and commitments (tied conceptually to collectivism); (3) and challenging social and institutional norms (tied conceptually to social praxis).

As Maldonado et al. (2005) state,

The goal [of SIRPs] is to eliminate institutional barriers to the matriculation of students of color. On the other hand, students, as historical agents, should come to redefine their education as a tool for social change through conscious engagement in a vital community. In the end, their vision of social change and the contribution they make to a democratic society should extend well beyond simply the scope of their collegiate careers. (p. 634)

In an attempt to offer a new conceptual framework emphasizing an empowerment perspective to cultural group aspects of identity and persistence, Maldonado et al. (2005) studied the qualitative studies programs at Berkeley and Madison. At both institutions, the goal was to build more democratic relations between students and their teachers—relations that share the ownership of knowledge and knowledge creation. Such collaborative relationships change the power structure and potential alienation among underrepresented students of color. Consistent with the APA Learner-Centered Psychological Principles, empowerment strategies as represented by student-initiated retention projects allow students to exercise a degree of control over their own academic support and recruitment initiatives.

The case study research by Maldonado et al. (2005) highlights how learner-centered practices such as student-initiated retention projects can advance the necessary knowledge and skills for students to succeed in college by helping them connect with important social networks and systems of support, particularly in gaining the self-confidence to forge relationships with professors. Students are also able to develop a separate cultural consciousness about themselves within the dominant culture of the university context. Students are able to negotiate the social matrices of the larger academic culture through the strengthening of their connections to their cultural backgrounds and ethnic/racial communities. Their ties to family and community are increased as they strengthen their sense of cultural identify and social ties. Students are challenged to understand the cultural knowledge and social connections they need within the dominant culture. They then can engage with those university structures, policies, and practices that have marginalized their own knowledge and identities. Through problem-posing strategies, students become participants as agents of change in transforming education to become more self-directed and democratic.

Gurin and Nagda (2006) describe an intergroup dialogue model for engaging students in exploring commonalities and differences in group identities and experiences. In this approach, students learn to work constructively with intergroup conflicts and build collective identities as socially just people. This intergroup dialogue moves beyond most diversity initiatives because it addresses conflicts, rather than masking them. Such dialogue provides students with opportunities to understand commonalities as well as differences between groups, and it fosters active thinking about possible causes of inequalities. It is a promising model in educating for democracy by actively promoting inclusion and social justice.

Dealing With Inequities

In a book addressing the inequities in public schools that continue to plague many nations, including the United States, Kozol (2005) contends that the current dialogue, through the language of higher standards and expectations, is focused on "adequacy" rather than "equality." This adequacy dialogue has replaced what were once important parts of the school curriculum—i.e., ethical and moral standards that engage students in relevant and critical dialogue contributing to their development as citizens in a democratic society. The inequalities with which

Kozol is most concerned include disparities between public schools in poor and wealthy communities, such as funding and resources. He maintains that urban schools, in particular, increasingly resemble the factory production lines that many reformers have for decades worked to replace with more ecologically and scientifically valid models. How to move beyond the market-driven model of today's schools will require significant changes in thinking and practice to offset the disturbing trend toward growing school segregation, which has arisen from the growing race and class inequality over the last two decades. More than fundamental school transformation is needed—reform must also include social and economic reforms that provide basic housing, employment, and health care to those who need it the most.

In a review of two recent books describing historical underlying causes for inequality in public schools (Gresson, 2004; Perlstein, 2004), Mulcahy (2006) points out that racial pain is felt by both black and white cultures and involves a felt absence of power and the presence of guilt and shame. He maintains that, to move forward, critical pedagogy must provide a framework for critical multiculturalism where students can be individually engaged to transform themselves and larger social systems. By failing to recognize the experience of students, little progress can be made toward social and racial healing. Of perhaps greater significance in Mulcahy's review, however, is his recognition that a major stumbling block to progress in school reform is the labeling of such practices as encouraging students' innate curiosity to interpret and make meaning of the world as practices linked to a liberal political agenda. This particular stumbling block rests on a failure to build schooling and learning on research-validated principles of learning, motivation, development, and individual differences, which not only places students in the role of passive learners, but also violates what we know to be true about the nature of learning and systems.

Another school inequity concern raised by Mulcahy (2006) is that one of the issues with the current fundamentalist politics underlying educational policies and practice is that it neglects the individual in favor of corporate gain. For centuries, educators have been arguing that a one-size-fits-all model focusing on standardizing curriculum and enforcing tests violates biological and ecological principles. Mulcahy, among others, believes that what is needed are many alternatives within any given system. For Mulcahy, the democratic educator working to promote a functioning democracy has the responsibility to critically engage students in an education that ensures the stability and longevity of democracy.

Chiu & Khoo (2005), in a study that examined how resources, distribution inequality, and biases toward privileged students affected performance, had fifteen-year-olds from forty-one countries complete a questionnaire and tests in mathematics, reading, and science. Their results indicated that schools with more privileged students typically had more resources (books, teacher attention, family income) and that privileged student bias (parent job status) was related to student performance, suggesting that without equal opportunity there will always be inequalities in student achievement. Chiu and Khoo argue that their results support the view that reducing distribution inequality will improve students' academic performance; however, their findings also show that increasing resources for privileged students at the expense of underprivileged students will decrease overall student performance. Thus, reducing privileged student bias at the classroom, school, and school system levels helps all students reach higher achievement levels in mathematics, reading, and science.

The concern with addressing the requirements of high-need versus resource-rich schools crosses the urban and rural school boundaries. Truscott and Truscott (2005) show that when resources are at the center of discussions about higher student achievement, both rural and urban communities have a common set of issues, and by banding together, they can increase their political power. In spite of their differing circumstances, urban and rural communities face similar struggles, such as increasing poverty and decreasing employment that adversely affect school funding levels. Truscott and Truscott further argue that traditional classifications of schools based on population levels in their communities is no longer useful given shifts of segments such as the middle class from urban to suburban to rural and back to gentrified city centers. Some of the common issues include childhood poverty, segregation by socio-economic status, serious fiscal challenges, plus finding and keeping good teachers.

THE LEARNING PARTNERSHIPS AND NETWORKS THAT WE NEED

Many of us are not aware of the vast networks we already have that can serve us in leading others toward a new educational vision and toward the creation of learner-centered educational models. As we have maintained throughout this book, the living systems framework, the Learner-Centered Principles, the Learner-Centered Model, and the various self-assessment and reflection tools we have presented—all can help guide the new school leader in his or her work. With the ubiquitous nature of technology today, many of the networks we have and know about are virtually at our fingertips.

The Role of Technology

Whether technology becomes the primary delivery mechanism for the educational system of the future or whether it is one of the major tools used in the teaching and learning process will require collaborative planning by all constituents involved (McCombs, 2000b). This includes students, parents, teachers, administrators, community members, and policymakers at local and national levels. By using the best knowledge available on how people learn, what enhances learning and motivation for diverse learners, and how best to support learning and change in inclusive and respectful dialogue, the best answers will emerge. And from a learner-centered perspective, they won't be the same answers for all learners or all learning communities. With technology, therefore, comes the promise of providing the tools and capacity for networked learning communities that can expand and transform ideas about learning and schooling in ways that produce healthy and productive lifelong learners.

The learner-centered framework adds a constant reminder that the human element cannot be left out of even the most advanced technology-supported networked learning communities. Further, aside from people, one of the biggest factors contributing to the success of information technologies in learning is establishing a context of safety and support for learning. As Green and Staley (2000) report, technologies such as computer conferencing can provide an effective learning tool if they attend to constructing a safe context and genuine interpersonal rapport. Our challenge is how to design educational systems in which technology is in service to, values, and supports diverse learners and learning contexts, which results in viewing the evaluation of learning from a new perspective. We suggest that evaluation will be centered on understanding how technology can contribute to individual growth and development and on assessing the personalized learning goals that arise from shared visions for learning in the larger learning community and society. Assessment methodologies will be those that support nonlinear learning and match the natural learning and motivation processes that occur in life. Rather than assessing the benefits of technology, the focus of technology assessment will be to explore how to enhance those benefits by matching them to learner needs combined with information on how learning best occurs.

Students as Partners

A largely untapped resource for all school leaders is their students and their creative responses to technology. Students know how to connect with technology and how to form networks of connections with their peers in and outside of their schools. Technology is clearly a tool of innovation that is underutilized and inequitably distributed in public schools. The need for today's students to create the future requires that they be knowledgeable, competent, and inventive. They should be able not only to reach high standards but to set even higher standards for themselves. Today's students need an educational system that allows all to succeed and time to be allowed to vary. When students become learning partners, it is possible to tap into their experiences and work with them to form the networks and partnerships needed.

Forming Networked Learning Communities

Online learning communities are fast becoming a reality that can transform thinking and practice beyond today's traditional models and boundaries of schools and educational systems. In learner-centered, networked learning environments, all people associated with the system are learners whose status changes from novice to expert as tasks and goals change (Hannum & McCombs, 2008). The boundaries are limited only by imagination and need for access to expertise as learning needs and opportunities change in response to dynamic curriculum objectives. Content can be digitally constructed and customized to meet individual learner needs, abilities, interests, goals, and other characteristics—including their dynamic and changing roles from novice to expert learners. Concepts such as "just-in-time learning" and "learning anytime, anywhere" describe the dynamic learning environment and online learning communities that revolve around and evolve from inquiry-based learning tasks.

In the context of online learning and networked learning communities, the learner-centered perspective contributes a balanced focus on

- the individual learner (the changing role of that learner from novice to expert, from learner to teacher);
- the learning process (the dynamic, self-directed, and often social nature of that process); and
- the learning context (the environment, climate, and community that supports the learner and the learning process).

This balance is essential within the learner-centered perspective because of the same factors we mentioned earlier with respect to learner-centered practices in general. That is, learner-centered practices

- address learner needs as well as learning needs in general;
- provide a whole-person view that includes cognitive/metacognitive, affective/motivational, social/developmental, and other individual needs;
- balance academic and nonacademic concerns that are part of learning and achievement goals for 21st-century learners; and
- acknowledge the importance of the context and learning community that supports both individual learners and the social nature of the learning process.

THE LEARNING PARTNERSHIPS YOU WILL NEED

We have talked throughout this book about the kinds of learning partnerships and networks school leaders of the future will need. We now invite you to think about your personal partnerships and networks that will help you move toward creating the learner-centered educational systems we need. We designed the exercise in Box 6.4 as a way for you to not only identify these partnerships and networks but to think about some new possibilities.

SELF-REFLECTIONS

You now have an opportunity in Box 6.5 to integrate what you have read and thought about in this chapter. As promised in the exercise at the beginning of this chapter, you will have a chance to refine your vision and the outcomes you will be pursuing in your school leader role.

Box 6.4   What Learning Partnerships Will You Need?

Drawing on the information about learning partnerships and networks in this section, journal your responses to the prompts below.

1. Identify the technological resources you have available in your school, district, or agency. Then identify the people who would be the best partners for you in your work to create the best technology-supported networked learning communities for the learners in your setting.

2. Outline a plan for creating collaborative teams with students to develop learning networks in your school, district, or agency. Include how the teams will incorporate professional and peer networks both within and outside of your setting.

3. Describe the structure of three types of online, networked learning communities you can create for your school, district, or agency. Include the role students will play.

4. Identify the face-to-face learning partners you can rely on as you create your vision for a learner-centered school, district, or agency.

5. Identify the online networked partners you can rely on as you create your vision for a learner-centered school, district, or agency.

Box 6.5   Reflections on Vision, Outcomes, and Partnership

1. In Box 6.2 on page 182, you responded to a series of questions stemming from a set of statements about the nature of learning and systems. Taken together, your statements summarize your *vision* for your school, district, or agency. In Box 6.1 on page 174, you described the *outcomes* you hope for in eight areas of practice. Describe here how your vision dovetails with and deviates from the outcomes you hope for.

2. In Box 6.3 on page 187, you addressed how the *outcomes* you described in Box 6.1 aligned with your state's learning standards. Describe here how your *vision* for your school, district, or agency aligns with your state's learning standards.

3. Describe how you can use the learning partnerships you described in Box 6.4 to help you realize your vision for your school, district, or agency.

WHAT'S NEXT

In Chapter 7, we take what have been many complexities and attempt to reduce them to their simplicity so that you as a school leader have a clear roadmap for designing the learner-centered educational systems we need for the future. We begin the chapter by presenting some new ideas from the living systems and ecological sciences that deal directly with one of the most important qualities of the new school leader—developing capacity from within. We encourage you to use these ideas to explore how you can form new partnerships with students and all stakeholders. We stress the simplicity of processes we discussed throughout this book that may have seemed complex from a research validation standpoint. At their most basic, they are premised on trusting in people, their capacities, and the emergence of new ideas, practices, and structures that can arise from commonly-held values, beliefs, and learner-centered principles. They provide the means for becoming new networked learning communities that can transform education. This final chapter concludes with a summary of the simpler principles and practices that can provide you with the foundation for your journey in creating the learner-centered educational systems we need for the future.

7

How We Develop Leadership Qualities From Within

... orderly change within social systems is in the direction of integration and holism; further, ...the social-change agent has as his major function to work with and in an organization so that it can change consistently with the changing dynamic equilibrium both within and outside the organization. This requires that the system become conscious of alienated fragments within and without so it can bring them into the main functional activities by processes similar to identification in the individual. First, there is an awareness within the system that an alienated fragment exists; next that fragment is accepted as a legitimate outgrowth of a functional need that is then explicitly and deliberately mobilized and given power to operate as an explicit force. This, in turn, leads to communication with other subsystems and facilitates an integrated, harmonious development of the whole system.

—Arnold Beisser (1970, p. 3)

In this chapter, we will describe findings and insights about leadership from brain research that can help us prepare for the future. We explore some additional leadership ideas from the living systems and ecological sciences that apply directly to the essence of leadership—developing leadership capacity from within. We give details regarding the origin of these concepts, with their basis in trusting people and their capacities. The result is the emergence of ideas, practices, and structures that arise from commonly-held values, beliefs, and evidence-based principles.

We acknowledge that you will most likely encounter leadership challenges, but we believe we can meet them by applying the combination of ideas from this book that best matches your unique needs and setting. We encourage you to explore how, as you create new partnerships with students and all stakeholders, you can begin leading networked learning communities that transform education. We address how capacity from within can be developed to take transformations in your systems to scale, using the power of new technologies that can help bring forth the new paradigm.

We conclude the chapter by presenting the simpler principles and practices that will help you, in your leadership role, to implement the learner-centered tools and practices we have described thus far in our journey. You will then be well on your way to becoming one of those most-needed future school leaders.

We journey now into a closer look at some ideas and leadership concepts regarding the essence of how to develop leadership qualities needed from within. These ideas and concepts will help you to better understand the principles we have described throughout the book and to engage in the learner-centered practices for transforming our current paradigm.

NEW IDEAS FROM BRAIN RESEARCH

Pink (2005) describes one of the major changes in thinking that is beginning to gain momentum among leaders. He calls this a switch from a predominant worldview based on the left brain functions that handle sequence, reason, and analysis to a focus on right brain functions. Pink argues that the information age is being replaced by a conceptual age that will be ruled by artistry, empathy, emotion, and the ability to see the big picture and transcend current thinking and paradigms.

Using recent findings from neuroscience and brain research, Oliver and Ostrofsky (2007) conclude that the mind is more of a valuing device than a reasoning engine. They describe a dynamic balance between what people believe, value, and strive toward; their personality; and the ecological systems in nature. Significantly, all fields of science and social science are beginning to converge on an understanding of the organic and ecological nature of individuals and systems.

Leadership Implications From the Neurosciences

Rock and Schwartz (2007) underscore the recognition that today's leaders will have to understand recent conclusions from cognitive science. They emphasize that these recent breakthroughs will help leaders influence "mindful change" that provides for a transformation of organizations. Such mindful change takes into account what has been learned about the brain and the ways the physiology of the brain can predispose people to resist or accept different forms of leadership. The authors maintain that recent developments in cognitive and neuroscience suggest that, for leaders to manage change, they will need to combine science, art, and craft and remain mindful of these factors:

- **Change is pain**. Organizational change is unexpectedly difficult because it provokes sensations of physiological discomfort.
- **Behaviorism doesn't work**. Change efforts based on incentive and threat (the carrot and the stick) rarely succeed in the long run.
- **Humanism is overrated**. In practice, the conventional empathic approach of connection and persuasion doesn't sufficiently engage people.
- **Focus is power**. The act of paying attention creates chemical and physical changes in the brain.
- **Expectation shapes reality**. People's preconceptions have a significant impact on what they perceive.
- **Attention density shapes identity**. Repeated, purposeful, and focused attention can lead to long-lasting personal evolution (Rock and Schwartz, 2007, pp. 1–2).

In elaborating on these conclusions, Rock and Schwartz (2007) point out that in humans, working memory is engaged when people encounter something new. An energy-intensive process compares the new information with the old. Changes that involve routine, familiar activities and habits are difficult to change, because they require a lot of effort and can lead to feelings that many people find uncomfortable, causing them to avoid change. Change is also hard because the brain detects perceived differences between what was expected and what actually happen. Energy is drawn away from the prefrontal region of the brain, which promotes and supports higher-intellectual function, to lower regions that can result in people becoming emotional and acting more impulsively. Put more simply, trying to change routine behaviors sends messages to the brain that something is not right, which can overpower rational thought (Rock & Schwartz).

The Role of Human Will

For both individual and organizational change, a strong will is required to push past this brain phenomenon. Leaders need to understand that change amplifies stress and discomfort, which means they must not underestimate the challenges in implementing new processes or directions. Rock and Schwartz (2007) explain that the human brain pushes back automatically when told to change because the natural state of any living thing is toward equilibrium and away from change. A limitation of person-centered and humanistic approaches is that they tended to be too unstructured and too focused on self-actualization. From a neuroscience and cognitive science perspective, a better approach for changing behavior is to focus on the holistic and emergent realization of self, for example, allowing people to solve problems for themselves—an approach used in leadership coaching (Rock & Schwartz).

In leadership coaching, the coach asks pertinent questions and supports people in finding their own solutions. This approach takes advantage of both the brain's socially-oriented structure and its pattern-making functions, which foster an innate desire to create novel connections. In other words, authentic inquiry, rather than persuasion, helps people realize that it is in their own interest to change.

The Role of Focusing Attention

In discussing the importance of focus, Rock and Schwartz (2007) report findings from quantum physics that have been applied to neuroscience, one of which is that brain circuits are strengthened and stabilized through the mental act of focusing attention. Attention then works to reshape brain patterns, with the result that paying attention and practicing new ways of thinking and behaving cause people to actually start thinking differently. Being a specialist in different fields and being exposed to how people in that field think and act lead ultimately to physiological differences that prevent people from seeing things in the same way. They report that new expectations, mental maps, theories, attitudes, and beliefs are known to change deep brain centers—resulting in people experiencing what they expect to experience (Rock & Schwartz). When leaders understand the implications of this finding, they can find ways to expose these expectations and beliefs by creating and cultivating "moments of insight." These insights change peoples' mental maps by provoking incongruities or creating a form of mental dissonance that helps people to more dramatically and quickly change their attitudes and expectations.

Rock and Schwartz (2007) contend that, when individuals have a moment of insight, the brain creates a complex set of new connections that have the potential to enhance mental resources and overcome the brain's resistance to change. This happens only when there are deliberate efforts on the part of leaders to "hardwire" these insights by giving them repeated attention and facilitating people's "ownership" of the changes for the changes to actually be successful and long-lasting.

Rock and Schwartz (2007) advise leaders who want to effect change in people's thinking or behavior to intensify individual and team insights by recognizing, encouraging, and deepening these insights. The adrenaline-like rush that accompanies genuine insights—those generated by each individual or team and not given to them as conclusions—are generated from within through the process of making the connections for themselves. This energizing experience is central to facilitating change and helps fight against any internal and external forces that may try to prevent the change, including fear.

The Leadership Challenge of Attending to the Self

According to Rock and Schwartz (2007), knowing how the brain operates helps leaders be "spectators" of their own behavior, observing their own thinking and behaviors. This metacognitive recognition is necessary in order to authentically help others come to their own insights. By paying close attention to oneself, attention density is increased and our thoughts and actions become a more intrinsic part of our identity, including who we are, how we perceive the world, and how our brain works. Rock and Schwartz refer to this capacity

Figure 7.1   A Hypothetical Case of Facilitating Change

A school superintendent wants to change the thinking of people throughout his school district so they will be more accepting of an increase in poor and minority children caused by a district rezoning. In the past, he would have simply done a cultural survey to identify current attitudes. Because he has studied the latest cognitive and brain research, he now understands that a better approach is to lay out a big picture view of what the new system will look like and how it will function—without identifying any individual or system changes that will need to be made. The goal is for individuals to picture the new behaviors in their own minds and develop energizing new mental maps. The superintendent would then follow up with helping all staff and teams within the district to focus attention on their own insights by facilitating discussions and activities around what it would mean to be a truly equitable school district committed to the success of all students. This would be followed up by regularly providing "gentle reminders" that facilitate the process of the new mental maps becoming dominant pathways along which new ideas, energy, and information can flow. The superintendent must stay vigilant and make sure the individuals and teams don't get side-tracked. If they do, he must gently bring them back—releasing the power of the focus and maintaining that power through attention.

—Rock and Schwartz, 2007, p. 6

as "self-directed neuroplasticity," or the capacity to learn through many media by paying increased attention to new ideas. Through the leader's ability to inspire others to closely and frequently focus their attention on specific ideas for a long enough time, true insights and changes in thinking and behavior can occur because new pathways in the brain have replaced older dominant pathways. Leaders can also make a big difference by reminding people about their useful insights and increasing their attention to them. This kind of encouragement builds rather than prunes brain synapses (Rock & Schwartz).

As an example of how these scientific principles might work in practice, consider a hypothetical case in Figure 7.1.

For Rock and Schwartz (2007), the leadership style exhibited in this example provides what the brain wants and leads to lifelong learning, resilience in the face of crises, the willingness to change, and the ability to continually improve oneself and our world.

PREPARING FOR THE FUTURE

In reviewing writers describing how change happens in schools, Coleman and Rud (2007) conclude that change is difficult because it is people rather than programs that are the critical factor. In order to introduce, gain support for, and sustain change, leaders need a network of strong relationships and clear and effective communication. Most current theories—including those of Marshall (2006), Scapp (2006), and Supovitz (2006) as reviewed by Coleman and Rud (2007)—hold that the greatest potential for major system change and transformation involves system instability or some sort of imbalance or crisis.

As we've discussed throughout this book, most current leadership theories also hold that, to challenge the status quo, constant dialogue about vision and strategy must occur (Coleman & Rud, 2007). This dialogue must address perceptions and misperceptions about the change, including any fears about the change itself or its direction. Building a future vision together through dialogue can create the critical connections necessary for change in any given living system. Coleman and Rud stress the fact that most of the writers they surveyed say the job of providing the vision is most important, followed by finding ways to promote the vision without mandating it. This balancing act means that change happens slowly, as leaders must naturally deal with the concerns, conflicts, and sense of loss that come with new practices. To effectively lead change, then, one of the most important roles for school leaders is to create a culture of learning where learning is continuous and cuts across all levels of learners in the system.

How do effective leaders bring about change? One person who has studied this issue is Otto Scharmer, the founder of Theory U.

Theory U and the Concept of "Presencing"

Theory U was developed by Otto Scharmer, a cofounder of the Leadership Lab for Social Responsibility in Business at the Massachusetts Institute of Technology Sloan School of Management. In an interview with Scharmer, Brown (2005) reports that Theory U resulted from eight years of research and interviews with 150 leaders on innovation and leadership. From his research, Scharmer found that these leaders created the mental environment most conducive to creativity and profound insight. This environment, which supports the hidden sources of idea generation, relies on an art Scharmer calls "presencing." Instead of focusing on process and structure, these leaders focused on the people dimension—how people think and behave in all its social complexity.

Consistent with other theories we have described, this model also holds that, for effective leadership in large-scale institutional change, leaders must create spaces where people can reflect, sense, experiment with, and implement innovative solutions. Scharmer says that the process begins by leaders asking themselves "...who is my self and what is my work? Your self doesn't mean your ego, but your highest future possibility. By 'work' we mean 'what is your purpose?'" (Brown, 2005, p 3).

Presencing

Scharmer (2003), who introduced the concept of presencing and its implications for leadership, relates this concept to a blind spot of leadership and says,

> This blind spot concerns the inner place from which an action—what we do—originates. In the process of conducting our daily business and social lives, we are usually well aware of *what* we do and what others do; we also have some understanding of the process: *how* we do things, the processes we and others use when we act. And yet there is a blind spot. If we were to ask the question, 'Where does our action come from?' most of us would be unable to provide an answer. The blind spot concerns the

(inner) *source* from which we operate when we do what we do—the quality of attention that we use to relate to and bring forth the world. (p. 2)

In deriving the concept of presencing, Scharmer (2003) explains that he realized most leaders operated from an experiential learning theory based on reflecting the experiences of the past. From his perspective, what was needed was a different source of learning that was deeper and involved sensing an emerging future. The invisible field beneath the surface can be the blind spot that structures the attention of individuals, groups, or organizations. These blind spots can be habits of thought, what we observe, and how all of these get embodied into new practices. In Scharmer's U-Process of Presencing, the goal is to move to a point where one is presencing—perceiving from the source of highest future possibility, which allows one to

- see and act from a future vision and intent;
- begin to dialogue about emerging possibilities; and
- bring forth new practices, routines, and infrastructure.

When leaders are presencing from this higher source, they engage their will in accessing their self, their emotions, and their ignorance. Scharmer (2003) contends that the most important tool for the leader is the self—his or her capacity to shift to that inner place to bring forth the highest future possibility at an individual and collective level.

Scharmer (2003) describes presencing, comprised of three stages of awareness, as emerging at both individual and collective levels but beginning with the inner journey of awareness:

- opening up to and becoming one with the world outside;
- opening up to and becoming one with one's inner world and deepest source of future possibility; and
- bringing these emerging futures and possibilities into being.

Senge, Scharmer, Jaworski, and Flowers (2004a) discuss what it means to have the capacity as leaders to "presence." They define this capacity as the ability to become present to what is emerging as our future in order to be our highest purpose and potential. In the process of presencing, people imagine alternative futures, even negative ones, in order to open themselves up to different possibilities. Senge et al. contend that the change that will really make a difference is the transformation of the human heart.

In further explaining the concept of presencing in an interview with Leeb (2002), Scharmer describes it as being able to free one's perception from past thinking so that it operates from the field of the future, which requires being able to act from full presence in the now through widening, deepening, and expanding one's perspectives. It includes focus on the development of consciousness about overall socioeconomic systems, underlying learning theory (including learning through reflecting on the past), and considering the spiritual dimension of social processes so that one can become present to the highest future possibility.

Leeb's interview shows Scharmer advocating for a technology of freedom in which we move past the technology of control—a process that includes a greater emphasis on and openness to the spiritual dimension of leadership.

Implications for Leading and Learning

Senge, Scharmer, Jaworski, and Flowers (2004b) conclude that if we are to create a new world, all of us must be willing to participate in changes that are both deeply personal and inherently systemic. They call for generative learning in which leaders focus not only on what they do and how they do it, but also on who they are and the inner source from which they operate individually and collectively. Senge et al. advocate for a living- and self-organizing-systems view of ourselves in which we are continually growing and changing along with others. Senge's view is that we consider the whole (the system) as the organizing pattern for understanding the parts (the people inhabiting the system). From this perspective one can see neither individual nor social identity threaten the life of the larger organism. In other words, just as in fractals, the individual parts mirror the larger whole, while the larger whole mirrors the individual parts.

Senge et al. (2004b) lend their voices to our contention that the Industrial Age model of schools must give rise to a living-systems view that is continually recreating itself as a function of individual and collective levels of awareness. These authors argue that we must move from a world governed by reactive and habit-driven thinking to one that integrates flexible, creative thinking, through which we become more aware of the dynamic whole—what is emerging and our part in it. An inner journey is required to release creativity and presence in leading—a state of being open to what comes and consciously participating in the larger field for change. Such openness and conscious participation cause the field to shift along with the forces shaping a situation so that, rather than continually re-creating the past, new manifestations or an emergence of a new future can be realized.

Senge et al. (2004b) maintain that the possibilities of larger fields for change must come from many perspectives, most important being the perspectives offered by

- the emerging science of living systems;
- the creative arts;
- profound organizational change experiences; and
- direct contact with nature's generative capacities.

Imagining various positive and negative scenarios of alternative futures can open people's thinking and perspectives and alter their awareness of present realities, which acts as a catalyst for profound change. The key in this approach is that the generation of these alternative futures helps people see that they have choices and that their choices matter. Participants begin to realize that separation from one another, our highest selves, and the generative processes of nature is a myth (Senge et al., 2004b).

Implications for New Kinds of Leaders

In the commentary following the Senge et al. (2004b) article, Darcy Winslow, Head of the Global Footwear, Women's Performance division for Nike, Inc., points out that women and youth are leading some of the best efforts to sustain change efforts (pp. 12–13). From her experience, they are the natural carriers of the message of long-term, systemic change, but, for change to actually occur, all of us must become better listeners and be open to these sources. Winslow also points out that when decisions flow from a clear set of principles, they are more widely honored than if they are based on economic metrics (as cited in Senge et al., 2004a).

In another commentary, Elena Diez Pinto, Director of the United Nations Development Programme's Democratic Dialogue for Latin America and the Caribbean, describes her experience that a conscious process of connecting people with each other and with themselves allows social and personal transformations to take place (Senge et al., 2004a, p. 14). She also has found that being open to the larger world of living systems sustains us and helps us create meaningful and lasting change. Based on her experience, she believes that dialogue is also a necessary process for making connections visible among people through listening, thinking together, and trying to understand the whole.

Robert Fritz (composer, filmmaker, and organizational consultant) comments that authentic listening, which he believes comes from focusing on reality without an agenda, acts as a source of breakthrough from traditional prejudices and allows us to see the universe in a new way (as cited in Senge, 2004a, pp. 15–16). He believes this process will help people see reality for what it is: a universe of parts in relationship to each other and to the entire whole—i.e., a dynamic and organic universe that is continually shifting, evolving, and emerging.

Research has found that women face more challenges to becoming successful leaders than men—challenges including sex discrimination, home responsibilities, and in some cases, their own failure to believe in themselves (Martin, 2007). Martin reports that this perception of "weakness" is often due to showing signs of femininity, such as warmth and supportiveness, that often conflict with people's perceptions of characteristic male qualities such as decisiveness and toughness. Because of these challenges, social networks are essential in providing emotional support to women and in helping them gain information that may otherwise be unavailable, including organizational problems and emerging projects or promotions. Martin further states that women can undermine themselves in leadership positions by failing to talk favorably about their accomplishments in an effort to avoid disapproval from others who may think it "unseemly" for women to bring attention to their achievements and skills. Martin suggests that women leaders engage in more subtle self-promotion by asking others to react to their clearly superior ideas or by modestly thanking others who have helped them. Martin concludes by saying that a thorough understanding of the qualities and characteristics of a good leader is essential in order for organizations and society to reduce barriers that favor men over women.

Tying These Concepts Back to Theory U and the Leader's Inner Journey

Scharmer (2004) explains that Theory U suggests that all human and social entities have a variety of sources and attention fields from which they can operate (p. 3). He states that the crises of our time relate to not being aware and not fully actualizing this variety of sources and qualities of attention. He claims that the source of our attention and action remains invisible to our normal mode of observation; that is, the source of our attention resides in our collective blind spot. Schamer believes that studying the evolving self helps us understand the inner source from which our agency originates and how we individually and collectively bring forth our realities or views of the world. To create profound system transformations, leaders need to become more aware of this inner place. Leaders may also need to change that inner place so that it is enlarged enough to include both personal and systems and even planetary issues.

Scharmer (2004) argues that we are in a global crisis that can be defined by the widening social, ecological, and cultural divides that separate individuals, groups, and societies. To pass into the future, leaders must move from a focus, albeit unconscious, on the past to an attention to the future through seven actions:

1. Paying attention: beginning to open up
2. Seeing: the view from outside
3. Sensing: the view from within
4. Presencing: the view from a surrounding presence
5. Crystallizing vision and intent
6. Prototyping living microcosms
7. Performing and embodying the new (Scharmer, 2004, p. 8)

These seven actions define the U, with actions one through three leading down to the bottom of the U, which is action four or presencing. From there the U goes upward so that a leader is able to actually perform and embody the new vision. More importantly, the leader is then able to empower others through the same process and actions.

As we said above, presencing is the key process and can occur at both the individual and collective levels. For any system to be transformed, presencing, at the bottom of the U, is both an action (a view) and the location of the self that can move to the final action of performing and embodying the new (Scharmer, 2004). The entire process is evolutionary and is characteristic of emerging systems.

Scharmer (2004) believes that, to meet today's challenges, leaders must engage in three different "movements of awareness":

1. Co-sensing: opening up to the world outside and activating a capacity of seeing in which the observer is no longer separate from the observed;
2. Co-presencing: opening up to what wants to emerge, and accessing a capacity of stillness that no longer separates what wants to emerge from who we are; and
3. Co-creating: bringing the new into reality by activating a capacity for co-creation that no longer separates the intelligence of head, heart, and hand. (p. 10)

To help you reflect on and process these ideas, we have designed the exercise in Box 7.1.

Leadership Challenges

We've seen that the biggest challenge for new school leaders is to open to the unknown, to their own higher presence and self, and to an emerging future field, all of which violates most people's assumptions about being separate entities, where knowledge originates, and how innovation occurs. In Scharmer's (2004) view, innovation occurs when we start acting before we fully understand what we're doing. Scharmer goes on to say,

> I believe that it requires a new form of collective leadership: Leaders must develop the capacity to shift the inner place (the source) from which a system operates. That is what leaders do—and what the most effective leaders have always done: reconfigure the focus and structure of collective attention. (p. 12)

In essence, for Scharmer (2004), leadership is about paying attention moment to moment. It is about opening the mind, the heart, and the will. When the mind is opened through a process of appreciative inquiry, judgmental reactions are suspended. When the heart is opening to sensing, emotional reactivity is reduced. When the will is opened to one's higher self, we can let go of old intentions and identities. The result, Scharmer believes, is a new form of leadership: a social technology of freedom. Instead of manipulation and control, diverse groups of people are freed to see, sense, and create together new solutions and systems that go beyond past patterns and that actualize future possibilities. The leader's self, or capacity to shift his or her inner space, is the most important tool in this process.

Scharmer (2004) recommends a "field walk" through three domains of the leadership process:

1. the individual consciousness of the self (phenomenology—first person), inner dialogue with the self;
2. second person point of view: the collective second person that cultivates people's abilities to listen individually and collectively; and
3. collaborative action research (third person point of view) in the enactment of institutional patterns and structures.

Box 7.1   Preparing for the Future

1.   Describe what kind of event you can envision to be the first in a series designed to establish the type of dialogue we have described in this chapter—i.e., how do you envision authentic dialogue happening in your school, district, or agency, and how do you envision it becoming an ongoing process?

2.   Describe your "blind spot."—i.e., what are the habits of thought from which you operate in your role as a leader?

3.   How do you think your "blind spot" hinders you as a leader? Describe specific steps you can take, alone or with others in your school, district, or agency to imagine alternative futures (possibilities).

4.   Of the following four perspectives, which one (or combination) do you think holds the most potential as a way for the people in your school, district, or agency to see their system differently?
     • Living systems
     • Creative arts
     • Experiences of change within the system
     • Direct contact with nature's generative capacities

     Describe how you can utilize this perspective (or perspectives) to move your school, district, or agency toward transformational change.

Through this field walk, ego boundaries collapse, and people experience a decentering of their spatial experience and a slowing down of time or the temporal experience of stillness. As a result, people experience increased individual energy and commitment and an enhanced field quality of collective presence and energy that can lead to profound long-term changes and innovations in the systems in which they operate (Scharmer, 2004). A different social reality is created that integrates all systems levels, and new dimensions of knowledge, innovation, and leadership are illuminated.

The Time Is Now

According to Scharmer (2006), the old social structure is dying, which represents a collective crisis of our time. All leaders are feeling the pressure of an ever-increasing workload and pressure to do even more. Scharmer believes the biggest issue in education is that these systems have not been able to develop people's innate capacity to sense and actualize their future. Scharmer argues that, without this capacity, people will not be able to adequately face this century's issues. In response to this crisis and these issues, people are either trying to return to some past order, are arguing to maintain the status quo and do more of the same, or they are advocating transformational change. It is this latter group that Scharmer argues is needed to make the kind of changes required in our current global situation.

Leaders for transformational change pay attention to future possibilities for themselves and others. Scharmer (2006) reports his study of how this hidden dimension of leadership can be accessed more consciously and reliably. He contends that to connect the observer to the observed requires a relationship between the two. To be reliable, leaders must not only access their inner source from which perceptions operate, but they must also engage others in a collective process of seeing what could be and not just what is. Scharmer states,

> The key insight that has emerged from my explorations and investigations is that there are four fundamentally different field structures of attention that manifest in four levels of perception, sense-making, action, and consciousness (from shallow to deep). The four field structures differ in the place from which attention (and intention) originates. Every action by a person, a leader, a group, an organization, or a community can be enacted in four different ways—from four different places (relative to one's personal or organizational boundary). (pp. 7–8)

The four ways are

1. listening by confirming habitual judgments;
2. listening by paying attention to factual and disconfirming data;
3. listening empathically, shifting into the place from which the other person is speaking; and
4. listening from the emerging field of the future that requires an open heart and open will to connect to the highest future possibility that wants to emerge.

The final two levels present the greatest challenge for leaders as institutions reinvent themselves. Nonetheless, to effect transformational change, leaders and their institutions will need to operate at all four levels (Scharmer, 2006).

Scharmer states that leaders also need to observe what is going on outside themselves and to open themselves and connect to what is going on outside, all of which allows one's inner knowing to emerge, open up, and connect to what is within. The process of leading and learning can then bring the new into reality so that one can act in an instant from the embedded wisdom that exists in local contexts. Such leading represents a collective leadership technology that allows access to a more basic level of learning and change requiring an open mind, heart, and will (Scharmer, 2006). According to Scharmer, leaders must be on guard against the voice of judgment, cynicism, the emotional act of distancing, and fear of letting go of what we have and who we are.

Understanding the Main Work of Transformational Leaders

To some readers, Scharmer's work may seem particularly complex in spite of his message of simplicity, but therein lies one of the paradoxes of new school leadership. The main work is an inner journey that spreads out to others in the system. Beginning with the inner journey, the transformational leader moves to create infrastructures for facilitating

> . . .a shared sensing and seeing of what is actually going on (co-sensing). Leader must encourage deep reflection and silence that facilitate a connection to the authentic source of presence and creativity—both individually and collectively (co-presencing). There must also be the fast-cycle prototyping of microcosms of strategic future opportunities—in other words, places that promote discovery by doing (co-creating). (Scharmer, 2006, p. 14)

He further states,

> *Leadership in this century is global leadership and means shifting the structure of collective attention from the individual (micro) and group (meso) to the institutional (macro) and global system level (mundo). Eventually this leads to co-evolving and co-developing. . . a larger innovation ecosystem that connects people and their institutions across boundaries and that interweaves the different spheres of activity and relationship through seeing from the whole* [emphasis ours]. (Scharmer, 2006, p. 15)

As an indication that this work is being recognized at a national level and merits the attention of leaders, Mates (2007) describes efforts by the Robert G. Hemingway Foundation to inquire about how to use limited resources to unleash human potential for the benefit of all. Of high interest to this foundation are efforts that enhance connections to one another and allow us to become more fully present to ourselves and what matters to us individually and collectively. Mates reports that the foundation's work is being guided by the U Process described by Scharmer and others, as well as Wheatley's work in the Art of Learning-Centering.

The exercise in Box 7.2, based on Scharmer's concept of presencing and its relationship to leadership, helps you identify how to attend and how you can be more aware of ways in which your attentional patterns affect your leadership abilities.

OTHER CHARACTERISTICS OF THE NEEDED FRAMEWORK

We now ask you to consider a few more factors as you continue on your inner journey. In describing the difficult tasks we all face in our world today, Cohen (2007) summarizes a discussion with leading futurists: Don Beck, Brian

Box 7.2   Levels and Types of Attending

To help you become more aware of how you attend, try the following.

1. Select a typical day in your setting. Each time you interact with another person or with information/data, take a moment afterward to identify the nature of your attending by tallying the number of times you engage in each of these four types of attending:

    a. confirmed my habitual judgments;

    b. focused on factual and disconfirming data;

    c. put myself into the shoes of the person speaking; and

    d. listened with an open heart and will to become aware of possibilities.

2. Using the responses you generated regarding your attentional preferences in Box 5.2 on page 144, respond to the following prompts.

    a. For the pattern that received the highest score, describe three ways you can use it to become more aware of possibilities and less focused on how you habitually pay attention and solve problems.

    b. Now describe how you can listen empathically to a person for whom this particular pattern of attention is *not* a strength.

    c. For the pattern that received the lowest score, describe three ways you can use it to become more aware of possibilities and less focused on how you habitually pay attention and solve problems.

    d. Now describe how you can listen empathically to a person for whom this particular pattern of attention is a strength.

Swimme, and Peter Senge. Their discussion identifies a number of important issues we as leaders need to be aware of in our global world.

-   A new kind of thinking is beginning to permeate in discussions of various sorts of institutions and organizations. Some people are calling it systemic thinking; others are calling it integral, second tier, or holistic thinking. Regardless of terminology, this way of thinking is emerging as a means by which visionaries can look beyond the complexities that seem to render many global dilemmas too difficult or unwieldy to solve.
-   These futurists—visionaries—are realizing that the highest form of knowledge emerges in dialogue that attempts to integrate our present world with our future world. Dialogue is viewed as a way to work through major conflicts involving a clash between differing value systems

and to move toward large-scale transformations with a higher level of consciousness that can help people to embrace our unique human potential by expressing a "comprehensive compassion" for all of life.

- These visionaries are seeing that our current crisis centers on understanding and interacting with a world of complexity that has not previously existed and that represents all the conflicts that have occurred in human history, all happening at the same time. These complexities have been shaped by different worldviews that have fragmented our world, the solution to which is to give birth to a wisdom in which we see that we need a holistic view to take responsibility for the entire planet and not just our local issues. We have also reached the point where the rapid increase in technology has moved past our ability to cope with it. America is seen by many in the world as the biggest perpetrator of many of these problems, the result being that ecological and social imbalances are worsening. At its core, the current crisis is one of perception in which people look at the same basic events, evidence, or experiences and cannot reach consensus on what they mean.

- To address this current crisis, these three futurists are seeing that "[i]n terms of the practical capacity we need, it would be something like *learning how to think like a planet*. The practical challenge is to become a mode of a complex planetary community" (Cohen, 2007, p. 5). In other words, we have to understand complex systems in order to reinvent our basic institutions to build an integral Earth community. This is difficult because people are at different levels of development, and what is needed are new levels of psychological emergence in individuals and cultures such that new social, political, and economic life conditions are created from an understanding of the clash in value systems. The crises we face must be recognized as collective and caused by collective rather than individual actions; thus the solutions and responses must also be collective.

- These three visionaries agree that collective responses must involve big corporations that span national boundaries and are less constrained than state or government institutions. These big corporations must take on the role of setting standards that guide a new awareness and capacity to transform systems in the service of all humans. Religion is another institution that can provide essential resources for helping people and cultures make a developmental shift to higher levels of thinking. As Beck states, "The shift that we need to bring about is from embracing a single expression of religion and spirituality *to recognizing the evolutionary flow of religious experiences*" (as cited in Cohen, 2007, p. 7). That is, religions need to deinstitutionalize so that a new sensibility can emerge in combination with a new science that addresses the moral, ethical, and spiritual issues that can meet the challenges of our existing life conditions.

- These three believe that science can help, as the spirituality that will emerge will be more closely tied to science than in the past. There will be a reintegration of science, spirituality, and religion that recognizes that people are at different developmental stages in their understanding and capacity for complex thinking. Science will help people see a new definition or spirit tied to the nature of life and to the nonlinear dynamics and adaptive intelligence that is the force of life itself. Senge states, "So I think the spirituality of the next millennium will be one that somehow reintegrates what we would call 'science' today, which at its best is about skepticism and an absolutely rigorous belief in experience" (as cited in Cohen, 2007, p. 9).

- The three futurists believe that the universe itself is in development at a cosmic level. Quantum science is discovering the inseparability of the inner and outer world, and it might be that there is a deeper reality of seamlessness where everything is inseparable from the whole. It might be that individuality and the perception of separation are illusionary, and we really are the whole evolving in the service of life. Swimme says,

> So in this new framework, we would need to understand *ourselves* as the *way* in which the universe is making fundamental decisions about the quality of life that it wants to blossom forth. And these decisions aren't just being made for humans or for a particular society but for the whole dynamic, pulsating, throbbing planetary community. (as cited in Cohen, 2007, p. 10)

Cohen concludes the discussion by taking the leadership challenge back to the ultimate moral purpose of the new school leader—the spiritual dimension of leadership. He states,

> And so, therefore, this new framework would have to illuminate the fact that it indeed is we who have created the past and who will create the future. It would have to emphasize not only the global context of human incarnation in the twenty-first century but also the evolutionary context. As you so beautifully described, we are all playing a crucial role in a developmental process that, for the most part, we remain unconscious of. So the significant task of a new spirituality would be to oblige us to become conscious of that fact. And most importantly, in this context, the task of a new spirituality would be a perennial one—to awaken as many of us as possible to the ultimate truth that there is only One and that we are all that One. Obviously we have come to a point where the divisions in the way that we think about life and the way we live life need to be urgently questioned. Our very survival depends on it. Indeed, what it means to be a human being in the twenty-first century is one issue at this point! (pp. 10–11)

How can we meet these challenges with the tools and information we now have? We invite you to see the challenges as opportunities to open your mind and heart and to have the will to create the type of transformational systems we are describing here.

FURTHER LEADERSHIP CHALLENGES IN CREATING LEARNER-CENTERED MODELS

John Hoyle (2001), an influential and visionary scholar in the area of leadership, has written about the fundamental importance of leading with love—defined as an unselfish concern and caring for others' good—as one leads with love in visioning, communicating, team working, empowering, mentoring, and evaluating. He sees caring for others as primary to the ability of organizations to reach their potential. Hoyle (2001) believes that effective leaders must first become aware of and comfortable with their own spirit in order to reach the hearts and souls of their employees. Hoyle (2006) argues that one of the roles of leaders is trying to figure out what is likely to happen in the future—or futuring, which requires creativity, passion for what they do, vision, and persistence. Hoyle (2006) believes that the real task of leaders is to transform top-down organizations "ruled" by authorities into bottom-up, empowered organizations that emphasize relationships. Future leaders must also nurture other future leaders through the processes of

- understanding the likelihood and possibility of different futures, and the opportunity to shape those futures;
- enhancing flexibility in policy making and implementation;
- broadening perspectives; and
- encouraging creative thinking (about possible, plausible, probable, and preferred futures and their potential impacts). (Burton, 2003, p. 5)

In his discussion of leading change, Hoyle (2006) points out that collaborative, working groups that have trusting relationships and clear and inclusive communication networks can reduce the amount of pain in change by empowering others and sharing the job of leadership. In such a context, change occurs when individuals share common beliefs, have quality information, strong professional development, and work together for a common cause.

How We Can Prepare Future Leaders to Respond to These Challenges

Good leadership preparation programs not only educate future educational leaders in the latest theories and practices, but they also provide real-world experiences in applying these theories and practices. Joseph Murphy (2007) is among those arguing that many universities have flawed programs. His basic argument is that many universities, particularly research universities, have constructed their programs using academic materials that do not emphasize the *practice* of leadership. The authentic problems of practice require "just-in-time" knowledge that can address these problems and engagement in the work of the profession. Future leaders need to understand the purpose and processes of schooling and what these processes mean for the practice of leading a school or other educational system. Murphy believes it more important to learn things they can apply to their job than to produce a dissertation that is scrutinized and evaluated by a committee of people typically not themselves practicing as school leaders. He suggests more attention be given to using stories from schools to improve action-oriented learning, making practice the center of preparation so that future leaders are prepared to cope with the complexities of learning and leading in schools.

The Leadership Role in Teacher Preparation

Given the significant role teachers play in the learning of children and youth, many have turned their attention to what defines quality teacher education. In 2001, the American Educational Research Association (AERA) formed the Panel on Research and Teacher Education (Cochran-Smith & Zeichner, 2005). Their charge was to uncover the evidence-based effective practices and policies in preservice teacher education in the United States. The general conclusion was that little is known about the most effective programs and qualities of teachers produced in these programs, thereby necessitating a major research agenda in this area. Others, however, contend that there are areas of professional development that can significantly influence teachers' classroom practices and, in turn, lead to improved student learning (Holland, 2005). According to these latter researchers, the areas of professional development that matter are

- knowledge about how students learn particular subject matter;
- knowledge and skills with instructional practices related to the subject matter and how students understand it; and
- knowledge of specific subject-matter content (Shulman, 2001).

Other studies on the impact of teachers on student achievement have found that teachers are responsible for between four and eighteen percent of changes in student test scores (Zurawsky, 2004). When additional professional development areas are included in the results, teachers have more impact, particularly if these areas include

- understanding the developmental stages of student learning;
- using multiple types of student assessment data; and
- revising instruction frequently to meet individual student learning needs (Emerick, Hirsch, & Berry, 2004).

Another area that promotes teacher leadership is preparing them to make decisions about teaching and learning, using dialogue and collaboration with other teachers as a source of information (Chrisman, 2005).

McCombs (2004a) has shown that learner-centered instruction as part of preservice teacher education is having a positive effect on the quality of teacher decisions. Further, Borko (2004) argues that effective programs help teachers create a community of learners among themselves and their students, which provides a powerful context for teacher learning and an increase in their understanding of how to create critical dialogue, establish trust, and maintain a balance between respecting individual community members and critically analyzing issues in their teaching. The highly effective Professional Development School (PDS) in North Carolina blends a focus on judgment-focused teaching based on assessments of student progress; problem-driven instruction to provide high-challenge tasks in collaborative groups; and practice-based learning that gives students ample time to learn (Miller, Duffy, Rohr, Gasparello, & Mercier, 2005). The authors report that this model has significantly improved student achievement and helped reduce the achievement gap.

School leaders interested in creating learner-centered education systems would do well to study models such as the North Carolina PDS in order to develop an understanding of how to identify natural teacher leaders and inspire them to identify and incorporate student leaders as an integral part of the system. The people within the resulting systems can then define the learning agenda needed for the future.

Addressing Leadership Challenges at an International Level

The Centre for Human Ecology (CHE) is a new international organization recently formed to create action, research, and education for personal development, ecological sustainability, and social justice (Wilding, 2007). Their aim is to find solutions to human problems by examining underlying causes, using respect, empowering people, and restoring nature in ways that validate individual identity, belonging, and purpose. Wilding describes human ecology as focused on connections between individual actions, social systems, and the ecology of the planet as a whole. The Centre seeks to find new and better ways to deal with individual lives and systems in ways that can reduce poverty and inequality, while also reducing the resources used and restoring the environment. The result is that quality of life is improved for all people now and into the future.

The approach of CHE is to address the whole person—head, heart, and hand—by providing personal development in knowledge and critical thinking, insight and compassion, and skills for effective action at three different levels: personal, local, and the wider society (Wilding, 2007). Their work centers on engaging people with others in real issues, bringing global perspectives to the work, and influencing change in the wider society. Information about this group can be accessed at http://www.che.ac.uk.

This seems a good spot for you to stop for a few moments and again reflect on what you have been reading and integrating by doing the exercise in Box 7.3.

WHAT IT MEANS TO DEVELOP CAPACITY FROM WITHIN

We've now seen that we have a storehouse of tools and knowledge to apply to the development of school leaders' inner capacity to create learner-centered educational models. We have explored some of the challenges and opportunities. We have documented the value of learner-centered learning communities as a way

Box 7.3   Revisiting Your Vision

1.   Several previous exercises have touched on your vision for your school, district, or agency. Incorporating what you've been reading so far, describe your vision in one or two paragraphs.

2.   List which of your beliefs are likely to stand in the way of achieving your vision.

3.   Describe how you can collaborate with the other stakeholders in your school, district, or agency, and in your community to fashion the LCP practices that are most appropriate to your school's needs and strengths.

to sustain the required system of ongoing learning, change, and improvement. Using the Assessment of Learner-Centered Practices school- and classroom-level surveys, it is possible to share the expertise and build capacity within the system. Connecting experts with each other through coaching and mentoring are proven ways of creating learner-centered support groups that keep learning and learners at the center of practice.

Taking the Capacity to Scale

From the Berkana Institute's work around the world with learning centers, Stilger (2005) has identified what he sees as six essential landmarks for inspirited leaders:

1. They work from a sense of true calling.
2. They journey in the company of others.
3. They live with a spiritual center.
4. They demand diversity.
5. Their lives are guided by reflective learning.
6. Their work is filled with ambiguity and uncertainty (p. 1).

Stigler's work (2005) shows that most important is that these leaders act from a place of spirit rather than a place of thought. When confronted with a particular situation, they look for the whole picture and the surrounding web of relationships and systems. Stilger states, "For these leaders, the search for spiritual grounding is accompanied by a continuous process of surfacing facts and impressions, revealing patterns and assumptions, examining actions and behaviors, and affirming or changing the course of action" (p. 4).

Wheatley and Frieze (2006) argue that connecting with kindred spirits helps us develop the new knowledge, practices, courage, and commitment needed to lead broad-based change. We form networks, which Wheatley and

Frieze contend are the only form of organization used by living systems on our planet. These networks are the result of self-organization, a process in which individuals or groups or species recognize their interdependence. They then organize in ways that support the diversity and viability of all in the network. Networks also create the conditions for the emergence of such things as new thinking and new systems.

Utilizing the Power of Technology

At the beginning of the 21st century, educational visionaries began to articulate the power of technology to aid in the school transformation process—something that can happen at either a conscious or an unconscious level. Carroll (2000) suggests that technology is becoming the tool for forming networked learning communities where members of all ages and positions can collaborate to achieve common goals and learn together as they solve common problems. The type of networked learning community that Carroll sees being a force of the future is focused on invention and knowledge generation. In this kind of community, change is perceived as good, and young and old work together collaboratively to learn and construct new knowledge. Carroll maintains that, if schools continue to focus on knowledge transmission, they will become marginalized learning places and will be replaced by parallel networked learning communities taking full advantage of modern communications and information technologies for knowledge adaptation and generation.

The advantage that Carroll (2000) cites for networked learning communities is that everyone can be an active learner. There is a reciprocity of roles between expert and novice learners depending on what knowledge is needed, and everyone has the chance to learn from each other given the different levels and areas of expertise in the community. Carroll predicts that the purpose of education will move from being curriculum-driven to being learner- and learning-driven. In other words, instead of being driven by a fixed, structured, and standardized curriculum, education will be driven by knowledge work in a networked learning community. Education will become customized and move from the standard, one-size-fits-all model. Perhaps most exciting, Carroll imagines a system in which the boundaries of schools classrooms, grade levels, and class time will no longer be relevant.

Bringing Forth the New Paradigm

In discussing what is necessary to bring forth a new paradigm, Horwitz and Vega-Frey (2006) contend that it must maintain a complex relationship with history so that we remember and learn from the past while also bringing forth new forms and ways of being. One of the new paradigms they believe is emerging is one called "spiritual activism" or a broader understanding of freedom. Horwitz and Vega-Frey identify forms that promote liberation or freedom:

- collective struggle in the form of grassroots movements, unions, and locally-based organizing;

- farms, food cooperatives, and community-supported agriculture models;
- religious and spiritual communities that call forth ecstatic expression, nurture contemplative refuge, and build strong community;
- justice-centered retreat centers that offer an oasis for incubation;
- creative protests that convey urgent messages in unexpected forms;
- *experiential and direct education that values students as experts of their own experience;* [emphasis ours]
- artistic venues that capture reality in compelling and unchartered ways;
- forms of communication that leave us feeling animated and inspired rather than drained and beaten up;
- local businesses founded in an ethic of fair economics and community interest; and
- communal and intentional living experiments (p. 3).

A SUMMARY: MOVING FROM COMPLEXITY TO SIMPLICITY

Throughout this book, we have been urging school leaders to understand the challenges we are currently facing within our Industrial Age educational paradigm. We have presented evidence from a variety of sources demonstrating that this paradigm is fundamentally flawed. Therefore, all of us who feel called to a school leadership role must be part of a network of school leaders ready to take on the challenge of transforming—not reforming—this current model. As we have urged throughout, we must be the enlightened leaders to a future that is rapidly changing and becoming increasingly diverse and global. This rapid change places a sense of urgency on our calling as school leaders to create something new for the future of our children, for us, and for our global society. As we have argued, we must build a system that is responsive to the best information from research and experience about human potential, human learning, and the living-systems principles upon which a learner-centered model of education is based.

In the next chapter, we summarize the main points from each chapter in order to distill from this complexity the simpler principles and practices that we hope will guide all of us as school leaders into a more creative and flexible future. In the summary that follows we stress the main points that we have made throughout this book. We conclude this summary with a set of simple principles and practices. As promised in our title to this book, these principles and practices are what we believe new school leaders will need to move from complexity to simplicity.

SUMMARY

At the outset, we said we believe that, at this moment in time, we are at the edge of a momentous shift in thinking about the many systems that influence our daily lives, including our thinking about educational, judicial, health care, social justice, welfare, and other systems that support human well-being nationally and globally.

We also said that for a number of years we have lived through a time during which education, in particular, has been subjected to the industrial, corporate, or business model emphasizing narrow content standards and curriculum, frequent high-stakes testing, and student achievement as the sole indicator of learning. After experiencing the failure of this model, we are now ready to enter a kinder, more respectful age of valuing diversity, natural learning principles, and innate human potential—from the very young to the very old—to learn and lead.

Further, we argued that the Industrial Age practice of viewing students as workers—and their achievement as products—creates an environment that has unintended and detrimental effects, because:

- the curriculum narrows, and real learning needed for life in this complex information and conceptual age suffers as students are pressured to achieve and are given instruction on how to take tests;
- the emphasis on testing student achievement in basic reading and math skills results in cutting short or eliminating students' meaningful and creative experiences with science, health (physical and mental), economics, art, music, and drama; and
- the practice of basing instruction on one-size-fits-all curricula reflecting the content of the achievement tests required to show accountability shortchanges students' diverse talents as well as their introduction to and immersion in the types of learning, inquiry, thinking, and reflecting that underlie the creativity necessary for flexible problem solving in an increasingly mobile world.

In short, we have argued throughout this book that the model of education currently in place needs drastic change because it is based on outdated assumptions about human capacity and ignores evidence-based natural learning principles. The consequences are that this current model actually deprives students of the information and skills necessary to live meaningful lives as productive citizens in a global community. Even further, a colleague (O'Connell, personal communication, August 30, 2007) believes that the community at large suffers because the strong educational models we need are absent. People are no longer active, thinking participants of a community and are more willing to let others (the more powerful) create their world.

On the other hand, Kalmon, one expert of many working on transformational models, contends that virtually no one believes that our current system of public education is preparing our children for their future (personal communication, August 30, 2007). More and more people are ready to re-think the entire system, and there is growing support for system transformation. Kalmon believes that what is needed is a national dialogue aimed at re-visioning public education. His advice is that we remain patiently urgent while this transformative process emerges.

Box 7.4   My Responses to the Questions Posed in Each Chapter

Journal your personal responses to the questions posed in each chapter so far, incorporating what you have learned from reading the chapters.

I.   Why do I believe this is a time of change?

2.   What do I know about learning and leading?

3.   What does the Learner-Centered Model mean for my practice?

4.   What tools do I need for my journey?

5.   What can the Learner-Centered Assessment tools accomplish for me in my setting?

6.   How do I move toward new student and system outcomes?

7.   What do I need to do to identify my blind spot and to shift my focus to fashioning my school, district, or agency as a living system based on learners and learning?

Now that you have read our summary of the questions throughout the book, take a few moments to complete the exercise in Box 7.4.

Simpler Leadership Principles and Practices to Prepare Us for Our Calling

Our integrative approach in this book has been intended to give you at least a brief glimpse of the best evidence in leading and creating learner-centered educational systems. We've covered a lot of material from a lot of sources, all of which converge to a set of learner-centered leadership principles, shown in Table 7.1, and practices, shown in Table 7.2, that show how even the complexities of school leadership are undergirded by a simple set of principles. The practices that are derived from these principles also form a simple set of guidelines for school leaders as they prepare to lead and create new learner-centered educational systems for the future.

Table 7.1   Leadership Principles That Take Us From Complexity to Simplicity

In reviewing all the principles we have presented in the previous six chapters, we see that they can be integrated into the following:

1. Leadership begins with an inner journey guided by deep truths about human capacity and research-validated learner-centered principles defining natural learning. This includes seeing the "big picture" of our human condition and the need for fundamental changes in how not only our organizations but our entire world is run.

2. Leaders have clarity about their deepest and most cherished purposes and values for themselves and their organizations. They are open to looking deeply at their higher purposes and willing to step outside the realm of conditioned thinking to empower others in the system to discover their agency over thinking and their purpose in creating together a new vision of learner-centered schooling.

3. Leaders have a moral foundation that leads to their abilities for courage, openness, reflection, risk-taking, and habits that include inquiry, future-focusing, connection, and inclusiveness. They are able to engage in moral leadership that focuses on emotions, group membership, sense and meaning, morality, duty, self-sacrifice, responsibility, and caring.

4. Leaders are able to see the systemic nature of the process and the big-picture vision of how in living systems, as the process proceeds, solutions not initially seen may suddenly emerge. They are able to understand the natural coexistence of opposites and go in seemingly opposite directions at once in order to innovate and find even better solutions.

5. Leaders know the best answers and new leaders will emerge when they use the best knowledge available on how people learn, what enhances learning and motivation for diverse learners, and how best to support learning and change in inclusive and respectful dialogue. They understand that dialogue is the essential process for facilitating sustainable change.

6. Leaders know the central role of people in establishing the personal and system climate for schooling, along with a visualization of the reciprocal role of learning and change in living systems. They understand and focus on school culture—the values, norms, attitudes, beliefs, and relationships of all members of the school community.

7. Leaders understand that nothing important happens quickly and that they need to adopt a personality of change that is passionately committed to knowing oneself, the context, the ideas from the wider community, and the skills that are important at different points in the lifecycle of change. They trust in living-systems principles of emergence when all constituencies are striving for shared schooling visions and lifelong learning competencies.

8. Leaders see the moral imperative of schooling is to help all learners understand who they are and their identities in a cultural, political, and moral sense by learning through knowledge to master themselves and contribute meaningfully to the betterment of life for all. They are able to act on the fact that people only support what they create and offer purposeful work as the necessary condition for people to engage fully.

9. Leaders engage in an ongoing process of self-assessment and reflection—a thoughtful and inquiry-driven process that leads to community building, dialogue, and openness among all stakeholders. They understand that our beliefs and values guide the decisions we make that support teaching and learning throughout all aspects of the educational process and system.

10. Leaders understand that learning and change are flip sides of the same psychological process—each is about "changing your mind." They know from deep within their own experiences that what needs to be sustained in learner-centered educational models is an *attitude of ongoing learning, change, and improvement.*

Table 7.2   Leadership Practices That Take Us From Complexity to Simplicity

As with the overarching principles shown in Table 7.1, we have also identified the best and most learner-centered leadership and schooling practices from those presented in the preceding six chapters. These include:

1. designing programs that build capacity for authentic learning to flourish through processes such as reflection, exploration, imagination, and connectedness. Intentionally creating the generative conditions for learning that embody the creative processes for learning and life.

2. helping people see ways to understand a complex situation through conceptual leadership rather than presenting a fixed solution. Identifying together with all key constituencies the valued life competencies for students to achieve as outcomes toward which the system must strive.

3. ensuring that all teachers and staff are respected, autonomous, committed, capable, as well as morally responsible for making the school work better for its students. Making the difference between risk and resilience through the quality of relationships between teachers and students—a hallmark and foundation of the learner-centered classroom and school.

4. replacing old assumptions and practices with new principles and practices based on learner-centered and leading principles for living systems. Using an inclusive and respectful dialogue process that builds trust and starts with a willingness for each leader to be him- or herself and to share their personal stories, purpose, and vision.

5. through learner-centered self-assessment and reflection tools identifying assumptions and practices assist staff and students, learning to share the responsibility for achieving valued learning outcomes and contributing to the development of professional lifelong learning communities.

6. engaging all learners—students, teachers, administrators, and parents—through quality relationships built on caring connections, personal relevance, empowering learners through choices, increasing opportunities for success, providing immediate and accurate feedback, and providing multiple ways to recognize and celebrate successes.

7. looking for the match or mismatch of practices with learner-centered learning principles, but also their match or mismatch with learners and their diverse needs.

8. making instructional practices flexible and varied from day to day while also adhering to learner-centered concepts of providing for choice, relevance, responsibility, challenge, control, connection, respect, competence, cooperation, and relationships.

9. constructing the curriculum around the questions of life and how our existing educational, economic, political, social, and other systems function in a student-directed inquiry process structured around elements of a story they can readily understand.

10. changing the role of teachers to that of co-learners and contributors not only to the academic, but also to the social and interpersonal development of students through partnerships in which students become responsible for their own learning and participate equally in determining what, how, and when they learn.

11. encouraging the development of teacher leaders who are skillful communicators, knowing how to create a positive climate and how to develop a sense of community, letting go of control, and trusting in the self-organizing principles of humans.

12. listening to what students want where instruction is personalized and students are allowed to actively process their experiences by using well-formed questions that guide them to reach intended skills and competences. Encouraging risk taking and failure that can lead to creative and authentic learning—without punishing or penalizing failure.

(Continued)

Table 7.2   (Continued)

13. forming the most advanced technology-supported networked learning communities while not overlooking the human element—the need for personal relationships and connections. Encouraging all teachers and staff how best to integrate technology into the learning process by understanding who students are, recognizing what technologies they know and use frequently, and partnering with students in deciding how these technologies can be used in their education.

14. providing opportunities for staff to think together and reflect on what they are learning and ways to expand the web with new and different people. Facilitating a change process that begins with people identifying a crisis because it helps develop awareness that change is needed. This awareness generates a will to change and to take ownership of the need to change for the benefit of all in the system, both individually and collectively.

15. building internal system accountability that focuses on aligning individual responsibility with collective expectations and data on student progress and performance on chosen life competencies. This leads to external accountability where visionary leadership integrates top-down and bottom-up approaches to achieve greater equality and prosperity.

Self-Reflection

Are there any leadership principles or practices you think are missing? Are there any you would change, modify, or even eliminate? Take a few minutes and jot your thoughts down in your journal and/or discuss these with your learning partner.

CONCLUSION

We conclude with an even simpler definition of leadership that grows out of the complexity of views we have explored. Wheatley (2005) defines leaders as anyone willing to help because they feel it is the right thing to do. In many ways, this book as been a challenge and a calling—for us and, hopefully, for many of you. For some of you reading this book, it's been an exciting re-affirmation of who you are and what you believe and feel called to act upon. For others, it is an awakening of what may have lain dormant: your inner awareness that there was something more you could do. And for yet others, it is an interesting and somewhat exciting possibility that you aren't quite ready to embrace. That's okay; we are not all at the same place at the same time. We all know, however, that we have something to do—individually and together—to further this vision and take on the calling to step forward as leaders. We will be the leaders of a new future and for a new future.

And what will that future look like? What kind of educational systems will promote the best possible future vision—one filled with love, understanding, wisdom, and learning. Most of all learning. Learning is the life force, and we are the leaders to a new tomorrow and a new paradigm of schooling that fosters the best of who we are and can become.

Box 7.5   Final Reflections

1. Describe the areas of common interest in your school (district, agency) and community that will form the basis for developing groups of networked learning communities. Include all the types of stakeholders you can think of (e.g., specific political figures, organizations, businesses, religious groups, and so on).

2. Describe a five-year plan for how you can turn your school, district, or agency into a group of networked learning communities.

3. Describe the specific steps you will need to take in the first year of your five-year plan.

SELF-REFLECTIONS

We have created a final reflection in Box 7.5 to help you pull together all that you have thought about and dreamed about in your new leadership role.

INTRODUCTION TO SUMMARY CHAPTER

You've been a wonderful learner and have covered a lot of information. We have a final tool for you in the form of a summary chapter. We invite you to use this tool to check your understanding of the major points we have made in each chapter. This tool can also provide a reminder of the major concepts and principles we have covered that reduces the complexity of leadership to these simpler concepts and principles.

INTRODUCTION TO ADDITIONAL RESOURCES

We have compiled a number of resources that will help you on your journey. There is a list of books, Web sites to explore, references, and a glossary of learner-centered terms. We also have a section that summarizes all the reflection exercises you have experienced.

8

Summary of Major Points in Each Chapter

When we focus attention on the learner and learning and we combine this with what we know about teaching, school, and classroom organization that best promote the highest levels of motivation and achievement for all students, then we are being learner-centered.

—Ruth Deakin Crick (2006, p. 4)

You've reached the end of a learning process and what the latest thinking is about leadership that produces learning-centered schooling. As a tool to help you check your understanding of the major points we've made in each chapter, we provide the following summary. This summary is also a tool for you to see how the complex topics of leadership can be reduced to simpler principles and concepts. We invite you to read this summary as your tool and guide to beginning a journey to a new form of leadership.

CHAPTER 1: WHY THIS IS A TIME FOR CHANGE

This is the time for a new educational paradigm because many converging forces indicate that the basic underlying assumptions of most of our human systems are simply wrong. Present-day educational models are out of balance and ignore the personal domains of human functioning, learning, and relationships. Current models are based on mechanical, Industrial Age, or economic business principles that privilege the technical and organizational aspects of the system, while ignoring the human and living-systems aspects that are critical components contributing to optimal learning and development of human potential.

Schools are living systems, not mechanical ones. Consequently, they must be based on research-validated principles of human learning and development. The Learner-Centered Principles, derived from over a century of research, help us understand that the concept of "learner-centered" means:

- each learner learns through a unique combination of genetic and experiential factors;
- focusing on the best available evidence about learning, how it occurs, and which teaching practices are most likely to result in the highest levels of student motivation and achievement; and
- the content of learning—the knowledge and skills needed for our future world and present realities—must equip learners with the capacity for complex and systemic thinking, for focused inquiry and reflection on who they are, and what the world needs through the use of authentic and real-life curricula.

This understanding of learner-centered principles and practices leads to the emergence of varied and flexible learner-centered educational models arising from ecological and living-systems principles. The Learner-Centered Model builds on the Learner-Centered Principles and integrates our best knowledge about learners and learning. First, it balances the educational system by making instructional decisions that focus first on individual learners and their learning needs, followed by the best available knowledge about learning. Second, it emphasizes the outcomes we value—the knowledge, skills, and life performances or competencies we want all learners to acquire during the schooling process.

The school leader's role in learner-centered, living-systems educational models is primarily knowing who they are as learners and as leaders and valuing everyone involved as learners. Such leaders possess an understanding that diversity and difference mean greater opportunities for everyone in the system, and they value the personal growth and development in all learners.

CHAPTER 2: WHAT WE KNOW ABOUT LEARNING AND LEADING

To take on the primary leadership role introduced in Chapter 1, school leaders must understand the latest knowledge, integrated with their personal wisdom and experience, about learning and leading. As we state in Chapter 2, people in leadership positions are increasingly pointing out the need to recognize our moral obligation to serve all students well by educating them holistically. The focus is on learning by recognizing students' unique learning strengths and needs. We also assert that, because schools are defined in large part by moral purposes and values, they require a special kind of leadership that focuses on creating a set of goals, purposes, values, and commitments that motivate people to do what is necessary for every student to achieve. We point out that, although the way learner-centered leadership looks will vary from school to school and from leader to leader, a common thread is a focus on learners and learning.

In Chapter 2 we also provide a review of leadership models and contrast outdated, bureaucratic, hierarchical, and top-down models with the new paradigm models being promoted by numerous scholars and researchers writing on the topic of school leadership. The new models being advocated are transformative, empowering, invitational, and driven by personal values, moral purpose, and vision. New school leaders are defined by the processes of critical reflection, networking, and authentic willingness to share and distribute the leadership role. The writers we include believe that future leaders need a holistic, big-picture view of human capacity and learning as a natural process, and they need to first understand themselves as learners to genuinely comprehend their role in leading and creating the new models of education needed in our global world.

One of the biggest challenges for new school leaders is for them to understand how to motivate others to join them in an ongoing process of continuous learning, change, and development. We indicate that the process of motivating people is not only to inspire them to pursue common goals but also to invite them to participate in the decision making and leadership processes. For this to happen, leaders must be highly sensitive and reflective about the dynamic interplay between leaders and other team members. The leadership required includes wisdom, creativity, emotional and integrative intelligence, moral purpose, self-awareness, self-regulation, motivation, empathy, and social skills. School leaders for the future need to understand

- how their own and other people's belief systems drive their personal and professional behaviors;
- change and why many people resist it; and
- organizations, how systems operate, and how they are reciprocally influenced by people.

The new school leader is a servant leader who first wants to serve, draw out, inspire, and develop the best and highest within people—from the inside out rather than imposed from the outside in. Two of the most important qualities of a servant leader are the ability to make sense out of a complex situation, and to help people see ways to understand it—conceptual leadership—rather than presenting a fixed solution. Servant leadership requires both the kind of organizational learning that is collective capacity-building, and a recognition that learning requires change. Servant leadership is about community and participation throughout the organization in ways that increase the capacity of the human community to shape its future. Servant leaders responsible for sustainable learning systems acknowledge that learning is about knowing, doing, being, living together, and living sustainably—for a better future and world. In essence, the new leader engages in enlightened leadership, using the wisdom that comes from within, which comprises the life-enhancing energy of mind, body, and spirit that arises from the interconnectedness and interrelatedness of life.

In describing the evidence-based learner-centered principles, we situate them within the larger framework of human and systems functioning. The learner-centered educational model is an ecological one—an open system that is complex, its elements able to adapt in a dynamic and interdependent way because of its diversity. In a learning ecology, a diversity of learning options is produced and delivered to students (including teachers) by way of opportunities they can use to receive learning through the methods and means that best support their unique situations, needs, and interests. To develop their human potential, students need opportunities to study real-world problems and to learn for understanding in self-directed ways.

The fourteen Learner-Centered Principles we describe in Chapter 2 provide a set of principles, validated through a series of research studies, that define the whole person and provide the foundation for a balanced educational model based on knowing learners and learning. Empirical evidence supporting practices derived from the Learner-Centered Principles underscores the importance of the Learner-Centered Model as a framework focusing on the whole learner that leads to improvements in student motivation and lifelong learning. This research also verifies that the relational domain—i.e., practices that establish positive student-teacher and student-student relationships within the context of a positive climate for learning—is essential to being learner-centered in the eyes of students. Community building and relationships are essential components of learner-centered leadership practices. Within learner-centered systems, leaders form a networked learning community within which learners—students, teachers, other school staff, families, and community members—form relationships and networks in order to collaborate in ways that serve everyone involved.

CHAPTER 3: WHAT THE LEARNER-CENTERED MODEL MEANS FOR PRACTICE

In Chapter 3 we provide more detail about what the Learner-Centered Model means for practice. We begin by saying that putting the Learner-Centered Model into practice will require leaders—in fact, everyone connected to the system—to be authentically committed to putting learners and learning at the core of schooling and to designing delivery systems that stem naturally from that core. It will also require leaders who trust in the natural learning capacities and the ability of all stakeholders, including students, to join together in developing systems that nourish all learners. The resulting systems will be sustained because of the meaningful relationships and networks of support that are created by the emerging community of learners.

We also describe in more depth the qualities that create sustainable learner-centered leadership. Others studying this topic have found that sustainability requires courageous leaders who are inclusive and committed to creating opportunities for communication and for sharing their realities and dreams. These characteristics produce the emotional connections and shared responsibility that lead to desired learning outcomes. The work of everyone in the school is a problem-solving endeavor focused on sustaining success for all students. To achieve this ongoing success, everyone involved needs to develop and maintain the relationships necessary to engage all learners—students, teachers, administrators, and parents.

New school leaders need to see schools as social organizations and moral communities rather than formal organizations with bureaucratic authority. In viewing schools as social organizations, leaders focus on shared orientations, shared beliefs, and networks of social relations. They see schools as learning and caring communities with a culture of traditions, rituals, and norms that define its character and competence. These leaders protect and promote the institutional values that arise because, out of these values, a shared commitment, connection, and moral authority emerge. In schools that are moral communities, the leader helps facilitate moral connections among all learners and helps them all to become self-managing. This type of leadership communicates that all teachers and staff are respected, autonomous, committed, and capable, as well as morally responsible for making the school function better for its students. New leaders are willing to risk failure and believe in the power of people to bring about significant changes through their collective and collaborative efforts.

We describe the concept of emergence in living systems as a fundamental aspect of change. We argue that change always happens through emergence and cannot be mandated in plans or strategies from on high. When small local actions begin to have powerful effects, known as emergent phenomena, new levels of capacity are built that have more power and influence than are present in separate, isolated efforts. Because they are constantly changing, emergent phenomena can't be predetermined, and system-wide change must begin by working locally. School leaders must encourage local experiments, watch for and nourish supportive beliefs and community building efforts, and encourage building connections with those who tend to work in isolation. The main role of leaders is strengthening connections, which requires providing institutional resources, opportunities for staff to think together and reflect on what they are learning, and ways to expand the web and social network with new and different people.

In examining what the Learner-Centered Model means for practice, we review evidence of what has been found with models based on the Learner-Centered Principles. We maintain that the role of the new leaders needed to transform our educational paradigm in the direction of the Learner-Centered Model moves from moral, ethical, and spiritual dimensions to an appreciation of what the future will hold for all of us. In implementing the Learner-Centered Model, the work of becoming "learner-centered" starts with connecting people through the honest and open exchange of values, beliefs, and perceptions through the use of a dialogue model that promotes inquiry into future possibilities. Implementation of the Learner-Centered Model begins with basic shifts in how we think and interact. We review research findings showing that such changes require a personal transformation that can occur only within the safety of a learning community because, within the community, people are able to identify any faulty thinking habits and to commit to making the changes necessary for everyone to experience ongoing learning.

In Chapter 3 we introduce you to the Learner-Centered Model self-assessment and reflection tools (the Assessment of Learner-Centered Practices surveys) and examples of what can happen when these tools are used at different levels of school systems. From our own research using the surveys, we have learned that the learning that occurs in learner-centered professional development often leads to comprehensive change. These tools help people to literally "change their mind." They begin to view their professional development as an ongoing learning and change process; that is, they embark on a lifelong journey that inspires and renews them, at the same time increasing their professional competence. We redefine leadership in the context of professional development as a focus on change from within using compassionate interventions that lead to renewal in mind, body, heart, and spirit.

CHAPTER 4: THE TOOLS NEEDED FOR THE JOURNEY

The learner-centered self-assessment and reflection tools we present in Chapter 4 range from those you can use personally to discover your deepest purpose and values, to those that help you understand your leadership role. They enlighten you as to the influence of your thinking, feelings, or conflicts, which, then provides a vehicle for identifying your own and your staff's beliefs, values, and perceptions of actual practices in your school, district, or agency. We begin the chapter by explaining that the journey within oneself is the first step needed for today's school leaders. We also explain that a big part of knowing who we are starts with increasing our awareness of our own thoughts and emotions. Investigating who we are and increasing our awareness of our thoughts, feelings, and emotions leads to greater self-awareness from which we can begin to transform organizational cultures while also actualizing individual and organizational potential.

We focus on what is required to lead in a time of change, with all its uncertainties and complexities. There is growing consensus that leading in a time of change requires an understanding of the different realities of all major stakeholders in the system, particularly the teachers and students, as they face the challenges of change. School leaders must make a conscious effort to understand a situation from multiple perspectives and the realities of various constituencies in the system before finding new ways to handle any given situation. They must also understand the importance of building more effective relationships so that together, people can face crises that arise with new meaning, trust, and faith. Forming a shared moral purpose and vision from common values provides stability and a sustainable direction for change. A necessary first step in beginning the change process is a perceived crisis that is shared. Inclusive and respectful dialogue is an essential tool that school leaders need throughout the change process.

In dialogue regarding change, it will be important for school leaders to recognize the value of including diverse cultural groups. Conversations must be kept constructive while minimizing the tendency for any individual or group to dominate. The new leader must provide a context of safety, security, and certainty so that individuals are free to ask questions of each other at any time in the conversation. This requires skillful handling of the emotions that may at times cause people to want to return to the familiar in an effort to self-protect their positions. Exhibiting higher-order metacognitive processes of self-assessment and reflection help school leaders become models for others in their systems. The leadership role in this process is to help all staff reflect in detail on why their perceptions differ and what approaches would be recommended as the basis for better bringing all staff into communities of learners and practice.

We describe the Assessment of Learner-Centered Practices surveys at the school- and classroom-level as concrete tools that school leaders can use, and we describe how these tools can lead to considered thinking about the kinds of practices that will be needed to prepare students for a global world. Such thinking involves considering curriculum and instruction as an inquiry-driven process for experiencing authentic questions about living in a fast changing world and for being a citizen in a democratic society. Further, we describe how technology can become a tool for learner-centered education in which students have more of a voice and partnership role in their educational process. We also describe how learner-centered practices at the school and classroom level lead to higher levels of lifelong learning skills in students.

We conclude Chapter 4 with a review of the tools needed to intensify our inner journey to becoming learner-centered school leaders. We emphasize understanding that learning and change are flip sides of the same psychological process. We present the stages of change individuals and systems undergo to help you form an overall picture of the change process. We end with a number of questions which we use to clarify moral purpose and which you can use to begin a dialogue to achieve

- *clarity* about what needs to be done;
- *courage* to take the next steps;
- *commitments* to support each other in these steps; and
- *capacity* needed to get the job done.

We urge school leaders to model what we believe is the most important quality of all—the authentic understanding of what it takes to move from complexity to simplicity through knowing principles of self, of learning, of leading, and of living systems.

CHAPTER 5: WHAT THE LEARNER-CENTERED ASSESSMENT TOOLS CAN ACCOMPLISH

To understand what learner-centered assessment tools can accomplish, we begin Chapter 5 by setting the context for why a new paradigm of learner-centered education is needed. This context is one in which people are becoming increasingly cognizant of the negative consequences of our current educational paradigm and policies associated with No Child Left Behind (NCLB). We present evidence from recent public polls and educator comments that national educational policies governing schools currently present an insult to children by not honoring them as unique people. These policies do this by forcing content to be taught as a standardized curriculum rather than individualized and inquiry-based units. Those advocating for more learner-centered models that combine academic and natural learning see that the most effective way for students to learn is to create environments in which students can pursue the questions that most interest them. While keeping curriculum goals and outcomes in sight, the teaching process responds to student choices and integrates students' interests into a curriculum focused on high standards of learning needed for life.

For school leaders who want to generate learner-centered educational models, we emphasize the need to understand

- what it takes to expand the learning agenda beyond testing;
- how to meet diverse student needs, including those living in poverty;
- how to focus on improving the quality of student-teacher relationships; and
- which approaches are most effective for students from impoverished backgrounds.

We discuss some of the most pressing issues facing school leaders in today's policy environment, including

- student disengagement and dropout;
- urban school inequities; and
- relying on research evidence.

Our recommendations in all these areas are consonant with learner-centered principles and conform to what we know about the principles of natural learning. We also emphasize that, in order to bring existing or new models of learner-centered education into line with current knowledge about learning and learners requires a deep understanding of ecological approaches and the role of human purposes and values in living systems.

We describe the school leader's role in staff development as one supporting an inside-out process using the Learner-Centered Principles and the Assessment of Learner-Centered Practices self-assessment and reflection tools. We say that the purpose for developing the Assessment of Learner-Centered

Practices surveys was to help educators at all levels of the educational system understand how the Learner-Centered Principles translated into practice and systemic educational transformation. After we review the development and validation of the classroom- and school-level Assessment of Learner-Centered Practices surveys, we provide you with an opportunity to experience the short form of the School-Level Assessment of Learner-Centered Practices and the kind of feedback it provides. This feedback allows you to identify discrepancies between your values and the reality you perceive in your school context. At the conclusion of Chapter 5, we invite you to use what you learn to identify changes that you may want to make in either your goals or your perceptions of actual practices.

CHAPTER 6: HOW WE CAN MOVE TOWARD NEW STUDENT AND SYSTEM OUTCOMES

Knowing what can be accomplished with learner-centered assessment tools marks the beginning of knowing how to move toward new student and system outcomes. In Chapter 6 we argue that the content-driven outcomes of the current paradigm must be replaced with outcomes that prepare students and all learners in schools for the future with a new set of life competencies. These competencies must be grounded on simple principles and truths about human capacities and learning potentials.

We begin the chapter with a description of present knowledge about the new directions needed and some of the innovative educational models beginning to emerge. You explore answers to these questions:

- What are the current imbalances and flaws that must be addressed?
- What are the outcomes we need?
- What is possible in schools of the future?

We argue that the primary areas that must be addressed in new learner-centered education designs are

- revamping curriculum and assessment systems;
- involving students more deeply in their own life inquiries;
- finding new ways for everyone in the system to be accountable and responsible for global citizenship; and
- balancing the system with more attention to the personal and interpersonal human functions.

We indicate that some of the more important student outcomes include that students be

- innovative;
- culturally aware;
- able to communicate and collaborate in sophisticated ways;

- in-depth analysts of concepts;
- interpreters of their own understanding; and
- critical, evaluative thinkers.

To realize these outcomes, we say that teachers will need to be partners with students and parents in tracking students' development and academic growth in the skills needed for productive lives in a global society. These adults will need to foster the critical thinking and communication skills that develop interdisciplinary thinking. They will also need to help students to use their new knowledge in an ethically- and globally-conscious manner and to reflect on and understand their rights and responsibilities in a global society. In this way teachers will help students prepare for lifelong engagement with the world.

We argue that school systems will need to place student engagement at the center of learning based on current events and issues relevant to students. School systems will also need to embed language, collaboration, and technology skills across the curriculum. We believe this can be accomplished by finding new ways for meaningful interactions, visits, and teacher exchanges as a focus for nourishing global sensitivity. In short, new educational systems must educate the whole child for the whole world.

In exploring what is possible in schools of the future, we describe several new initiatives aimed at transforming today's educational paradigm. These initiatives are consonant with learner-centered principles and truths about human capacity and are designed to encourage an open and inclusive public dialogue that engages all constituencies in exploring what education and education policy could look like. We believe such a dialogue needs to address the flaws in the current paradigm and move to what is possible when learner-centered natural learning principles and truths about human capacity are used as the foundation for schools and schooling.

As a personal exercise, you have the opportunity to examine your own school and state-level standards and outcomes against the Learner-Centered Principles and information presented in Chapter 6. You also have the opportunity to identify ways in which these outcomes could be changed to better reflect the outcomes valued by your school staff, students, parents, and community.

We then invite you to consider ways in which you could address diversity issues and system inequities using a learner-centered lens. We conclude the chapter with a discussion of how technology plays a role in creating learning networks and partnerships, how students could be authentic partners in the redesign process, and how technology could support the formation of networked learning communities that expand the boundaries of learning and schooling. In the final exercises, you will have the opportunity to

- identify the learning partnerships you have and will need in your transformational school-leadership role;
- describe how you can use those learning partnerships to create the learning networks in your setting; and

- reflect on your vision for your setting, the outcomes you hope to achieve, and how to use the partnerships you identified to help you achieve them.

CHAPTER 7: HOW WE CAN DEVELOP LEADERSHIP QUALITIES FROM WITHIN

In this final chapter, we challenge you to increase your understanding of what is required to develop leadership qualities from within. We review recent findings from brain research that can help leaders understand how human brain functions can be used to support the development of inner capacities in oneself and in others. We then review new work on leadership from Otto Scharmer. His Theory U and concept of presencing are described as further tools the new school leader will need for transforming the current educational paradigm and creating learner-centered educational systems.

We review Scharmer's concept of presencing, which he formulated from extensive interviews with and analyses of a group of the most effective leaders in the United States Scharmer's concept of presencing comprises three stages of awareness:

1. opening up to and becoming one with the world outside;
2. opening up to and becoming one with one's inner world and deepest source of future possibility; and
3. bringing these emerging futures and possibilities into being.

In the next section, we describe the implications presencing has for leading and learning, including the need for openness and conscious participation as part of a living system. We situate the idea of living systems within the context of leadership as an inner journey, from which leaders derive the ability to establish the relationships and networks he or she needs in order to bring about transformational change.

We iterate a series of leadership challenges, including opening to the unknown, to one's own higher presence and self, and to an emerging future field that comprises what we do next in our schools. We describe four ways in which leaders take action, including

- listening by confirming habitual judgments;
- listening by paying attention to factual and disconfirming data;
- listening empathically, shifting into the place from which the other person is speaking; and
- listening from the emerging field of the future that requires an open heart and open will to connect to the highest future possibility that wants to emerge.

In considering the challenges we describe, we ask how we can meet the challenges of the leadership we present with the tools and information we now have, following with our response to some ways in which this might unfold. We include a discussion of how we can prepare future leaders to respond to these challenges and describe some critical aspects of leadership training models.

One of the most important questions we pose in this chapter is what it means to develop capacity from within, by which we mean developing our capacity to act from a place of spirit rather than from a place of thought. We also include a discussion of the importance of utilizing the power of technology to develop networked learning communities to replace the traditional, site-specific models currently in place.

This chapter ends with a final self-reflection exercise that we hope provides an opportunity for you to integrate what you have learned from reading this book with what you already know to continue you on your journey toward effecting transformational change.

Appendix

Descriptions of the Eight Patterns of Attending and Learning*

Note: These descriptions include a wide range of the characteristics of each pattern. Very few people exhibit all of them, even when a particular pattern is a person's preferred way of attending and learning. Most of us exhibit more characteristics of a pattern if it is one we naturally use to attend and learn and fewer characteristics of a pattern if it is one we do not use as easily or fluidly. Almost everyone has one or two (or even three) preferred patterns for attending and learning. Consequently, almost everyone has one or two (or even three) patterns that are not naturally easy ways for them to attend and learn.

Interpersonal
People oriented toward the interpersonal understand what makes other people function as they do. These people naturally empathize with others and can easily put themselves into others' shoes to see the world from their perspective. They can see how a particular set of interactions will result in a foreseeable consequence and adjust their interactions accordingly.

These people make good collaborators because they like to work within a consensual framework, and they prefer working in a group setting. They are good at giving and receiving feedback and like to teach others something new. They know how to conduct interviews because they are intuitively aware of others' feelings.

People oriented toward the interpersonal lead through negotiation, facilitation, consensus, and friendship. Because they enjoy functioning in a group, they enjoy technology that enables communicating with friends, colleagues, and strangers: internet chat, e-mail; text messaging, blogging, and sites where they can interact in real time with peers.

Linguistic
People who attend and learn linguistically tend to enjoy language in a variety of ways. They enjoy words, their meanings, their roots, and uses. These people enjoy playing with words through their sounds, meanings, double meanings, literal and figurative meanings, and so on. They learn language and languages easily and enjoy figuring out how language works through grammar (syntax), meaning (semantics), sounds (phonology), and variations in social usage (pragmatics). They like hearing and/or telling stories and appreciate the various aspects of narratives.

If these people live in a culture in which reading is valued, they find reading easy and pleasurable, as well as informative. They may engage in reading as a way to reduce stress or to relax. They find it easy to glean information and knowledge through reading and writing, and they may use writing to solve problems and/or develop self-understanding. Many of these people collect books, magazines, and/or articles. They are among the first to download software that enables them to access the written and spoken word. Their most-used computer software is usually a word processing application.

Those oriented toward linguistic attending and learning like to play with language, enjoying and producing various sorts of humor, such as puns, riddles, jokes, and double entendres.

Musical

Those who attend and learn musically are attuned to melodies, harmonies, and the unfolding of songs over time. They feel and respond to rhythm and meter, and they appreciate a variety of themes in music. They play music in their heads and can create musical combinations of their own. They are sensitive to the sounds in their environment, particularly if those sounds are musical or if they are disharmonious.

People oriented toward music like to study or learn something new while listening to music, and they often have a music player, radio, or TV turned on to play music. They typically have extensive music collections and enjoy listening to widely different styles. They are the first to download music and the software necessary to operate their music players. Their most-used computer software is usually an application to create and record music, play music, and make music podcasts.

These people tend to be able to discern minute variations in a variety of patterns of sounds, not just musical. For example, when cardiologists perform a physical examination and listen to the heart, they are able to identify normal patterns of cardiac activity and to detect any minute variation that might constitute a problem or anomaly. Similarly, engine mechanics can often discern subtle differences in engine functioning from listening to it at differing speeds and loads.

People oriented toward musical attending and learning enjoy playing with music, as, for instance, the composer PDQ Bach (Peter Schiekele), who, according to Wikipedia (2007), combines parodies of musicological scholarship, the conventions of Baroque and classical music, and elements of slapstick comedy.

Logical

People oriented toward the logical tend to develop organizational schemes, patterns, and categories for their experiences, thoughts, and feelings and for the physical world. These people like to organize their belongings for ease of retrieval and interaction—organizing their closets, for instance, according to color, function, and/or seasonal use.

People who find logical learning easy prefer to organize their time into discrete intervals and activities and will often maintain a time slot even for relaxing or "goofing off." They have a system they use to pack a suitcase or a car for traveling, to decorate a home for a holiday, or to host a dinner party for friends. They like using calendars and/or lists to help them think and act.

These people enjoy games that employ logical thinking (e.g., chess, checkers, Go, and strategy-based computer games). They find the scientific method to be the most reasonable way to proceed to investigate phenomena, and they often rely on induction and/or deduction as a way to solve problems. They much prefer argumentative discourse to narrative discourse because they see argumentative discourse as more systematic and reasoned. They are among the first to download software that enables them to organize their time and projects.

People oriented toward logical attending and learning often like to play games of logic that utilize strategic thinking.

Quantitative

People oriented toward quantitative attending and learning easily understand numeric concepts and calculations and often find numbers more reliable and less fuzzy than words. They use mathematical symbol systems to think, ask questions, and solve problems. They prefer keeping their checkbooks balanced to the penny, and they enjoy applying mathematical tools and ideas to real-world problems.

In everyday life, they like to measure quantity; volume; length, width, and depth; speed; various sorts of ratios; time; acceleration; and so on. They prefer numeric descriptions to verbal ones and will "run the numbers" to determine a cost-benefit ratio on virtually any phenomenon. Engineers, economists, and computer programmers typically exhibit quantitative abilities. They download software to play with supersymmetry, generate scripting language, create fractals, and set type using typesetting engines.

Spatial

Those oriented toward the spatial focus on how things look. They are highly aware of how their surroundings appear, where they are in space, and what the physical landscape looks like. They easily find their way when traveling, often visualizing where they are going or have been in order to orient themselves. They use maps as a way to represent the physical world, and they employ graphs, charts, and models (2-D or 3-D) to represent visual information. They are the first to download computer applications such as Google Earth; painting, drawing, coloring and design programs; animation programs; graphics and illustration programs; and multimedia programs.

These people usually enjoy looking at and/or producing art of various types and notice color, line, texture, balance, composition, and medium. In their everyday lives, these people costume themselves with attention to visual effect. They notice the interior design of homes and businesses and are able to visualize how interiors and exteriors would look with different configurations. Many can take apart and put together again various machines.

People oriented toward the spatial prefer the graphic novel to the "standard" format used in written books. They see their world as a series of short visual snapshots or videos, running like a movie. At a film, the cinematography and costumes stand out for them. They prefer computer games with rich visual detail.

Physical

People oriented toward the physical are aware of their body and how it feels. They attend to keeping their body healthy through nutrition, rest, and exercise. They enjoy moving their body, getting a massage or facial, and taking a leisurely bath and/or soaking in a hot tub. They take pleasure in using lotions, oils, fragrances, and emollients to cleanse and soften their skin.

Many are active in sports, some competitively, some not. They enjoy learning physical skills and putting them to use in complex, strategic ways. They know how to pace themselves so they can minimize injuries and how to recover if they do suffer an injury. Many of these people study yoga, Feldenkrais, Pilates, or other mind-body practice. The software they are likely to download is related to whichever practice or fitness program they study.

Many people oriented to the physical enjoy watching dance and/or professional sports and appreciate the talent and skill that dancers and professional athletes display. Others, such as chiropractors, physical and occupational therapists, and massage therapists are drawn to helping other people rehabilitate from injury or stress. They are able to enter into other people's perceptions of their own physical self to support them in making physical changes that will increase their health and well-being.

Intrapersonal

Those oriented toward the intrapersonal are attuned to their own processes, ideas, feelings, experiences, and growth. They are often committed to personal growth and developing their spirituality. They make time for the solitude necessary to reflect and engage in the practices that lead to mental and spiritual health. They have a clear understanding of their motivations and goals and often keep a journal or diary about their thoughts and feelings.

These people are aware of their own strengths, as well as their human shortcomings. They hold realistic views of what they can and want to do, and they know where to go if they need help. They can predict how they will react to varying events and experiences, and they know which things they need to avoid. Others are drawn to them because they don't usually botch an activity or undertaking.

They tend to hold strong personal convictions, though they are willing to examine the implications of their convictions and make changes that lead to greater health. These people tend to lead by example, rather than through group facilitation and consensus-building. They tend to prefer working alone and don't mind going to a restaurant or public event by themselves.

People oriented toward the intrapersonal often show an affinity for pursuits that involve thinking, such as psychology, philosophy, writing, and theology. They tend to download self-help and wellness software.

---

* These descriptions are based on those used by Miller and Miller (1994) and are used with permission.

Resources

MUST-READ BOOKS

Borman, G. D., & Overman, L. T. (2004). Academic resilience in mathematics among poor and minority students. *Elementary School Journal, 104,* 177–195.

Bracey, G. W. (2002). International comparisons: An excuse to avoid meaningful educational reform. *Education Week, 21*(19), 30–32.

Houston, P. D., & Sokolow, S. L. (2006). *The spiritual dimension of leadership: 8 key principles to leading more effectively.* Thousand Oaks, CA: Corwin Press.

Lazarus, R. S. (2000). Toward better research on stress and coping. *American Psychologist, 55*(6), 665–673.

Marshall, S. P. (2006). *The power to transform: Leadership that brings learning and schooling to life.* San Francisco, CA: Jossey-Bass.

McCombs, B. L., & Miller, L. (2007). *Learner-centered classroom practices and assessments: Maximizing student motivation, learning, and achievement.* Thousand Oaks, CA: Corwin Press.

McCombs, B. L., & Whisler, J. S. (1989). The role of affective variables in autonomous learning. *Educational Psychologist, 24*(3), 277–306.

Pellicer, L. O. (2007). *Caring enough to lead: How reflective thought leads to moral leadership* (3rd ed.). Thousand Oaks, CA: Corwin Press.

Williams, B., & Imam, I. (2007) (Eds.). *Systems concepts in evaluation: An expert anthology.* Point Reyes, CA: EdgePress of Inverness.

WEB SITES TO EXPLORE

Links to Learner-Centered Psychological Principles

http://www.apa.org/ed/cpse/LCPP.pdf
http://www.apa.org/ed/lcp2/lcp14.html

Examples of Learner-Centered Schools

http://sc.jeffco.k12.co.us/education/components/scrapbook/default.php?
sectiondetailid=149335&pagecat=553
http://www.eaglerockschool.org/home/index.asp
http://www.dist113.org/

Example of an Early Learner-Centered Educator

http://www.follettfoundation.org/mpf.htm

Example of Systems Thinker Resources and Newsletter
http://www.pegasuscom.com/

Examples of Living Systems Resources
http://www.stephaniepacemarshall.com/books.html
http://www.margaretwheatley.com/
http://www.berkana.org/

Example of Sustainability Principles Site
http://www.centerforsustainablechange.org/

Examples of Learner-Centered Professional Development Materials
http://www.peaklearn.com/professionaldevelopment.html
http://www.inspiredteaching.org/

Example of Learner-Centered Student Potential Materials
http://www.pathfinderusa.com/

Example of Network to Keep the Public Informed
http://www.publiceducation.org/index.asp

Example of Resources in Servant Leadership
http://www.greenleaf.org/

Examples of Learner-Centered Uses of Technology
http://www.techforlearning.org/index.html
http://genyes.com/

Examples of Learner-Centered Dialogue Resources
http://appreciativeinquiry.case.edu/
http://www.appreciative-inquiry.org/

Examples of Learning Communities Sites
http://www.creatinglearningcommunities.org/index.html
http://www.communitiesofthefuture.org/

Example of State Level Efforts to Transform Education
http://c21l.org/

Example of Learner-Centered Foundation
http://www.hopefoundation.org/hope/index.php?option=com_frontpage&Itemid=1

Example of Learner-Centered School Resources
http://www.bigpicture.org/index.htm

Example of Futurist Systems Thinker
http://ottoscharmer.com/

Example of New Learner-Centered School Reform Initiatives
http://www.futureminds.us/

Glossary of Learner-Centered Terms

LEARNER-CENTERED: SOME DEFINITIONS©

Culture: The dynamic, deeply-learned confluence of language, values, beliefs, and behaviors that pervade every aspect of a person's (and/or organization's) life. Also refers to the operating norms of any group or organization that reflect different values, beliefs, etc. of that group.

Domains of Change: Aspects of living systems that occur simultaneously at various levels of system functioning. In educational systems, the levels of functioning include classroom, school, district, community, and society. The domains of change operating throughout all these levels are:

- *personal*, which supports the personal, motivational/learning, and interpersonal needs of those who serve and/or are served by the system (e.g., students, teachers, administrators, parents);
- *organizational*, which provides the organizational and management structures and policies that support the personal and technical domains, and ultimately, learning and achievement for *all* learners); and
- *technical*, which specifies the content and performance standards, curriculum structures and processes, instructional approaches, and assessment strategies that best promote learning and achievement of *all* students and learners in the system.

Honoring the Person as an Individual: The belief that *individual learners are unique and learn best when this uniqueness is honored and accommodated*. Individual differences include:

- cultural heritage;
- gender;
- profiles of intelligences;
- socio-economic status;
- educational background;
- family structure and dynamics; and
- life experiences and their interactions for each person.

Intrinsic Motivation: Motivation inherent in human beings. It naturally emerges and flourishes in learner-centered contexts.

Learner-Centered(ness): *Respecting the person as a learner and honoring the person as an individual.* Holding beliefs, attitudes, practices, principles, etc. that reflect the assumptions and principles of the *Learner-Centered Psychological Principles*:

- learners are unique, and this uniqueness must be respected and attended to;
- learning is holistic and constructive in nature;
- a positive social context and relationships enhance learning; and
- learning and motivation are natural processes for all learners.

Learner-Centered Practices: Teaching and learning approaches, processes, communication styles, and school and classroom management strategies that are consistent with the *Learner-Centered Principles* and definition of "learner-centeredness."

Learner-Centered Psychological Principles: Fourteen principles that summarize findings from a century of research on learning and learners. The *Principles* were produced by the American Psychological Association's (APA) Presidential Task Force on Psychology in Education and the Mid-continent Regional Educational Laboratory, published in January 1993, and revised and published by the APA in 1997. The principles are categorized into four domains of factors impacting learning for each individual:

- Metacognitive and Cognitive;
- Motivational and Affective;
- Developmental and Social; and
- Individual Differences.

Lifelong Learners: People who value and are committed to ongoing learning and growth throughout the lifespan. Understanding that learning is change and change is learning.

Living Systems: A description of systems whose fundamental goal is to serve humans and their unique needs and capacities (e.g., educational, family, and social systems); those systems whose operation is best understood by principles describing the particular processes relevant to the functions and purposes of the system. For educational systems, processes are related to learning and the individual learner across personal, technical, and organizational domains.

Personal Change Process: A transformation process in which there is a substantial and sustainable change in beliefs, attitudes, knowledge, emotions, and behaviors resulting in a "shift" in practice. Begins with the individual and progresses to the group or cultural level. Stages in the personal change process include four phases:

- I —developing awareness, will to change, and ownership of need to change;
- II—observing models and building understanding of personal domain practices;
- III—adapting strategies, building skills, and developing personal responsibility for continuous learning and change; and
- IV—adopting and maintaining attitudes and practices that contribute to continuous learning and professional development.

Psychology of Learning and Psychology of Change: Understanding that change and learning are synonymous and occur within the "heads and hearts" of individuals as a result of transformations in thinking, feeling, and behaving.

Respecting the Person as a Learner: The belief that *all individuals learn and are motivated to learn* when their basic capacities, talents, abilities, and needs are known, respected, and accommodated in supportive teaching and learning practices. The most important accommodations include providing opportunities for

- personal choice;
- control;
- connections;
- responsibility;
- cooperation;
- competence;
- voice;
- respect;
- trust;
- relevance; and
- challenge.

Systemic Change: Shifts in society, organizations, and individual behavior that occur as a result of the dynamic patterns of thinking and relationships between people and their environment. Change in one domain of a system automatically and always results in changes in other domains of that system. A holistic and comprehensive way of thinking about and bringing about change through the simultaneous consideration of the personal, technical, and organizational domains of living systems.

Transformation: A process in which a fundamental shift in understanding emerges that results in a new way of thinking, feeling, and behaving; occurs in response to significant experiences which alter existing perceptions and understandings.

Voice: Each individual's expression of thoughts, feelings, and interpretations or perceptions of reality at any point in time; an expression of uniqueness that must be honored and respected in learning.

Whole Person: A term that acknowledges all aspects of a person: physical, social, emotional, intellectual, and spiritual.

References

Alexander, P. A., & Murphy, P. K. (1998). The research base for APA's learner-centered psychological principles. In N. Lambert & B. L. McCombs (Eds.), *How students learn: Reforming schools through learner-centered education* (pp. 25–60). Washington, DC: American Psychological Association.

Allen, S. W., & Schwartz, J. M. (2007a). Lead your brain instead of letting it lead you. *The Complete Lawyer, 3*(3), 1–5. Retrieved August 1, 2007, from http://tcl.thecompletelawyer.com/volume3/issue3/article.php?ppaid=2439

Allen, S. W., & Schwartz, J. M. (2007b). Law students: Create a well-rounded life. *The Complete Lawyer, 3*(3), 1–7. Retrieved August 1, 2007, from http://tcl.thecompletelawyer.com/volume3/issue3/article.php?ppaid=2432

Amrein, A. L., & Berliner, D. C. (2003). The effects of high-stakes testing on student motivation and learning. *Educational Leadership, 60*(5), 32–38.

APA Task Force on Psychology in Education. (1993, January). *Learner-centered psychological principles: Guidelines for school redesign and reform*. Washington, DC: American Psychological Association and Mid-Continent Regional Educational Laboratory.

APA Work Group of the Board of Educational Affairs. (1997, November). *Learner-centered psychological principles: A framework for school reform and redesign*. Washington, DC: American Psychological Association.

Association for Educational Communications and Technology (AECT). (2007). *Future minds: Transforming American school systems*. An initiative of AECT. Draft document released in August 2007.

Azzam, A. M. (2007). Why students drop out. *Educational Leadership, 64*(7), 91–93.

Babbidge, T. (2006, February 10). Anti-CSAP group argues its case. *Rocky Mountain News*, 44A.

Bartholomew, B. (2007). Why we can't always get what we want. *Phi Delta Kappan, 88*(8), 593–598.

Barton, P. E. (2006). The dropout problem: Losing ground. *Educational Leadership, 63*(5), 14–18.

Beisser, A. (1970). Paradoxical theory of change. In J. Fagan and I. L. Shepherd (Eds.), *Gestalt therapy now*. New York: Harper & Row. Retrieved July 23, 2007, from http://www.gestalt.org/arnie.htm

Benninga, J. S., Berkowitz, M. W., Kuehn, P., & Smith, K. (2006). Character and academics: What good schools do. *Phi Delta Kappan, 87*(6), 448–452.

Bennis, W. (2007). The challenges of leadership in the modern world. *American Psychologist, 62*(1), 2–5.

The Berkana Institute (2007). *Annual Review 2006*. Spokane, WA: Author.

Berkana Institute and The Art of Hosting. Retrieved July 27, 2007, from http://www. artofhosting.org/home

Berliner, D. (2005, April). *Ignoring the forest, blaming the trees: Our impoverished view of educational reform.* AERA Distinguished Lecture at the Annual Meeting of the American Educational Research Association, Montreal.

Blankstein, A. M. (2007). Terms of engagement: Where failure is not an option. In A. M. Blankstein, R. W. Cole, & P. D. Houston (Eds.), *Engaging every learner* (pp. 1–28). Thousand Oaks, CA: Corwin Press.

Boaler, J. (2006). Promoting respectful learning. *Educational Leadership, 63*(5), 74–78.

Bolman, L. G., & Deal, T. E. (2002). *Reframing the path to school leadership: A guide for teachers and principals.* Thousand Oaks, CA: Corwin Press.

Borko, H. (2004). Professional development and teacher learning: Mapping the terrain. *Educational Researcher, 33*(8), 13–15.

Bottoms, G. (2007). Treat all students like the "best" students. *Educational Leadership, 64*(7), 30–37.

Boyle, A. (2007). Compassionate intervention: Helping failing schools to turn around. In A. M. Blankstein, R. W. Cole, & P. D. Houston (Eds.), *Engaging every learner* (pp. 147–172). Thousand Oaks, CA: Corwin Press.

Brady, M. (2008). Cover the material—or teacher students to think? *Educational Leadership, 65*(5), 64–67.

Bransford, J., Brown, A., & Cocking, R. (Eds.). (1999). *How people learn: Brain, mind, experience, and school.* Committee on Developments in the Science of Learning Commission on Behavioral and Social Sciences and Education National Research Council. Washington, DC: National Academy Press.

Brown, E. (2005, July). Otto Scharmer: Theory U: Presencing emerging futures. *MIT Sloan School of Management News Briefs.* Retrieved July 31, 2007, from http://mitsloan.mit.edu/newsroom/newsbriefs-0605-scharmer.php

Brown, J. S. (1999). *Growing up digital: Learning, working and playing in the digital age.* Paper presented at the American Association of Higher Education 1999 Conference on Higher Education, March 23, 1999.

Bruner, J. (1996). *The culture of education.* Cambridge: Harvard University Press.

Burton, L. E. (2003). Out of the blue: The teachable moment. *Futures Research Quarterly.* World Future Society. Bethesda, MD: Spring, 2003.

Cacioppo, J. T., Hawkley, L. C., Rickett, E. M., & Masi, C. M. (2005). Sociality, spirituality, and meaning making: Chicago health, aging, and social relations study. *Review of General Psychology, 9*(2), 143–155.

Caine, G., & Caine, R. (2006). Meaningful learning and the executive functions of the human brain. In S. Johnson & K. Taylor (Eds.), *The neuroscience of adult learning.* New Directions for Adult and Continuing Education, No. 110, S. Imel and J. M. Ross-Gordon (Eds.), pp. 53–62. San Francisco: Jossey-Bass.

Caine, R. (2008). How neuroscience informs our teaching of elementary students. In Block, C., Parris, S., & Afflerbach, P., (Eds.), *Comprehension instruction* (2nd ed. pp. 127–141). New York: Guilford Press.

Caine, R., & Caine, G. (2006, September). The way we learn. *Educational Leadership, 64*(1), 50–54.

Caine, R., Caine, G., McClintic, C. & Klimek, K. (2005). *12 brain/mind learning principles in action.* Thousand Oaks, CA: Corwin Press.

Carroll, T. G. (2000). If we didn't have the schools we have today, would we create the schools we have today? *Contemporary Issues in Technology and Teacher Education, 1*(1), 117–140.

Cervone, D., Shadel, W. G., Smith, R. E., & Fiori, M. (2006). Self-regulation and personality science: Reply to commentaries. *Applied Psychology: An International Review, 55*(3), 470–488.

Cheng, Y. C. (2007, April). *Educational research in the Asia-Pacific region: Paradigm shifts, reforms and practice.* Invited presentation at the Presidential Session of the Annual Meeting of the American Educational Research Association, Chicago.

Chin, E., & Young, J. W. (2007). A person-oriented approach to characterizing beginning teachers in alternative certification programs. *Educational Researcher, 36*(2), 74–83.

Chiu, M. M., & Khoo, L. (2005). Effects of resources, inequality, and privilege bias on achievement: Country, school, and student level analyses. *American Educational Research Journal, 42*(4), 575–603.

Chrisman, V. (2005). How schools sustain success. *Educational Leadership, 62*(5), 16–21.

Church, M., Bitel, M., Armstrong, K., Fernando, P., Gould, H., Joss, S., et al. (2003). *Participation, relationships and dynamic change: New thinking on evaluating the work of international networks.* Working Paper No. 121. ISSN 1474-3280. London: Department Planning Unit, University College London.

Clem, F., & Simpson, E. (2007). Viewpoint. Meeting students where they can learn and have a profound effect on education. *eSchool News, 10*(2), 27.

Cochran-Smith, M., & Zeichner, K. M. (2005). *Studying teacher education: The report of the AERA Panel on Research and Teacher Education.* Mahweh, NJ: Lawrence Erlbaum.

Cohen, A. (2007). *The challenge of our moment: A roundtable discussion with Don Beck, Brian Swimme, & Peter Senge.* Retrieved July 27, 2007, from http://www.wie.org/j23/roundtable.asp?pf=1

Coleman, K., & Rud, A. G. (2007). The change process in a culture of learning: An essay review. *Education Review, 10*(7). Retrieved August 2, 2007, from http://edrev.asu.edu/essays/v10n7index.html

Coles, M. J., & Southworth, G. (Eds.). (2005). *Developing leadership: Creating the schools of tomorrow.* Buckingham: Open University Press.

Combs, A. (1974). *The professional education of teachers: A humanistic approach to teacher preparation.* Boston: Allyn & Bacon.

Combs, A. W. (1962). A perceptual view of the adequate personality. In A. W. Combs (Ed.), 1962 ASCD yearbook, *Perceiving, behaving, becoming: A new focus for education* (pp. 50–64). Alexandria, VA: Association for Supervision and Curriculum Development.

Combs, A. W. (1986). What makes a good helper? A person-centered approach. *Person-Centered Review, 1*(1), 51–61.

Combs, A. W. (1991). *The schools we need: New assumptions for educational reform.* Lanham, MD: University Press of America, Inc.

Combs, A. W., Miser, A. B., & Whitaker, K. S. (1999). *On becoming a school leader: A person-centered challenge.* Alexandria, VA: Association for Supervision and Curriculum Development.

Corbett, D., Wilson, B., & Williams, B. (2005). No choice but success. *Educational Leadership, 62*(6), 8–12.

Cornelius-White, J. (2007). Teachers who care are more effective: A meta-analysis of learner-centered relationships. *Review of Educational Research, 77*(1), 113–143.

Covey, S. R. (2002). *Principle-centered leadership.* New York: Simon & Schuster.

Covington, M. V., & Teel, K. M. (1996). *Overcoming student failure: Changing motives and incentives for learning.* Washington, DC: APA Books.

Csikszentmihalyi, M. (1996). *Creativity.* New York: Harper Collins.

Cushman, K. (2006). Help us care enough to learn. *Educational Leadership, 63*(5), 34–37.

Daniels, D. H., Kalkman, D. L., & McCombs, B. L. (2001). Individual differences in young children's perspectives on learning and teacher practices: Effects of learner-centered contexts on motivation. *Early Education and Development, 12*(2), 253–273.

Daniels, D. H., & Perry, K. E. (2003). "Learner-centered" according to children. *Theory into Practice, 42*(2), 102–108.

Darling-Hammond, L., & Ifill-Lynch, O. (2006). If they'd only do their work! *Educational Leadership, 63*(5), 8–13.

Darling-Hammond, L., LaPointe, M., Meyerson, D., & Orr, M. (2007). *Preparing school leaders for a changing world: Lessons from exemplary leadership development programs.* Retrieved August, 8, 2007, from http://seli.stanford.edu/research/sls.htm

Davis, H. A. (2006). Exploring the contexts of relationship quality between middle school students and teachers. *Elementary School Journal, 106*(3), 192–224.

Davis, S., Darling-Hammond, L., LaPointe, M., & Meyerson, D. (2005). *School leadership study: Developing successful principals.* Stanford, CA: Stanford Educational Leadership Institute.

Davis, S. H. (2007). Bridging the gap between research and practice: What's good, what's bad, and how can one be sure. *Phi Delta Kappan, 88*(8), 569–578.

Day, C. (2000). Effective leadership and reflective practice. *Reflective Practice, 1*(1), 113–137.

Deakin Crick, R. (2006). *Learning power in practice: A guide for teachers.* London: Paul Chapman Publishing.

Deakin Crick R. (2007) Learning how to learn: The dynamic assessment of learning power. *Curriculum Journal, 18*(2) 135–153.

Deakin Crick, R., Broadfoot, P., & Claxton, G. (2004). Developing an effective lifelong learning inventory: The ELLI Project. *Assessment in Education, 11*, 248–272.

Deakin Crick, R., & McCombs, B. L. (2006). The assessment of learner-centered practices surveys (ALCPs): An English case study. *Research and Evaluation Journal, 12*(5), 23–444.

Dewey, J. (1938). *Experience and education.* New York: Macmillan.

Do, S. L., & Schallert, D. L. (2004). Emotions and classroom talk: Toward a model of the role of affect in students' experiences of classroom discussions. *Journal of Educational Psychology, 96*(4), 619–634.

Dweck, C. S. (1999). *Self-theories: Their role in motivation, personality and development.* Philadelphia: Taylor and Francis/Psychology Press.

Eisner, E. (2005). Back to whole. *Educational Leadership, 63*(1), 14–18.

Emerick, S., Hirsch, E., & Berry, B. (2004). Does highly qualified mean high-quality? *ASCD Infobrief, 39*, 1–10.

Farson, R. (2007). The case for failure: Risk, innovation, and engagement. In A. M. Blankstein, R. W. Cole, & P. D. Houston (Eds.), *Engaging every learner* (pp. 173–191). Thousand Oaks, CA: Corwin Press.

Forbes, S. (1999). *Holistic education: An analysis of its intellectual precedents and nature.* Unpublished dissertation, University of Oxford: Green College.

Fredrickson, B. L., & Losada, M. F. (2005). Positive affect and the complex dynamics of human flourishing. *American Psychologist, 60*(7), 678–686.

Freeman, M., deMarrais, K., Preissle, J., Roulston, K., & St. Pierre, E. A. (2007). Standards of evidence in qualitative research: An incitement to discourse. *Educational Researcher, 36*(1), 25–32.

Fuhrman, S., & Lazerson, M. (Eds.). (2005). *The public schools.* New York: Oxford University Press.

Fullan, M. (2001). *Leading in a culture of change.* San Francisco: Jossey-Bass.

Fullan, M. (2003). *The moral imperative of school leadership.* Thousand Oaks, CA: Corwin Press.

Fullan, M. (2006). *Turnaround leadership.* San Francisco: Jossey-Bass.

Gabriel, J. G. (2005). *How to thrive as a teacher leader.* Alexandria, VA: Association for Supervision and Curriculum Development.

Garner, R. (2007, July 13). Classroom revolution as curriculum embraces modern life. Retrieved July 14, 2007, from http://www.independent.co.uk/news/education-news

Green, D. A., & Staley, A. (March, 2000). *Using information technology in traditionally "soft" subjects.* Paper presented at the International Conference on Learning with Technology, "Does Technology Make a Difference?" Philadelphia, Temple University.

Greenleaf, R. K. (1977). *Servant leadership: A journey into the nature of legitimate power and greatness.* New York/Mahwah, NJ: Paulist Press. 25th Anniversary Edition (2002).

Gresson, A. D. (2004). *America's atonement: Racial pain, recovery rhetoric, and the pedagogy of healing.* New York: Peter Lang.

Gurin, P., & Nagda, B. R. A. (2006). Getting to the what, how, and why of diversity on campus. *Educational Researcher, 35*(1), 20–24.

Guterman, J. (2007). Where have all the principals gone? *Edutopia, 3*(3), 49–52.

Hadjioannou, X. (2007). Bringing the background to the foreground: What do classroom environments that support authentic discussions look like? *American Educational Research Journal, 44*(8), 370–399.

Hannum, W., & McCombs, B. L. (2008). Enhancing distance learning with learner-centered principles. *Educational Technology, 48*(3) 11–20.

Hargreaves, A., Earl, L., Moore, S., & Manning, S. (2001). *Learning to change: Teaching beyond subjects and standards.* San Francisco: Jossey-Bass.

Hargreaves, A., & Fink, D. (2004). The seven principles of sustainable leadership. *Educational Leadership, 61*(7), 8–13.

Hargreaves, A., & Fink, D. (2006). *Sustainable leadership.* San Francisco: Jossey-Bass.

Harper, D. (2002, March). *Generation www.Y White Paper.2.* Olympia, WA: Generation Y Organization.

Harter, S. (2006). *The cognitive and social construction of the developing self.* New York: Guilford Press.

Hassan, Z. (2005, July). *The six or seven axons of social change: Margaret Mead's gift.* Retrieved July 6, 2007, from at http://www.berkana.org/articles/axions.htm

Hawley, W. D., & Valli, L. (2000). Learner-centered professional development. *Research Bulletin No. 27.* Bloomington, IN: Phi Delta Kappa Center for Evaluation, Development, and Research.

Hermans, H. J. M., & Dimaggio, G. (2007). Self, identity, and globalization in times of uncertainty: A dialogical analysis. *Review of General Psychology, 11*(1), 31–61.

Hoffman, L. & Burrello, L. (2002). *Can moral purpose overcome the limits of leadership?* Paper presented to the University Council for Educational Administration, November 1, 2002.

Holland, H. (2005). Teaching teachers: Professional development to improve student achievement. *Research Points, 3*(1), 1–2, 4.

The Hope Foundation (2007). *Coyote Ridge Elementary School (Broomfield, CO).* Retrieved May 17, 2007, from http://www.hopefoundation.org/hope/index.php?option=com_content&task=view&id=147&Itemid=154

Horwitz, C., & Vega-Frey, J. M. (2006). *Spiritual activism and liberation spirituality: Pathways to collective liberation.* Retrieved July 6, 2007, from http://www.berkana.org/articles/spiritual_activism.htm

Houston, P. D. (2007). Out-of-the-box leadership. In P. D. Houston, A. M. Blankstein, & R. W. Cole (Eds.), *Out-of-the-box leadership* (pp. 1–9). Thousand Oaks, CA: Corwin Press.

Houston, P. D., & Sokolow, S. L. (2006). *The spiritual dimension of leadership: 8 key principles to leading more effectively.* Thousand Oaks, CA: Corwin Press.

Hoyle, J. R. (2001). *Leadership and the force of love: Six keys to motivating with love.* Thousand Oaks, CA: Corwin Press.

Hoyle, J. R. (2006). *Leadership and futuring: Making visions happen.* Thousand Oaks, CA: Corwin Press.

Jain, M., & Stilger, B. (2007). *Reflections on now activism.* Retrieved July 6, 2007, from http://www.berkana.org/articles/Now_Reflecion.htm.

Just for the Kids. (2003). *Promising practices: How high-performing schools in Texas get results.* Austin, TX: Just for the Kids.

Kanfer, R., & McCombs, B. L. (2000). Motivation. In H. F. O'Neil Jr., & S. Tobias (Eds.), *Handbook on training* (pp. 85–108). New York: Macmillan.

Kim, J. S., & Sunderman, G. L. (2005). Measuring academic proficiency under the No Child Left Behind Act: Implications for educational equity. *Educational Researcher, 34*(8), 3–13.

Kofman, F., & Senge, P. M. (1993). Communities of commitment: The heart of learning organizations. *Organizational Dynamics, 22*(2), 5024.

Kohn, A. (2005). Unconditional teaching. *Educational Leadership, 63*(1), 20–24.

Korten, D. (2006). The great turning: From empire to earth community. *YES! A Journal of Positive Futures, Summer,* 12–18.

Kozol, J. (2005). *The same of the nation: The restoration of Apartheid schooling in America.* New York: Crown Publishers.

Lambert, L. (2000). Framing reform for the new millennium: Leadership capacity in schools and districts. *Canadian Journal of Educational Administration and Policy, 14,* 1–5. Retrieved August 17, 2007, from http://www.umanitoba.ca/publications/cjeap/articles/lambert.html

Lambert, L. (2002). Beyond instructional leadership: A framework for shared leadership. *Educational Leadership, 59*(8), 37–40.

Lambert, L. (2003, November). Eye on leadership. Seminar presented at the 2003–2004 Annual Seminar Series, "Eye on Education: Innovation, Integration, Isolation and Inspiration." University of Calgary, Canada.

Lambert, L. (2005). Leadership for lasting reform. *Educational Leadership, 62*(5), 62–65.

Lambert, N., & McCombs, B. L. (Eds.). (1998). *How students learn: Reforming schools through learner-centered education.* Washington, DC: APA Books.

Lave, J., & Wenger, E. (1998). *Communities of practice: Learning, meaning, and identify.* Cambridge: Cambridge University Press.

Legault, L., Green-Demers, I., & Pelletier, L. (2006). Why do high school students lack motivation in the classroom? Towards an understanding of academic amotivation and the role of social support. *Journal of Educational Psychology, 98*(3), 567–582.

Leeb, W. A. (2002). Presencing—A social technology of freedom: Interview with Dr. Claus Otto Scharmer. *Trigon Themen, 2*, 1–3.

Levine, M. (2007). The essential cognitive backpack. *Educational Leadership, 64*(7), 16–22.

Lieberman, A., & Wood, D. (2001). When teachers write: Of networks and learning. In A. Lieberman and L. Miller (Eds.), *Teachers caught in the action: Professional development that matters* (p. 184). New York: Teachers College Press.

Lin, X., Schwartz, D. L., & Hatano, G. (2005). Toward teachers' adaptive metacognition. *Educational Psychologist, 40*(4), 245–255.

Lindsey, D. B., & Lindsey, R. B. (2007). Culturally proficient equity audits: A tool for engaging every learner. In A. M. Blankstein, R. W. Cole, & P. D. Houston (Eds.), *Engaging every learner* (pp. 37–57). Thousand Oaks, CA: Corwin Press.

Maldonado, D. E. Z., Rhoads, R., & Buenavista, L. (2005). The student-initiated retention project: Theoretical contributions and the role of self-empowerment. *American Educational Research Journal, 42*(4), 605–638.

March, T. (2006). The new www: Whatever, whenever, wherever. *Educational Leadership, 63*(4), 14–19.

Marshall, H. H., & Weinstein, R. (1986). Classroom context of student-perceived differential teacher treatment. *Journal of Educational Psychology, 78*, 441–453.

Marshall, S. P. (2006). *The power to transform: Leadership that brings learning and schooling to life.* San Francisco: Jossey-Bass.

Martin, R. A. (2002, April). *Alternatives in education: An exploration of learner-centered, progressive, and holistic education.* Paper presented at the annual meeting of the American Educational Research Association, New Orleans.

Martin, S. (2007). The labyrinth to leadership. *Monitor on Psychology, 38*(7), 90–91.

Mates, B. (2007). Reflections from a community member: Philanthropy and social change. Retrieved July 6, 2007, from http://www.berkana.org/articles/philanthropy.htm

Mathews, J. (2004a, January 20). Turning strife into success. *Washington Post.*

Mathews, J. (2004b, February 17). Seeking alternatives to standardized testing. *Washington Post.*

McCombs, B. L. (1986). The role of the self-system in self-regulated learning. *Contemporary Educational Psychology, 11*, 314–332.

McCombs, B. L. (1988). Motivational skills training: Combining metacognitive, cognitive, and affective learning strategies. In C. E. Weinstein, E. T. Goetz, & P. A. Alexander (Eds.), *Learning and study strategies: Issues in assessment, instruction, and evaluation* (pp. 141–169). New York: Academic Press.

McCombs, B. L. (1989). Self-regulated learning: A phenomenological view. In B. J. Zimmerman & D. H. Schunk (Eds.), *Self-regulated learning and academic achievement: Theory, research, and practice*, pp. 51–82. New York: Springer-Verlag.

McCombs, B. L. (1991). Motivation and lifelong learning. *Educational Psychologist, 26*(2), 117–127.

McCombs, B. L. (1995a). Putting the learner and learning in learner-centered classrooms: The learner-centered model as a framework. *Michigan ASCD Focus, 17*(1), 7–12.

McCombs, B. L. (1995b). Alternative perspectives for motivation. In L. Baker, O. Afflerbach, & D. Reinking (Eds.), *Developing engaged readers in school and home communities* (pp. 67–87). Hillsdale, NJ: Lawrence Erlbaum.

McCombs, B. L. (1997). Self-assessment and reflection tools for promoting teacher changes toward learner-centered practices. *NASSP Bulletin, 81*(587), 1–14.

McCombs, B. L. (1998). Integrating metacognition, affect, and motivation in improving teacher education. In B. L. McCombs & N. Lambert (Eds.), *How students learn: Reforming schools through learner-centered education* (pp. 379–408). Washington, DC: APA Books.

McCombs, B. L. (1999a). What role does perceptual psychology play in educational reform today? In H. J. Freiberg (Ed.), *Perceiving, behaving, becoming: Lessons learned* (pp. 148–157). Alexandria, VA: Association for Supervision and Curriculum Development.

McCombs, B. L. (1999b). *The Assessment of Learner-Centered Practices (ALCP): Tools for Teacher Reflection, Learning, and Change.* Denver: University of Denver Research Institute.

McCombs, B. L. (2000a). Reducing the achievement gap. *Society, 37*(5), 29–36.

McCombs, B. L. (2000b, September). *Assessing the role of educational technology in the teaching and learning process: A learner-centered perspective.* Paper presented at the Secretary's Conference on Educational Technology: Measuring the Impacts and Shaping the Future, Washington, DC. Retrieved September 10, 2001, from http://tepserver.ucsd.edu/courses/tep203/fa04/a/articles/mccombs.pdf

McCombs, B. L. (2001a). What do we know about learners and learning? The learner-centered framework: Bringing the educational system into balance. *Educational Horizons, 79*(4), 182–193.

McCombs, B. L. (2001b, September). *The learner-centered framework on teaching and learning as a foundation for electronically networked communities and cultures.* Paper prepared for the PT3 Vision Quest on Assessment in e-Learning Cultures. Denver: University of Denver.

McCombs, B. L. (2002a, February). *Normative data for grades 4–8 ALCP surveys.* Denver: University of Denver Research Institute.

McCombs, B. L. (2002b, March). *ALCP college survey validation results.* Denver: University of Denver Research Institute.

McCombs, B. L. (2002c, May). *Normative data for grades K–3 ALCP surveys.* Denver: University of Denver Research Institute.

McCombs, B. L. (2002d, September). *Normative data for grades 9–12 ALCP surveys.* Denver: University of Denver Research Institute.

McCombs, B. L. (2003a, April). *Defining Tools for Teacher Reflection: The Assessment of Learner-Centered Practices (ALCP).* Paper presented in the Interactive Symposium Proposal, "Using Learner-Centered Tools to Assess and Address Teacher Dispositions," at the Annual Meeting of the American Educational Research Association in Chicago, IL.

McCombs, B. L. (2003b). Providing a framework for the redesign of K–12 education in the context of current educational reform issues. *Theory Into Practice, 42*(2), 93–101.

McCombs, B. L. (2003c). What really happens in school reform in the new economy:

It's more than simply changing classes. Review of "Changing Classes" by Martin Packer. *Contemporary Psychology, 48*(6), 796–800.

McCombs, B. L. (2003d). From credible research to policy for guiding educational reform. In W. M. Reynolds and G. E. Miller (Eds.), *Comprehensive Handbook of Psychology, Volume 7: Educational Psychology* (pp. 583–607). New York: John Wiley & Sons.

McCombs, B. L. (2004a). The Learner-Centered Psychological Principles: A framework for balancing a focus on academic achievement with a focus on social and emotional learning needs. In J. E. Zins, R. P. Weissberg, M. C. Wang, & H. J. Walberg (Eds.), *Building academic success on social and emotional learning: What does the research say?* (pp. 23–39). New York: Teachers College Press.

McCombs, B. L. (2004b, April). *The Case for Learner-Centered Practices: Introduction and Rationale*. Paper presented in the Interactive Symposium Proposal, "The Case for Learner-Centered Practices Across the K–12 and College Levels," at the Annual Meeting of the American Educational Research Association in San Diego.

McCombs, B. L. (2005). What do we know about learners and learning? In D. Kauchak, P. Eggen, & M. D. Burbank (Eds.), *Charting a professional course: Issues and controversies in education*. Columbus, OH: Pearson-Merrill-Prentice Hall.

McCombs, B. L. (2007). Affective domain: Student perceptions and motivation. In R. Seidel, & A. Kett (Eds.), *Workbook companion for: Principles of learning to strategies for instruction, a needs-based focus on high school adolescents* (pp. 323–337). Norwell, MA: Springer.

McCombs, B. L., & Bansberg, B. (1997). Meeting student diversity needs in poor, rural schools: Ideal practices and political realities. In M. C. Wang & K. K. Wong (Eds.), *Implementing school reform: practice and policy imperatives* (pp. 161–192). Philadelphia: Temple University Center for Research in Human Development and Education.

McCombs, B. L., & Lauer, P. A. (1997). Development and validation of the learner-centered battery: Self-assessment tools for teacher reflection and professional development. *The Professional Educator, 20*(1), 1–21.

McCombs, B. L., & Lauer, P. A. (1998, July). *The learner-centered model of seamless professional development: Implications for practice and policy changes in higher education.* Paper presented at the 23rd International Conference on Improving University Teaching, Dublin, Ireland.

McCombs, B. L., & Marzano, R. J. (1990). Putting the self in self-regulated learning: The self as agent in integrating will and skill. *Educational Psychologist, 25*(1), 51–69.

McCombs, B. L., & Miller, L. (2007). *Learner-centered classroom practices and assessments: Maximizing student motivation, learning, and achievement.* Thousand Oaks, CA: Corwin Press.

McCombs, B. L., Daniels, D. H., & Perry, K. E. (in press). Children and teachers' perceptions of learner-centered practices and student motivation: Implications for early schooling. *Elementary School Journal.*

McCombs, B. L., & Pierce, J. (1999). *The development of the college level Assessment of Learner-Centered Practices (ALCP): Tools for teacher reflection, learning, and change.* Denver: University of Denver Research Institute.

McCombs, B. L., & Pope, J. E. (1994). *Motivating hard to reach students.* In the *Psychology in the Classroom Series.* Washington, DC: American Psychological Association.

McCombs, B. L., & Quiat, M. A. (2002). What makes a comprehensive school reform model learner-centered? *Urban Education, 37*(4), 476–496.

McCombs, B. L. & Vakili, D. (2005) A learner-centered framework for e-learning. *Teachers College Record, 107*(8), 1582–1609.

McCombs, B. L. & Weinberger, E. (2001, April). *The impact of learner-centered practices on the academic and non-academic outcomes of upper elementary and middle school students.* Paper presented in the symposium, "Integrating What We Know About Learners and Learning: A foundation for Transforming PreK–20 Practices," at the annual meeting of the American Educational Research Association, Seattle, Washington.

McCombs, B. L., & Whisler, J. S. (1989). The role of affective variables in autonomous learning. *Educational Psychologist, 24*(3), 277–306.

McCombs, B. L., & Whisler, J. S. (1997). *The learner-centered classroom and school: Strategies for increasing student motivation and achievement.* San Francisco: Jossey-Bass.

McLuhan, M. (1989). *The global village: Transformations in world life and media in the 21st century.* New York: Oxford University Press.

McQuillan, P. J. (2005). Possibilities and pitfalls: A comparative analysis of student empowerment. *American Educational Research Journal, 42*(4), 639–670.

Meece, J. L., Herman, P., & McCombs, B. L. (2003). Relations of learner-centered teaching practices to adolescents' achievement goals. *International Journal of Educational Research, 39*(4–5), 457–475.

Meier, D. (2002). Standardization versus standards. *Phi Delta Kappan, 84*(3), 190–198.

Miller, L., and Miller, L. C. (1994). *The Quick Smart Profile.* Austin, TX: Smart Alternatives, Inc.

Miller, S., Duffy, G. G., Rohr, J., Gasparello, R., & Mercier, S. (2005). Preparing teachers for high-poverty schools, *Educational Leadership, 62*(8), 62–65.

Mills, R., & Spittle, E. (2001). *Wisdom Within.* Edmonton, Alberta, Canada: Lone Pine Press.

Mills, R. C. (1991). A new understanding of self: The role of affect, state of mind, self understanding, and intrinsic motivation. In B. L. McCombs (Ed.), Unraveling motivation: New perspectives from research and practice. Special issue of the *Journal of Experimental Education, 60*(1), 67–81.

Mills, R. C. (2005). Sustainable community change: A new paradigm for leadership in community revitalization efforts. *National Civic Review, 94*(2), 47–57.

Mills, R. C. (in press). *Creating the Optimal School Climate for Learning: School Administrator—Teacher Handbook.* Saratoga, CA: Center for Sustainable Change.

Mills, R. C., Dunham, R. G., & Alpert, G. P. (1988). Working with high-risk youth in prevention and early intervention programs: Toward a comprehensive model. *Adolescence, 23*(91), 643–660.

Mulcahy, D. E. (2006, January 9). The continuing quest for equal schools: An essay review. *Education Review, 9*(2). Retrieved February 15, 2006, from http://edrev.asu.edu/essays/v9n2index.html.

Murphy, J. (2007). Questioning the core of university-based programs for preparing school leaders. *Phi Delta Kappan, 88*(8), 582–595.

Murphy, P. K. (2007). The eye of the beholder: The interplay of social and cognitive components in change. *Educational Psychologist, 42*(1), 41–53.

National Commission on Excellence in Education. (1983). *A nation at risk: The imperative for educational reform.* Washington, DC: U.S. Department of Education.

National Study Group for the Affirmative Development of Academic Ability. (2004). *All students reaching the top: Strategies for closing academic achievement gaps.* Naperville, IL: Learning Point Associates.

Neill, M. (2003). The dangers of testing. *Educational Leadership, 60*(5), 43–46.

Nichols, S. L., & Berliner, D. C., (2007). *Collateral damage: How high-stakes testing corrupts America's schools*. Cambridge, MA: Harvard Education Press.

Niesz, T. (2007). Why teacher networks (can) work. *Phi Delta Kappan, 88*(8), 605–610.

Noddings, N. (2005). What does it mean to educate the whole child? *Educational Leadership, 63*(1), 8–13.

Noguera, P. A. (2004). Transforming high schools. *Educational Leadership, 61*(8), 26–31.

Noguera, P. A., & Blankstein, A. M. (2007). From vision to reality: Pedro Noguera discusses engaging every learner with Alan Blankstein. In A. M. Blankstein, R. W. Cole, & P. D. Houston (Eds.), *Engaging every learner* (pp. 29–35). Thousand Oaks, CA: Corwin Press.

O'Connor, E., & McCartney, K. (2007). Examining teacher-child relationships and achievement as part of an ecological model of development. *American Educational Research Journal, 44*(8), 340–369.

Oliver, L. E., & Ostrofsky, R. (2007). The ecological paradigm of mind and its implications for psychotherapy. *Review of General Psychology, 11*(1), 1–11.

Patterson, W. (2003). Breaking out of our boxes. *Phi Delta Kappan, 84*(8), 569–574.

Pellicer, L. O. (2007). *Caring enough to lead: How reflective thought leads to moral leadership* (3rd ed.). Thousand Oaks, CA: Corwin Press.

Penuel, W. R., & Riel, M. (2007). The 'new' science of networks and the challenge of school change. *Phi Delta Kappan, 88*(8), 611–615.

Perlstein, D. (2004). *Justice, justice: School politics and the eclipse of liberalism*. New York: Peter Lang.

Perry, K. E., & Weinstein, R. S. (1998). The social context of early schooling and children's school adjustment. *Educational Psychologist, 33*(4), 177–194.

Phillips, M. (1997). What makes schools effective? A comparison of the relationships of communitarian climate and academic climate to mathematics achievement and attendance during middle school. *American Educational Research Journal, 34*, 543–578.

Pierce, J. W., Holt, J. K., Kolar, C., & McCombs, B. L. (2004, April). *Testing the learner-centered model with data at the college level*. Paper presented as part of the interactive symposium, "The Case for Learner-Centered Practices Across the K–12 and College Levels," at the annual meeting of the American Educational Research Association, San Diego, California.

Pink, D. H. (2005). Revenge of the right brain. *Wired, 13*(2). Retrieved August 1, 2007, from http://www.wired.com/wired/archive/13.02/brain.html

Prensky, M. (2006). Listen to the natives. *Educational Leadership, 63*(4), 8–13.

Pugh, K. J., & Bergin, D. A. (2005). The effect of schooling on students' out-of-school experience. *Educational Researcher, 34*(9), 15–23.

Reeves, D. B. (2006). *The learning leader: How to focus school improvement for better results*. Alexandria, VA: Association for Supervision and Curriculum Development.

Rich, D. (2005). What educators need to explain to the public. *Phi Delta Kappan, 87*(2), 154–158.

Richardson, A. (2002). *An ecology of learning and the role of elearning in the learning environment*. Retrieved July 2, 2007, from http://unpan1.un.org/intradoc/groups/public/documents/APCITY/UNPAN007791.pdf

Richardson, W. (2006). The new face of learning. *Edutopia, 2*(7), 34–37.

Rock, D., & Schwartz, J. (2007). The neuroscience of leadership. *Strategy+Business, Management*. Retrieved August 1, 2007, from http://www.strategy-business.com/press/freearticle/06207?tid=2e0&pg=all

Rogers, C. R. (1961). *On becoming a person*. Boston: Houghton Mifflin.

Rose, L. C., & Gallup, A. M. (2007). The 39th annual Phi Delta Kappa/Gallup Poll of the public's attitudes toward the public schools. *Phi Delta Kappan, 89*(1), 33–48.

Rubalcava, M. (2005). Let kids come first. *Educational Leadership, 62*(8), 70–72.

Scapp, R. (2006). *Managing to be different: Educational leadership as critical practice.* New York: Routledge.

Scharmer, C. O. (2003, April). *The blind spot of leadership: Presencing as a social technology of freedom.* Unpublished Habilitation Thesis.

Scharmer, C. O. (2004, May). *Theory U: Leading profound innovation and change by presencing emerging futures.* Cambridge, MA: Massachusetts Institute of Technology. A paper based on the introduction of a book with the same title.

Scharmer, C. O. (2006, February). *Theory U: Leading from the emerging future: Presencing as a social technology of freedom.* Cambridge, MA: Massachusetts Institute of Technology. An excerpt from a book with the same title.

Schwahn, C. J., & Spady, W. G. (2006). *Total leaders: Applying the best future-focused change strategies to education.* Lanham, MD: Rowman and Littlefield Education.

Seligman, M. E. P., & Csikszentmihalyi, M. (2000). Positive psychology: An introduction. *American Psychologist, 55*(1), 5–14.

Senge, P. M., Scharmer, C. O., Jaworksi, J., & Flowers, B. S. (2004a). Awakening faith in an alternative future: A consideration of *Precence: Human purpose and the field of the future. Reflection, 5*(7), 1–16.

Senge, P. M., Scharmer, C. O., Jaworski, J., & Flowers, B. S. (2004b). *Presence: Human purpose and the field of the future.* Global network (www.solonline.org) and Cambridge, MA: Society for Organizational Learning.

Sergiovanni, T. J. (2007). An epistemological problem: What if we have the wrong theory? In P. D. Houston, A. M. Blankstein, & R. W. Cole (Eds.), *Out-of-the-box leadership* (pp. 49–68). Thousand Oaks, CA: Corwin Press.

Shapiro, H. S. (2006). *Losing heart: The moral and spiritual miseducation of America's children.* Mahwah, NJ: Lawrence Erlbaum Associates, Inc.

Shulman, L. (2001). Understanding teachers and their learning. *New Educator, 7,* 1–5.

Simon, H. (1983). *Reason in human affairs.* Stanford, CA: Stanford University Press.

Spady, W. (2001). *Beyond counterfeit reforms: Forging an authentic future for all learners.* Lanham, MD: Scarecrow Press.

Spady, W. (2006, November 8). *Fundamental unity leadership percepts.* Unpublished manuscript.

Spady, W. (2007, June). *Are we looking for reform, re-form, or transform education?* Keystone, CO: Unpublished working paper.

Spady, W., McCombs, B. L., Caine, R., Mills, R., Caine, G., & Brady, M. (2007, August). *The new possibilities network: Statement of truths.* Unpublished manuscript.

Sparks, D. (2007). What it means to be an outside-the-box leader. In P. D. Houston, A. M. Blankstein, & R. W. Cole (Eds.), *Out-of-the-box leadership* (pp. 11–29). Thousand Oaks, CA: Corwin Press.

Sroka, S. (2006). Listening to the whole child. *Education Update, 48*(1), 1–8.

Sternberg, R. J. (2007). A systems model of leadership: WICS. *American Psychologist, 61*(1), 34–42.

Stilger, B. (2005, June). Landmarks for leaders: In times of uncertainty and chaos. Retrieved July 6, 2007, from http://www.berkana.org/articles/landmarks.htm

Stilger, B. (2007, June). *Four roots: Work in progress.* Spokane, WA: Berkana Institute.

Stewart, V. (2007). Citizens of the world. *Educational Leadership, 64*(7), 9–14.

Stookey, C. W. (2003). *The container principle: Resilience, chaos, and trust.* Nova Scotia: The Nova Scotia Sea School.

Suarez, E. M. (1988). A neo-cognitive dimension. *The Counseling Psychologist, 16*(2), 239–244.

Suarez, R., Mills, R. C., & Stewart, D. (1987). *Sanity, insanity, and common sense: The groundbreaking new approach to happiness.* New York: Fawcett Columbine.

Suarez-Orozco, M. M., & Sattin, C. (2007). Wanted: Global citizens. *Educational Leadership, 64*(7), 58–62.

Sugrue, C. (Ed.). (2005). *Passionate Principalship: Learning from the life histories of school leaders.* Oxford, England: Routledge-Falmer.

Sugrue, C., & Furlong, C. (2004). The cosmologies of Irish primary principals' identities: Between the modern and the postmodern? *International Journal of Leadership in Education Theory and Practice, 5*(3), 189–210.

Summers, J. J., Beretvas, S. N., Svinicki, M. D., & Gorin, J. S. (2005). Evaluating collaborative learning and community. *Journal of Experimental Education, 73*(3), 165–188.

Supovitz, J. A. (2006). *The case for district-based reform: Leading, building, and sustaining school improvement.* Cambridge, MA: Harvard Educational Press.

Swanson, C. B. (2004). *Who graduates? Who doesn't? A statistical portrait of public high school graduation, Class of 2001.* Washington, DC: The Urban Institute.

Timm, J., & Stewart, D. (1990). *The thinking teacher's guide to self-esteem.* Tampa, FL: Florida Center for Human Development.

Tomlinson, J. (1999). *Globalization and culture.* Chicago: University of Chicago Press.

Truscott, D. M., & Truscott, S. D. (2005). Differing circumstances, shared challenges: Finding common ground between urban and rural schools. *Phi Delta Kappan, 87*(2), 123–130.

Vanhuysse, P. (2006). Bees and foxes, spiders and hedgehogs. *Education Review, 9*(1). Retrieved February 15, 2006, from http://edrev.asu.edu/essaus/v9n1/

Vroom, V. H., & Jago, A. G. (2007). The role of the situation in leadership. *American Psychologist, 62*(1), 17–24.

Wagner, T. (2003). Reinventing America's schools. *Phi Delta Kappan, 84*(9), 665–668.

The Wallace Foundation (2006). *Leadership for learning: Making the connections among state district and school policies and practices.* Retrieved August 8, 2007, from http://www.wallacefoundation.org/WF/elan

Wallis, C., & Steptoe, S. (2006). How to bring our schools out of the 20th century. *Time, 168*(25), 50–56.

Wass, H., & Combs, A. W. (1974). Humanizing the education of teachers. *Theory Into Practice, 13*(2), 123–129.

Waters, J. T., Marzano, R. J., & McNulty, B. (2004). Leadership that sparks learning. *Educational Leadership, 61*(7), 48–51.

Wheatley, M. (1999). *Leadership and the new science: Discovering order in a chaotic world* (2nd ed.). San Francisco: Berrett-Koehler Publishers.

Wheatley, M. (2000). *Disturb me, please!* Retrieved July 6, 2007, from http://www.berkana.org/articles/disturb_me.htm

Wheatley, M. (2001a). *Listening.* Retrieved July 6, 2007, from http://www.berkana.org/articles/listening.htm

Wheatley, M. (2001b). Restoring hope to the future through critical education of leaders. Retrieved July 6, 2007, from http://www.berkana.org/articles/restoring_hope.htm

Wheatley, M. (2002). *Supporting pioneering leaders as communities of practice: How to rapidly develop new leaders in great numbers.* Retrieved July 6, 2007, from http:// www.berkana.org/articles/pioneering_leaders.htm

Wheatley, M. (2005, June). *It's just our turn to help the world.* Retrieved July 6, 2007, from http://www.berkana.org/articles/our_turn.htm

Wheatley, M. (2006a). Leadership lessons for the real world. Leader to Leader Magazine, Summer 2006. Retrieved June 28, 2007, from http://www.margaretwheatley.com/ articles/leadershiplessons.html

Wheatley, M. (2006b). Relationships: The basic building blocks of life. Retrieved June 28, 2007 from http://www.margaretwheatley.com/articles/relationships.html

Wheatley, M. (2007). *Core practices of life-affirming leaders.* Retrieved July 6, 2007, from http://www.berkana.org/articles/core_practices.htm

Wheatley, M., & Frieze, D. (2006). *Lifecycle of emergence: Using emergence to take social innovations to scale.* Retrieved July 6, 2007, from http://www.berkana.org/articles/ lifecycle.htm

Wheatley, M., & Frieze, D. (2007). Beyond networking: How large-scale change really happens: Working with emergence. *The School Administrator,* Spring. Retrieved June 28, 2007, from http://www.margaretwheatley.com/articles/largescalechange. html

Wielkiewicz, R. M., & Stelzner, S. P. (2005). An ecological perspective on leadership theory, research, and practice. *Review of General Psychology, 9*(4), 326–341.

Wilding, N. (2007). *Centre for human ecology.* Retrieved July 6, 2007, from http:// pioneersofchange.net/ventures/che/document_view

Williams, B. (2003*). Closing the achievement gap: A vision for changing beliefs and practices* (2nd ed.). Alexandria, VA: Association for Supervision and Curriculum Development.

Williams, B., & Imam, I. (2007). (Eds.). *Systems concepts in evaluation: An expert anthology.* Point Reyes, CA: EdgePress of Inverness.

Wolk, S. (2007). Why go to school? *Phi Delta Kappan, 88*(9), 648–658.

Wraga, W. G. (2006). The heightened significance of *Brown v. Board of Education* in our time. *Phi Delta Kappan, 87*(6), 425–428.

Zmuda, A., Kuklis, R., & Kline, E. (2004). *Transforming schools: Creating a culture if continuous improvement.* Alexandria, VA: Association for Supervision and Curriculum Development.

Zurawsky, C. (2004). Teachers matter: Evidence from value-added assessments. *Research Points, 2*(2), 1–2, 4.

Index

CORWIN
PRESS

The Corwin Press logo—a raven striding across an open book—represents the union of courage and learning. Corwin Press is committed to improving education for all learners by publishing books and other professional development resources for those serving the field of PreK–12 education. By providing practical, hands-on materials, Corwin Press continues to carry out the promise of its motto: **"Helping Educators Do Their Work Better."**